3/23/89

The Evolution
of
Blitzkrieg Tactics

RECENT TITLES IN
CONTRIBUTIONS IN MILITARY STUDIES

The Evolution
of
Blitzkrieg Tactics

Germany Defends Itself Against Poland, 1918-1933

Robert M. Citino

Contributions in Military Studies, Number 61

GREENWOOD PRESS
New York • Westport, Connecticut • London

LIBRARY OF CONGRESS CATALOGING-IN-PUBLICATION DATA

Citino, Robert Michael, 1958-
   The evolution of blitzkrieg tactics.

   (Contributions in military studies, ISSN 0883-6884 ;
no. 61)
   Bibliography: p.
   Includes index.
   1. Germany—Armed Forces—History—20th century.
2. Germany—Military relations—Poland. 3. Poland—
Military relations—Germany. I. Title. II. Series.
UA710.C55 1987   355.4'22   87-5
ISBN 0-313-25631-4 (lib. bdg. : alk. paper)

British Library Cataloguing in Publication Data is available.

Library of Congress Catalog Card Number: 87-5
ISBN: 0-313-25631-4
ISSN: 0883-6884

First published in 1987

Greenwood Press, Inc.
88 Post Road West, Westport, Connecticut 06881

Printed in the United States of America

∞™

The paper used in this book complies with the
Permanent Paper Standard issued by the National
Information Standards Organization (Z39.48-1984).

10 9 8 7 6 5 4 3 2 1

For Roberta

Contents

Tables

Preface

Many historians tend to shunt aside military history. Certain historical events, however, are incomprehensible unless one studies their military aspects. One such phenomenon is the relationship of the German Weimar Republic to its Polish neighbor to the east. Germany, loser of the First World War, disarmed and weakened, was forced to cede most of Upper Silesia, Poznan, and West Prussia to the new Polish state. The regaining of these territories remained an underlying goal of Germany's interwar diplomacy. The German army (Reichswehr) also had its eyes on the eastern lands. Since German land forces were limited by treaty to 100,000 men, there was no hope for a forcible revision of the Versailles settlement. Military reality compelled the German army to plan for the defense of the borders against a possible attack by the Polish army. Elaborate maneuvers were staged in Germany which simulated Polish attacks upon Berlin or East Prussia. During the Weimar era, and indeed also during the first two years of the National Socialist regime, the Polish army was many times larger than the Reichswehr and conceivably could have launched a successful attack across Germany's eastern frontier. Therefore, the military situation was in many ways the primary determinant of the diplomatic relations of the two states. There has as yet been no comprehensive study of the military preparations taken by Germany and Poland along their common border. It is this gap in twentieth-century military history which this book is meant to fill.

The goal of this work is to determine the defensive measures taken by Germany along its eastern frontier from 1918 to 1933, that is, from the end of the First World War until the formation of the Hitler cabinet in January 1933. This latter event marked the end of Polish military ascendancy in the east, since Hitler soon tore up the military clauses of the Versailles treaty. The study will examine the defensibility of the border and the steps which the German army took to strengthen the defenses in the area. This question is particularly important given the weapons in use in the 1920s. Although the area between Berlin and Warsaw is basically a featureless plain, entrenched infantry with artillery support could quite possibly have held this line against a combined infantry-cavalry assault, that is, against precisely the sort of attack Poland could have launched. In addition, any Polish strike at Berlin would have to contend with a major river crossing, that of the Oder. This work will therefore determine just what kind of defense the <u>Reichswehr</u> planned to meet a Polish assault, and will show how prominently the line of the Oder figured in German plans. Finally, it will investigate German fear for the safety of East Prussia and defensive preparations in this detached province.

Apart from the geographical and tactical aspects of the question, however, the lack of manpower would force the German government to labor under strategic and operational constraints. Basically, the three divisions that Germany had stationed in the area should have been insufficient to defend against an attack by the fifteen divisions that Poland could have mustered. This work will examine the measures taken by the German army to rectify the manpower imbalance. These measures included the recruitment of irregular border guard formations, often made up of inhabitants of the border regions; the maintenance of a system of fortifications in East Prussia and on the Oder; and a thorough training program that would allow the quality of the German forces to compensate for their small numbers. The third method was by far the most important. In an age of increasing military sophistication, German officers felt that they could not rely on half-trained irregulars for border security. In the German officer corps, there were few advocates of a "nation in arms." Likewise, the development of heavy artillery had rendered even fixed fortifications of doubtful utility, a fact proven many times in the previous war. A lack of confidence in border guards and fortifications left German military leaders with no choice but to design a high-quality, mobile army to defend the state. The perceived challenge from Poland was the primary reason for the development of <u>Blitzkrieg</u> tactics.

No discussion of the German-Polish military balance would be complete without an analysis of the Polish army, particularly as it was seen from Berlin. It is an indisputable fact that the Polish forces on the German border enjoyed a numerical advantage. The extent of this advantage, about three to one in favor of the Poles, was potentially decisive. Cannon counting, however, is the most sterile form of military analysis. This work will show the German opinion of the actual condition and battle-worthiness of the Polish army. In the 1920s, as in the contemporary era, an army is only as good as its equipment. Modern military equipment is complex and expensive. Procurement of new weapons requires that the state have a technological base as well as a strong economy, neither of which Poland possessed. This study will show how Poland attempted to overcome its economic weakness and create a modern army.

This book is based primarily upon unpublished sources. The first major source was the large body of German Foreign Office documents captured by the U.S. Army at the end of the Second World War. These documents have been microfilmed and are available in the National Archives, Washington, D.C., under the microcopy designation T 120. Included in the huge number of documents is the official correspondence of the German foreign minister, state secretaries, and the various sections (<u>Abteilungen</u>) of the German Foreign Office. The National Archives collection includes many secret files (<u>Geheimakten</u>). Of particular interest to this study were the records of Section IV (Po) of the Foreign Office, which dealt

with Polish military and diplomatic affairs.   These records
include many reports from German officials about Polish military maneuvers, armament, and organization and form the basis
for the discussion of Polish military strength in chapter 3.
Besides its Foreign Office holdings, the National Archives
also possesses numerous collections of the personal papers of
German military leaders.   These, too, are available to the
public.   Of special importance to this study were the papers
of Generals Hans von Seeckt and Wilhelm Groener, the two most
important military leaders of the Weimar era.   The Seeckt
papers (Microcopy M 132) were most helpful for analyzing
German strategy at the time of the Russo-Polish war.   The
Groener papers (Microcopy M 137) form the basis for the
discussion of the Panzerschiff controversy in chapter 4.
Other captured records utilized in this study were the files
of the German navy which are to be found in the Naval
Historical Library, London.   A complete copy of these records
is located in the University of Michigan library in Ann Arbor.
This large collection of naval documents bears the serial
number 13-132849 and is available on restricted interlibrary
loan from the University of Michigan.   These documents form
the basis for the description of German naval planning against
Poland.   In particular, the detailed description in chapter 4
of German plans for an attack upon the Polish port of Gdynia
is based on these records.   In addition, these documents
describe in great detail the full program of maneuvers, battle
exercises, and wargames which the German navy undertook in
this period.
     The second principal source for this study consists of
the records of the American military attache in Berlin.   The
American attaches and their staffs reported on a wide variety
of topics of interest to the military historian, including
German army deployments, maneuvers, armaments, and much more.
These documents have only recently been collected and microfilmed by University Publications of America, Inc.   They
comprise 28 reels of film and are available under the title
Military Intelligence Reports: Germany, 1919-1941.   Since
these documents only became available in 1983, it is no
exaggeration to say that this book has been the first to
utilize this important source.   The description of the
fortress of Königsberg in chapter 2, the first to appear in
any English-language work, relied heavily upon the reports of
the American military officer who was permitted by the Germans
to visit the city.   The majority of the reports on German
fortifications are to be found on reel 24 of this collection.
The discussion of German army maneuvers in 1925 and 1928 was
based in large part on the reports of the American officers
who attended the exercises.   Reels 14, 15, and 19 were
especially helpful on the question of maneuvers.   In addition,
this collection contains many translations of articles by
German officers in the Militär-Wochenblatt, the leading
military journal in Weimar Germany.
     I would like to thank Professors Barbara and Charles
Jelavich of Indiana University.   It is difficult to put into
words what their scholarly expertise and friendship have meant
to me in preparing this work.   The years I spent as a graduate
student working with them will always remain the most reward-
ing of my life.   In addition, the suggestions, tolerance, and
encouragement I received from my wife Roberta during the
research and writing of this book were indispensable to the

finished product.   Finally, I should thank my daughter
Allison, whose imminent arrival gave me impetus to finish this
project.

1
The Uncertain Years, 1918-1921

The period from the end of the First World War until January
1921 was a very dangerous one for Germany. The German army
had collapsed in the summer of 1918, and hostile states had
appeared on Germany's eastern borders. Armed clashes between
Polish forces and remnants of the German army threatened
public order in the east. The Treaty of Versailles, which the
Germans signed in the summer of 1919, did nothing to stabilize
the situation along the German-Polish border. The treaty was
a French creation which disarmed Germany and awarded large
segments of former German territory to Poland. To such leaders of the German army as Generals Hans von Seeckt and Wilhelm
Groener, the purpose of the treaty was not to ensure the
peace, but to perpetuate French hegemony in Europe. The
treaty's principal means of subjugating Germany, according to
these military leaders, was the establishment of a strong
Poland on Germany's eastern flank. The collapse of the eastern empires in the war had allowed the Poles to reassemble
their state after more than a century of partition. Largely
through the efforts of two men, Roman Dmowski and Jozef
Pilsudski, a Polish state existed by the time of the peace
conference. At the conference, the French supported the Poles
in their claims on German territory.

    In the view of Germany's military leaders, the forced
dismantling of their army posed a great danger to Germany's
continued existence, particularly in light of the threatening
attitude of Poland. The historical legacy of invasion and
counterinvasion was, to them, justification for their demand
that the Allies permit Germany to maintain a large standing
army. In 1919, it appeared to Groener and others that Germany
was in a situation similar to that of Prussia in 1807. The
problem facing the German officers was how to form a cohesive
national army from the scraps of the force defeated by the
Allies. The material for a new army, to be sure, was available in Germany. Bands of military volunteers, the Freikorps,
had arisen in response to the eastern danger immediately after
the war. Neither Seeckt nor Groener, however, trusted these
unruly formations, which proclaimed loyalty only to their own
officers rather than to the state.

    The German leadership's success in forming a new army
would receive a stern test in 1920. In that year, the Russo-
Polish War brought with it great danger to Germany's exposed

eastern provinces. The collapse of the Polish army in Belorussia and the Soviet advance upon Warsaw caused a state of near panic in the eastern German territories. Because of its proximity to the theater of war and its physical detachment from the rest of Germany, East Prussia found itself especially threatened. It remained to be seen if the German army, once the finest army in Europe, would be able merely to protect Germany's borders. To determine the disadvantages under which the Germans had to operate, however, it is first necessary to discuss the military provisions of the Treaty of Versailles.

The terms of the Treaty of Versailles handed to the Germans on 7 May 1919 caused consternation among practically all political and social groups in Germany. General Hans von Seeckt, head of the German military mission to Versailles, later remarked that the contents of the treaty "fulfilled my worst expectations."[1] For Count Ulrich Brockdorff-Rantzau, leader of the German delegation to the peace negotiations, the thick text of the treaty was unnecessary: "It would have been simpler to declare 'Germany renounces her existence.'" The first cabinet of the Weimar Republic fell on 20 June as a result of a deadlock over the issue of ratification of the treaty. On 28 June Germany signed the treaty because of the threat by the Allies to resume their advance into the Reich.[2] A crucial factor in the decision to sign had been the statement by Field Marshal Paul von Hindenburg, chief of the General Staff and the Army High Command, that further military resistance to the enemy was hopeless.[3] General Wilhelm Groener, quartermaster general of the army, had seconded this advice, although he conceded that in the east, German forces could retake the lost province of Poznan and perhaps even seize Warsaw. In the west, however, the German armies would face an enemy ten times larger than they were and could offer resistance only behind the line of the Elbe. In a memorandum to General Headquarters at Kolberg, Groener characterized thoughts of further resistance at this time as "madness", which if realized would lead to a "war of annihilation by France against Germany."[4] Still, some members of the military and civilian leadership refused to accept the obvious. There was talk of a popular uprising in East Prussia to defend the area from Polish encroachments. Some officials in the eastern lands to be awarded to Poland considered seceding from the Reich so as to be in a position to deny the legal validity of the treaty. Groener intervened again to prevent a popular uprising in East Prussia. The military and civilian leaders of East Prussia had made detailed preparations for a "people's war" against Poland. The Social Democratic commissioner of the province, August Winnig, was very supportive of efforts to incite a popular rising. During this period, German Freikorps troops were in action against the Red Army in the Baltic states. In addition, remnants of the regular army grouped into the VIIIth Army Corps under General Rüdiger von der Goltz were fighting in the area.[5] A popular uprising against the Versailles treaty could have received some help from these regular and irregular German forces.

It was Groener who convinced the government that the prospects for success of armed resistance were "completely hopeless." Inevitable defeat in the west, he wrote in a memorandum on the military situation, would wipe away temporary gains in the east. Marshal Foch had over 5,000,000 men

at his disposal: 2,250,000 French; 200,000 Belgian; 2,500,000
British; 250,000 American.   On the Polish front, there were
70,000 men in the Haller army, 70,000 additional troops in
Poznan, and 100,000 men in "Congress Poland." Besides these,
there were about 100,000 recent recruits.   Polish forces on
the German border numbered 155,000 men with 296 field and 134
heavy guns: 59,000 men on the Upper Silesian front, 58,000
men on the Poznan front, and 38,000 men on the West Prussian
and East Prussian fronts.   The total numbers for an advance
from the west, he estimated, were 600,000 men immediately
available, with a second echelon of 250,000 men available in
four to six weeks.   In the East, the Poles and Czechs had
200,000 men immediately available.   In a short time, they
could raise a further 200,000 men.
        Opposite these,   there were the following German troops
available: in the west, 63,000 men; in Germany, 60,000 men;
in Bavaria, 10,000 men; in Saxony, 16,000 men; in the east,
240,000 men.   Available German forces thus totalled 389,000
men. The comparison of strengths, Groener argued, showed that
at first Germany would have numerical superiority in the east.
But in the west, German forces were so small that they could
only hinder an enemy advance for a few days.[6] This sensible
analysis led the German government to sign the treaty, a fact
which won him many enemies among his fellow military men.
        The treaty which brought forth such violent reactions
among the Germans was basically a French creation, that is,
the territorial and military clauses to which Germany most
objected were of French inspiration.   The final shape of the
treaty reflected the French desire for European hegemony,
which France could achieve only at Germany's expense. British
leaders, especially Prime Minister David Lloyd George, recognized the true nature of French aspirations.   From the beginning of the negotiations, disagreement arose between the
British and the French over how to treat conquered Germany.
The French favored a punitive peace.   Lloyd George strove to
limit French gains wherever it seemed reasonable to do so.
When British interests were at stake, Lloyd George did not
hesitate to secure them at cost to Germany, as for instance in
the question of what should be done with the German fleet.
The presence of the American president Woodrow Wilson, who
sided with the French more often than with the British,
further complicated the deliberations.[7]
        The provisions of the treaty demonstrated the French
desire to dominate Europe.   Taken individually, the separate
clauses do not appear harsh, but assembled into one package,
they had a devastating impact on Germany.   When Lloyd George
first read the treaty in its entirety, he doubted that the
Germans would sign it.   From the French point of view, the
purpose of the peace was to reverse the European balance of
power from that which had existed in 1914 to one in which
France stood as the only great power on the continent.
Germany had been the strongest military power before and
during the First World War, a fact confirmed by the effort
required to defeat it.   The Versailles treaty relegated
Germany to the third rank of powers and placed France in the
dominant position Germany had occupied.   Versailles negated
Germany's strategic advantages and magnified its disadvantages
as these had been revealed in the war.
        From 1914 to 1918, German armed forces had labored under
certain disadvantages.   On the grand strategic level, Austria-

Hungary had been a weak ally. More than once Germany had to
rush troops southward to stiffen Habsburg forces facing the
Russians. After 1914 what little offensive capability the
Imperial and Royal army had possessed at the war's opening had
disappeared as a result of the rout of Austrian forces in
Galicia.[8] Second, Germany's armies faced enemies with greatly
superior reserves of manpower. Battles of attrition such as
that of Verdun in 1916 worked to Germany's disadvantage in the
long run. The entry of America into the war in 1917 gave the
Allies a decisive superiority in manpower.

On the strategic level, Germany's obligation to fight a
war on two fronts--three, if one counts the German forces
fighting alongside the Austrians--was a crucial factor in its
ultimate defeat.[9] The plan of Chief of the General Staff
Alfred von Schlieffen to fight and win a two-front war had
grave deficiencies. Most damaging was his assumption that the
underdeveloped state of the Russian rail system would prevent
any Russian offensive against Germany until six weeks after
mobilization. The Russians invaded East Prussia before the
German armies could crush the French, and the great German
encirclement victory at Tannenberg could not disguise the fact
that the Schlieffen plan had failed its ultimate test.[10] The
other important strategic failure was the inability of the
German High Seas Fleet to counter the overwhelming sea power
of Great Britain. The long blockade of Germany's shores
caused starvation and a collapse of morale among the German
population.

On the tactical level, the development of rapid-fire
artillery and the machine gun gave the advantage to the
defense. The firepower which troops defending in entrenchments could bring to bear on an assaulting force made
attacking a foolhardy, bloody venture. Napoleon's dictum that
victory would always go to the "big battalions" was no longer
true. In the First World War, the big battalions merely
suffered higher casualties, since the large numbers of men
necessary to carry out an assault formed a larger target for
enemy fire. This tactical problem for the attacker made quick
decisive victories in the style of the French emperor
impossible. The grandiose Napoleonic sweep of the Schlieffen
plan foundered on tactical realities. In the east, although
the Germans dealt devastating blows to the Russian army in
1914 and 1915, they were not able to destroy it. Of course,
the tactical superiority of the defense worked to German
advantage on the western front after the stabilization of the
line in October 1914. Here, the onus of attacking was on the
Allies, since their goal was to drive the Germans from French
soil.

The most important German advantage was superior staff
work. The elder Helmuth von Moltke had formed the Great
General Staff during the 1860s.[11] Its task was to substitute
collective intellect for that of the individual genius, since
the Napoleonic character might not be available when his
country needed him. The effectiveness of this system was
evident during the wars of German unification, and the other
powers soon formed their own versions. In the First World
War, German staff work was instrumental in the annihilation of
the Russian army at Gorlice and in the rout of the Italians at
Caporetto.

By 1918, Germany's disadvantages far outweighed its
advantages. On 8 August, the German front in the west

collapsed.   The troops were dispirited by the failure of
General Erich Ludendorff's much-heralded spring offensives and
had suffered casualties which the High Command could no longer
replace.   Allied pursuit was swift,   spearheaded by tanks and
fresh   American   troops.   The Germans had no choice but to
request an armistice,   which they signed on 11 November.   The
aim of   the Treaty of Versailles was to make   permanent   this
temporary shifting in the military balance in Europe which had
occurred   on 8 August.   For all its idealistic language of
national   self-determination   and universal   disarmament,   the
treaty was really a military document.   Virtually every clause
in the treaty,   apart from those of a purely vengeful   character,   was intended to weaken Germany in a military sense.   To
the German generals,   even the pragmatic ones such as Groener,
the treaty was unacceptable since it did   not   even   permit
Germany the means to defend itself.
     Although   the Allies had promised Germany that   President
Wilson's   conciliatory   Fourteen Points would be the basis   of
the   peace,   the   treaty forced Germany   to   cede   territories
amounting to some 13 percent of its prewar area.[12]   In   the
west,   the   losses included Alsace-Lorraine to France and   the
small   districts of Eupen,   Malmedy,   and Moresnet to Belgium.
France   received the large coal fields of the Saar region   for
fifteen years as recompense for the destruction of French coal
mines during the war.   At the end of this period, a plebiscite
would take place to determine the wishes of the inhabitants as
to   future national affiliation.   In the north,   the Allies
ordered a plebiscite in Schleswig to determine the division of
the territory.   Through this process, Denmark regained a small
slice of Northern Schleswig lost to Prussia in 1864.
     In the east,   Germany had to give up large tracts of land
to   the new Polish state.   The treaty recognized the province
of   Poznan as part of Poland.   Germany also lost a   strip   of
West Prussian territory which secured Polish access to the sea
and   at   the same time cut off East Prussia from the   rest   of
Germany.   Danzig   and   the whole of Upper   Silesia   were
originally   part of the German cessions to Poland,   but Lloyd
George secured changes in those sections of the treaty   over
heated   French   and Polish objections.[13]   Danzig now became   a
free city under the auspices of the League of Nations.   Upper
Silesia   would   be the site of a plebiscite on 20   March   1921
which   almost led to a German-Polish war.   The   final   territorial   settlement in Upper Silesia took place on 20   October.
Poland   received 25 percent of the territory and 44 percent of
the   population.   To German dismay,   the areas   which   Poland
received   were by far the most significant industrial   sectors
of   the region,   including 80 percent of Germany's total   zinc
production   and   25 percent of the   coal   production.[14]
Plebiscites also took place in the Allenstein and Marienwerder
districts   of East Prussia,   and the results were small German
territorial   losses.   Germany lost the port of Memel,   which
came   under   the   administration of   a   League   commission.
Lithuania seized the city in 1923.   In human terms, Germany's
population   losses represented about 12 percent of its   prewar
population.   While   the   treaty stopped short of   the radical
French   solution   of   detaching   the   Rhenish   provinces   from
Germany,[15]   the territories lost contained a significant   part
of Germany's national resources.   In geostrategic terms, East
Prussia   was   now   a vulnerable German enclave   surrounded   by
Polish   territory   and cut off from land   communications   with

Germany.   In future German military planning, the problem of
East Prussia was to receive a great deal of attention.
     The recipient of the ceded eastern territories, as well
as of subsequent German enmity, was the resurrected state of
Poland.   Once one of the largest European states, Poland had
disappeared from the map at the hands of its stronger
Prussian, Austrian, and Russian neighbors in the partitions of
the eighteenth century.   Napoleon had seen fit to reestablish
a Polish state of sorts, the Grand Duchy of Warsaw, as a lure
to gain Polish recruits for his <u>Grande Armee</u>.   The defeat of
Napoleon by the three partitioning powers in 1815 caused
Poland to disappear once more.   At the Congress of Vienna,
Russia received the largest share of Polish territory, which
came to be known as "Congress Poland."   Several Polish
uprisings during the nineteenth century caused the partitioning powers to tighten their grip on Polish lands, although the
revolts did bring the "Polish question" to the attention of
the Great Powers.   In Germany, the government subjected the
Poles living in West Prussia, Poznan, and Silesia to a
Germanization campaign which included restrictions on language
and education.
     The outbreak of the First World War opened up opportu-
nities for Poland.   In an effort to win the Polish people to
their respective sides, both the Central and Entente Powers
promised to reestablish Poland in some form.   In November
1916, having cleared Polish territories of Russian troops in
the great offensive of the previous year, the emperors of
Germany and Austria-Hungary promised a "constitutional heredi-
tary monarchy" for Polish-speaking areas.[16] Two days later, a
Regency Council assumed leadership in Warsaw, although the
German military authorities continued to administer the area.
Neither of the Central Powers wanted to include any of their
own Polish lands in a new state, but only those seized from
Russia.
     Meanwhile, a struggle for power in the postwar Polish
state began to develop between two men: Jozef Pilsudski and
Roman Dmowski.   Pilsudski had begun his political career as a
revolutionary socialist.   He had founded and led the Polish
Legion which had fought on the side of the Central Powers in
the war.   During the latter part of the war the Germans had
imprisoned him at Magdeburg when it appeared that he was
thinking of changing sides.   He had something of the dreamer
about him, and he yearned to reestablish the great Poland of
the early modern period.   Dmowski, though no less of a
patriot, was somewhat more pragmatic.   He was the leader of
the National Democratic party and during the war had established a committee of Polish emigres in Paris.   This committee
attempted to win promises of Polish independence from the
Entente.   Dmowski had considerable success, and Poland received the promise of independence and access to the sea in
Wilson's Fourteen Points.
     The simultaneous collapse of all the partitioning powers
in 1917 and 1918 was the essential precondition for the
rebirth of Poland.   Into the chaotic situation created by the
dissolution of the Russian, German, and Austrian empires
stepped the recently freed Pilsudski.   He arrived in Warsaw
and established a Polish government on 14 November 1918.   On
13 December, in a move which boded ill for future German-
Polish relations, he broke off diplomatic relations with
Germany because "German authorities are acting in a   manner

injurious   to Polish interests."[17]   Meanwhile,   he reached   an
understanding with Dmowski's Paris Committee.   Dmowski became
Poland's chief representative at the peace conference.   One
other event occurred in this period which was to be of significance for the future.   On 27 December,   the Poles living in
the Poznan district rose up, disarmed the German garrison, and
seized control of the area.[18]

Through the efforts of Dmowski and Pilsudski, then, a
Polish state existed by the time the representatives of the
victorious powers met in Paris.   As representatives of an
associate power, the Polish delegation participated in the
deliberations and offered suggestions that were certain to
clash with German interests.   Since the Germans found the
doors to the conference locked, they became highly suspicious
of what was going on in the deliberations and could later
claim with justice that they had been treated unfairly.   Much
of their hostility was directed at the Poles, whom they
accused of fattening themselves at German expense.   The
German-Polish hostility of the 1920s originated at the
Versailles conference.

At least part of the blame must go to Dmowski.   The
Polish representatives made the most of their opportunity to
press claims on German territory.   Dmowski made persistent
and, for the Allies, often exasperating attempts to expand the
territorial limits of his state. Lloyd George commented that

No one gave more trouble than the Poles.   Having
once upon a time been the most formidable military
power in central Europe--when Prussia was a starve-
ling duchy--there were few provinces that Poland
could not claim as being historically her inheri-
tance of which she had been reft.   Drunk with the
new wine of liberty supplied to her by the Allies,
she fancied herself once more the resistless
mistress of central Europe.   Self-determination did
not suit her ambitions.[19]

Dmowski's presentation of the Polish territorial claims
took place on 29 January 1919.[20] Those demands took as their
departure point the Polish borders of 1772, that is, before
the first partition.   Since Poland lacked well-defined
boundaries, "the principle of including within those
boundaries only those territories where the Poles were in a
large majority must not be accepted altogether." Dmowski
asserted that the borders of 1772 would not satisfy Poland in
the west, as they would leave out Silesia, "where 90% of the
population . . . was strongly Polish," an absurd statement.
All of eastern Germany, he claimed, "was not naturally German
but Germanized." Danzig, where "at least 40%" of the population was Polish, should revert to Poland. With regard to East
Prussia, he stated that "some wrong would have to be done" to
the Germans there.   The best solution, as he saw it, was that
"this small island of German people should be made a republic
with its capital at Königsberg." In a previous letter to
President Wilson on 8 October 1918, he had been even more
explicit on the subject of East Prussia. At that time, he had
suggested that the German-speaking areas of East Prussia must
either unite with Poland on the basis of regional autonomy or
form an independent republic joined to Poland by a customs
union.   The economic union with Poland would have a beneficial

effect on this "thinly settled land" which would lead to further Polish settlement of the region. In time, he stated, the dominant position of the Germans in East Prussia would be destroyed.[21] In short, Dmowski was calling for nothing less than a partition of Germany. His exorbitant demands on German territory brought a rejoinder from Lloyd George:

> The proposal of the Polish Commission that we should place 2,100,000 Germans under the control of a people which is of a different religion and which has never proved its capacity for self-government throughout its history, must, in my judgment, lead sooner or later to a new war in the east of Europe.[22]

While Lloyd George attempted to limit Polish claims upon German territory, the Poles had found a patron in France. All through the negotiations, French support for Poland was the surest guarantee for Polish national interests. "All that we realized," Dmowski was to write, "we owe primarily to France."[23] To destroy Germany as a military threat, France needed a strong ally on Germany's eastern border. In 1914, the French could count on the aid of the Russian army in case of a war with Germany. Now the new Soviet government appeared to Paris as anything but a potential ally. The French feared that the Bolsheviks would attempt to export their revolution and viewed the westward advance of the Red Army with alarm. The German Freikorps battling the Soviet troops in the Baltic region could only be a temporary solution from the French point of view. On 13 June 1919 the Allies demanded the evacuation by the Germans of all territory which had belonged to Russia before 1914.[24] The solution to both French problems, the German and the Russian, seemed to be Poland. France viewed Poland both as a cordon sanitaire against the Soviet Union and as a more traditional counterweight to Germany. French premier Georges Clemenceau advocated accepting Dmowski's demands in toto, because only a Poland "forte, forte, et tres forte" would be able to perform the tasks which French strategy had required.[25] While for France the resurrection of Poland was in part a sentimental affair, the main motive for Franco-Polish cooperation was the interest both states had in keeping Germany under control. Lloyd George characterized French behavior at the peace conference well when he remarked, "A greater Poland suited French policy--and the greater the better.[26] The situation which arose from the confused negotiations at Versailles hardly augured well for the future peace of central Europe. In the first place, the alliance which had won the war seemed to be unraveling. The victorious Allied powers quarreled amongst themselves about the peace. France insisted on a prostrate Germany, while the British recognized that a strong Germany was necessary for the stability of Europe. Whenever possible, France supported the claims of the small states to territories formerly belonging to the Central Powers in order to secure its own position. Britain traditionally sought to maintain a balance of power on the continent and could not support France's actions. France then sought to strengthen the successor states even more as Britain's support waned.

In the case of Czechoslovakia, expansion of territory was easy because of the collapse of the Habsburg Empire at the end of the war.   The inclusion in one state of Bohemia, Moravia, Slovakia, and Ruthenia, all former Habsburg territories, hurt the interests of no great power, although twenty years later a German leader would make much of the "crime" committed at Versailles against the Sudeten Germans.   The French policy of creating powerful neighbors on Germany's borders was completely successful in the case of Czechoslovakia.   The new state had clearly defined and easily defended natural borders in the west and possessed a flourishing arms industry, the Skoda works.

The drawing of Poland's borders created problems not experienced in the formation of Czechoslovakia.   The new state was carved, for the most part, out of the territory of two temporarily powerless countries, Germany and Russia.   The Versailles treaty determined Poland's western borders and the Polish war with Russia determined the eastern.   It was obvious after 1919 that just as Poland and France shared a community of interests with regard to Germany, so did Germany and Russia with regard to Poland.   Throughout the interwar years Germany and the Soviet Union sought at least a reduction of Polish territory to its clearly defined ethnographic limits.[27]   Often they talked of Poland's destruction.   Seeckt's statement that "Poland's existence is unbearable" coincided with the Soviet view.[28]   Cooperation between Germany and the Soviet Union remained for Poland the greatest danger in the years after the war.

Germany   found   the   eastern   settlement   at   Versailles unacceptable.   It is interesting to surmise what the German reaction would have been if the Allies had accepted Dmowski's entire program, including the establishment of an independent East Prussia.   The slight scaling-down by the Allies of Polish demands did nothing to improve the chances for an accommodation between Germany and Poland.   Foreign Minister Hermann Müller proclaimed in July 1919 that "this dictated peace paid no heed to the vital interests of either nation." All of the political parties in Germany agreed with   Müller.   The Communist party of Germany stated that "the situation on Germany's eastern borders is untenable.[29] Especially galling to the Germans was the loss of Danzig, an indisputably German city.   In addition, the separation of East Prussia from the Reich by the Polish corridor appeared to many Germans as an act of naked power, a Gewaltakt without justification, which threatened the future of the area as a German province.[30] Romantic nationalist groups in Germany such as the Ostmarkenverein reacted very strongly to the loss of territory in the east. These groups criticized the Versailles treaty on both historical and economic grounds.   The treaty was an unfair imposition on the German nation, they argued, since all parties had agreed to the armistice, and by implication the peace, on the basis of the Fourteen Points.   One pamphlet of the Ostmarkenverein declared:

There is no indisputably Polish area in the east. Germans and Poles live so closely intermingled that it is impossible to divide the area by nationality. According to Wilson, however, peoples and provinces may not be transferred from one sovereignty to another, like chips in a game.[31]

Neither was the Polish government entirely satisfied with its gains at Versailles. The Allied decision to hold a plebiscite in Upper Silesia had dismayed Polish leaders. The establishment of Danzig as a free city appeared to many in Poland as the worst possible solution.[32] The Polish reaction to the announcement of the peace terms was muted, due no doubt to the high expectations which prevailed in the new state. In fact, the Poles as much as the Germans came to view the Versailles treaty as a Diktat which had ignored vital national interests. Polish minister Stanislaw Glabinski declared that "the treaty was really 'dictated' to 'victorious' Poland in the same way as it was to defeated Germany, which was compelled to accept the peace terms."[33]

Despite its dissatisfaction with the treaty, the Polish government made Versailles the basis of its foreign policy. Alexander Skrzynski, later Polish foreign minister, characterized the treaty as the "Maxima Charta" of Poland, "not only as far as the imagination and sentiments of the Polish nation are concerned, but even objectively in relation to the functions of the new political condition of modern Europe."[34] The Polish national interest, and national survival, demanded literal adherence to the provisions of the treaty. Poland was the cornerstone of Versailles, and a general collapse of the edifice erected in 1919 would crush the new state.

Just as Poland's goal was the maintenance of the treaty, Germany's was its revision. It would not be an exaggeration to characterize Germany's foreign policy throughout the interwar period as a series of attempts to revise those sections of the treaty which it found particularly obnoxious, especially the territorial settlement in the east. In the Locarno treaty of 1925, Germany would come to accept the arrangement on its western borders. Allied attempts to secure an "eastern Locarno" failed because of German unwillingness to renounce its former eastern territories.[35] Gustav Stresemann, German foreign minister from 1923, was a figure often associated with a conciliatory foreign policy. He also had only revisionist thoughts for the east.[36] Public opinion in Germany demanded nothing less than the restoration of the eastern borders of 1914. Agreement on this issue was one of the few unifying factors on the increasingly fragmented German political scene. It was only with the advent of a different system of government in Germany in 1933 that a rapprochement with Poland became possible.

Although revisionist aspirations were prevalent in Germany, the military means for realizing these goals were limited. National power is ultimately a function of military power, and in 1919 Germany possessed little military power. The French had designed the treaty to ensure that the strategic situation of 1919 would endure. The victorious powers gained two advantages by destroying German military capability. First, they knew that the verdict of the war had been, to use Wellington's words after the battle of Waterloo, "the nearest run thing you ever saw in your life." German military power, vanquished on the field after the costly struggle, should not be permitted to rise again. Second, the Allies were aware that Germany would never accept the territorial settlement they had arranged. A disarmed Germany, facing the combined military forces of the Great Powers and hopelessly inferior to such second-rank powers as Poland and Czechoslovakia, would have no recourse to arms as a means to revise the treaty. In terms of German-Polish relations, German disarmament made impossible any rapprochement between the two states. Germany could never come to terms with a Polish state holding West Prussia, Poznan, and half of Upper Silesia, and apparently threatening Pomerania, Brandenburg, and the rest of Silesia. German-Polish enmity, in turn, guaranteed to France a secure ally on Germany's eastern flank. The military clauses were the glue which held together the Versailles settlement.

The military restrictions placed upon Germany were the subject of a dispute between France and Britain. The British wanted to limit the Germans to a small professional army of long-term volunteers, that is, an army on the British model. The French favored a militia-style force based on short-term conscripts less susceptible to what the French viewed as German militarism. On 3 March 1919, Marshal Foch presented the French plan for a German army of 200,000 conscripts with a term of service not to exceed one year. It was to consist of fifteen infantry and five cavalry divisions organized into five corps. The British protested that this plan would allow Germany to train 3,000,000 soldiers over the next fifteen years and insisted on the adoption of their own plan, which called for a smaller force of long-term volunteers. While he feared that allowing the Germans a professional army would enable them to develop an effective officer cadre, Foch relented. Thereafter he concentrated on making the new German army as small as possible.[37]

German officers, of course, had their own ideas about a postwar army. In a cabinet meeting of 24 April 1919, Groener stressed the importance of keeping conscription. In general terms he outlined the need for military power if the state was to survive, and stated that "I cannot accept voluntary disarmament, for this would lead to the partition of Germany, to a Germany such as existed after the Peace of Westphalia."[38] Seeckt held similar views. In a telegram to Groener on 21 April, he stated:

> A one-sided commitment by Germany to disarmament must not be undertaken. However, Germany is ready, in accordance with the Wilson program, to give guarantees that her armament levels will be lowered to the minimum compatible with her security, provided that the other states, in particular our former enemies, give the same guarantees. If they do, Germany proposes: disarmament; retention of conscription, since mercenary armies are too expensive; size of at least 300,000 men; rejection of any control by foreign commissions; freedom in training and drilling; willingness to evacuate the left bank of the Rhine, if France and Belgium set up a corresponding demilitarized zone.[39]

While Seeckt's suggestions were reasonable from the standpoint of French security, especially his offer of a mutually demilitarized Rhineland, his proposals had no effect at Versailles, since they received no hearing.

On first seeing the treaty, Groener commented that since the provisions "were so laughable, they will also be easier to contest."[40] Later that evening, however, he stated to his colleagues that Germany lacked the power to resist the terms.

"Threats are meaningless," he stated, "if one cannot carry them out." The military terms were strict. They limited the German army to 100,000 volunteers organized into seven infantry and three cavalry divisions. In accordance with the British plan, an officer had to serve for twenty-five years, an enlisted man for twelve. The treaty allowed the Germans no aircraft, tanks, or heavy artillery. The General Staff, War Academy, and Cadet School were all dissolved. Allied troops were to remain in occupation of the left bank of the Rhine and the bridgeheads at Köln, Koblenz, and Mainz until German disarmament was complete. The treaty ordered the permanent demilitarization of the Rhineland, as well as of a fifty-kilometer strip on the right bank. The naval clauses of the treaty reflected prewar British anxiety about the German navy. The entire High Seas Fleet was to be turned over to the Allies and the Germans permitted to keep only a token force of ships under ten thousand tons with no submarines. The fortifications on Helgoland and Dune were to be destroyed, and Germany was forbidden to fortify the approaches to the Baltic Sea. No new land fortifications were permitted on any of Germany's borders. An Interallied Control Commission would operate on German soil to verify German compliance with the treaty. Germany also had to acknowledge guilt for starting the war. Finally, the former Kaiser and other high-ranking German leaders were to be handed over to the Allies to stand trial for war crimes.

The last clause was totally unnecessary and vindictive. Despite its lack of real significance, the issue of the Kaiser's extradition came to symbolize for many Germans, and especially for the military men, the gross inequities of the treaty. To Brockdorff-Rantzau, the crimes committed by the Allies, particularly the starving to death of thousands of innocent civilians by the naval blockade, were just as worthy of censure as anything the Kaiser had done.[41] Seeckt stated unequivocally that no officer would support any government which agreed to the Allied demands. The war-guilt clause was an added indignity. Inclusion of these "shame paragraphs" led many reasonable Germans to reject the treaty altogether.

Unlike the largely symbolic clauses regarding the Kaiser and war guilt, the military clauses struck at the heart of Germany's position as a world power. Groener believed that an army of 350,000 men was the minimum necessary for Germany's defense. Seeckt agreed, though he was willing to allow a reduction to 200,000 men, provided it was done gradually. Seeckt's figure represented a middle ground between Groener's demand and the 100,000-man army demanded by the Allies. With only 100,000 men, stated Seeckt, Germany would be powerless against her vindictive and heavily armed enemies. He summed up the situation curtly: "We are defenseless, our opponents aren't."[42]

Seeckt was correct. The military needs of a country in Germany's geographic position far outstripped the capability of a 100,000-man army. Traditionally, the North German Plain had been the parade ground for European armies. Most of the Thirty Years' War of 1618-48 took place on German soil, as the names of the famous battlefields of Breitenfeld, Lützen, and Nördlingen attest. The more ordered and civilized wars of the eighteenth century had perhaps been less destructive than the wars of religion, but had still caused great disruption to the German lands. The greatest campaigns of the nineteenth

century, those of the emperor Napoleon, had with one major
exception all taken place in German areas.   The names of the
major battlefields in the campaigns of 1805-6, 1809, and 1813
are all German: Austerlitz, Jena, Auerstädt, Wagram, and
Leipzig.   Napoleon's logistical system was regressive and
hearkened back to that of the seventeenth century. His troops
lived off the land; they foraged for food and clothing.[43] The
suffering of the German population was therefore very great
during the Napoleonic period.   The unification of Germany and
its development into the greatest continental military power
should be viewed against this historical backdrop of war and
invasion, especially French invasion, in central Europe.
France's cry in 1919 that German forces had invaded French
soil twice in a generation is true only in a limited sense.
In 1870, France had declared war on Germany and had an
offensive strategy.   Its forces bore the name "Army of the
Rhine" and possessed many maps of Prussian territory, almost
none of French.   In 1914, France's military plans called for
the invasion of Alsace-Lorraine with a view to rupturing the
German front and advancing to the Rhine and beyond.[44] In both
conflicts, France's offensives failed to achieve their goals
because of poor staff work and outmoded tactical doctrine.
Both times, German forces seized the strategic initiative, and
the French claimed that they had been invaded by Germany
without provocation.

When the Prussian or German army was weak, as for
instance in 1806, the result was a catastrophe.   After the
twin defeats at Jena and Auerstädt, Prussia ceased to exist as
an independent great power, and King Frederick William III had
to stand by meekly while Napoleon and Tsar Alexander I of
Russia disposed of his realm on the raft at Tilsit.   Much the
same situation faced Germany in 1919, or so thought German
officers.   The imperial army had vanished, the national borders appeared indefensible, and there arose in the east a new
state demanding large chunks of German territory.   Germany's
enemies had some 1,000,000 men in the field.   This was the
background for Groener's demand that Germany keep an army of
at least 350,000 men, plus 200,000 irregular troops.   To him,
the 100,000-man army was insufficient even to maintain order
at home.[45]   The unity of the Reich required a strong army.

Throughout this period, a low-intensity, undeclared war
was taking place on the German-Polish border, which reinforced
the worries of the German officers.   One British officer
described conditions on the Polish front during the summer of
1919:

> One could walk along the front for hours during the
> day without hearing a shot, but when groups of
> several men are seen, the Germans open fire.   Artil-
> lery is even more rarely heard.   At night, there is
> even more firing and fresh shell holes testify to
> recent artillery activity but there are few of them
> when judged by west front standards. . . .   All
> reports to the contrary, it does not appear that the
> Germans will attack.   If they once intended to
> assume an offensive, it is now probable that the
> Polish counter-preparations have made the Boche
> change his mind.   At present, the Germans probably
> fear a Polish attack as much as the Poles fear a
> German attack.[46]

For most German officers, forming a powerful army seemed the best way to deter the Poles from any thoughts of aggression.

Actually, the German army began to reorganize itself even before the Allies imposed the peace terms. On 1 March 1919, at the request of the General Staff, Seeckt drew up a memorandum on the army question. He suggested that the future German army should retain its separate contingents from Prussia, Bavaria, Saxony, Württemberg, and Baden. However, there should be a unified command structure under a war minister and a general staff. The army would consist of 200,000 men and twenty-four divisions. Service in the armed forces would be on a voluntary basis and would be of two years' duration. In addition, a militia (Miliz) would supplement the regular army. Service in the militia would consist of three months of training and a year of service.[47]

By this time the press of events had forced the German government to establish the framework for a new army. Unrest at home was complemented by the situation on the borders. The Freikorps, which had thus far carried on the struggle in the East, had proved unsatisfactory from the perspective of the High Command. While the irregulars had a great deal of fighting spirit, they lacked standardization. Their primary allegiance was to their own officers, rather than to the Reich. The military leaders, in particular Seeckt, did not consider them suitable material for the new army. Germany's needs of the moment required something more akin to the old imperial army, if nowhere near the size of that force. On 6 March, the Reichstag passed a law establishing a provisional army (vorläufige Reichswehr) organized into two corps and twenty-four brigades. The president of the Reich held supreme command in theory, although in fact the defense minister controlled the army. The enlistment period was six months, and the term was automatically extended if neither soldier nor government renounced it.[48]

The provisional army did not replace the Freikorps. Its creation was a response to the current danger which threatened the state with dissolution. In these circumstances the Freikorps continued to play an important role. Since they were among the few men willing to bear arms in Germany at the time, they formed the backbone of the new army. Estimates of their numbers vary, but the consensus is that there were around 400,000 Freikorps troops in 1919 organized into diverse groups of varying effectiveness. They formed an available pool of manpower and entered the provisional Reichswehr as whole units. The 18th Brigade, stationed at Bad Nauheim, consisted of Freikorps troops from Hesse. Likewise, the 24th Brigade was formed out of volunteer bands of security troops.[49] Leadership in the provisional Reichswehr remained in the hands of the imperial officer corps.

Since the new army was only provisional, it is difficult to determine its actual size or fighting efficiency. In all, the army raised forty-four brigades, with those numbered higher than twenty-four merged into the original brigades in October 1919. The provisional Reichswehr contained at its height more than 400,000 men. The entire system lasted only a few months, since German acceptance of the treaty meant that the army had to undergo an immediate reduction in strength. It had served its purpose of protecting Germany's borders. There was no repeat of the loss of Poznan, where an impotent Germany had no choice but to accept a Polish fait accompli.

In addition, the provisional force had successfully maintained order inside Germany.

The treaty had originally stipulated that the 100,000-man army be in place by 13 March 1920, but the Allies had extended this deadline. The new schedule dictated a reduction to 150,000 men by 1 October 1920 and then to 100,000 men by 1 January 1921. The Germans adhered to this schedule and by the later date had created the 100,000-man force which was to bear responsibility for the defense of the state from 1921 to Germany's rearmament in 1935.

The reduction of forces in Germany meant the dissolution not only of the provisional Reichswehr but of many of the volunteer bands as well. As we have seen, Seeckt never really trusted the men of the Freikorps. They lacked, in his words, a "strict military bearing," and often threatened the state as much as they protected it.[50] They reacted to the announcement of their dissolution in a predictable manner. Led by Lieutenant Commander Hermann Erhardt, the 2nd Naval Brigade staged a rebellion against the government in Berlin on 13 March 1920. This was the Kapp Putsch, named for the political figurehead whom the rebels wished to install in power. Opposition from high-ranking army officers,[51] as well as a general strike by the workers of Berlin, led to the withdrawal of the Erhardt Brigade and the collapse of the putsch by 17 March.

The Kapp Putsch found an echo in several key eastern cities, particularly Danzig, Stettin, and Swinemünde. A Western officer who toured these cities in late March 1920 sent the following report:

> In Stettin, the military counterrevolution was a complete success on Saturday, 13 March. The forces then were estimated to be 5,000 Freikorps and 5,000 Baltic troops. The military, by erecting wire defenses, gave the town the impression that the soldiers were afraid. The soldiers shot some harmless people who approached their wire out of curiosity. This aroused the crowd, especially against the Freikorps.[52]

As in Berlin, a general strike by the workers of the eastern cities succeeded in thwarting the putsch by the Freikorps. Luckily for the Germans, this period of severe military disorganization had occurred at a time when the Poles were more concerned with their own eastern border, as we shall see.

With the end of the Kapp Putsch, Germany had come through its most dangerous period. The plebiscite in Upper Silesia had not yet taken place, and a final border settlement with Poland would have to wait. The condition along the rest of the Polish-German border seemed secure. Poland would soon face its own trial by fire, while in Germany, government, army, and population had worked together to put down insurrection from both the Right and the Left. Germany's international position was still weak. The Reich was not "bündnisfähig,"[53] but in the eyes of German officers, the state no longer faced imminent dissolution, as it had in the years 1918 and 1919.

The first crisis for the security of Germany's eastern borders occurred in the summer of 1920, and came not from Poland but from the collapse of the Polish forces facing the

Bolsheviks.[54]   The German government had declared   neutrality
in the Russo-Polish conflict soon after Marshal Pilsudski's
invasion of the Ukraine in the spring.   Now, as troops of
General Mikhail Tukhachevsky's West Front pursued the broken
Polish army, the weak state of the defenses in East Prussia
became apparent to German military leaders.   The army,
undergoing the reorganization demanded by the Allies and
preoccupied with internal affairs in the wake of the failure
of the foolhardy Kapp Putsch, was unable to guarantee the
security of the East Prussian border.   The response of the
local authorities, with support but not direction from the
central government in Berlin, was the creation of irregular
units.   These forces were to consist of Ortswehren, local
militia responsible for the defense of their immediate surroundings, and Grenzwehren, whose task was to augment the
border defense forces which had arisen in the days immediately
following the war.
     The primary purpose of the formation of the two new
forces was to prevent Bolshevik troops from entering East
Prussia, since it appeared that the Polish army was finished.
The specter of invasion by the Russians alarmed a population
with vivid memories of the entry of the Russian army in 1914.
The secondary purpose was to preserve law and order among the
civilian population.   East Prussian Minister President Ernst
Siehr and other influential local politicians feared that the
approach of the Soviet forces would encourage "criminal
elements" in East Prussia to attempt a putsch with the goal of
establishing a Königsberg soviet.[55]   In addition, the collapse
of the Polish army raised the possibility that bands of
demoralized, routed Polish troops would cross the border into
East Prussia in search of food and shelter.   Already in July,
a band of two thousand Polish troops and forty officers had
crossed the border near Grajevo and been disarmed and interned
in the Reichswehr camp at Arys.[56]   The commissioner of
Allenstein feared that if the two brigades of the Reichswehr
currently stationed in East Prussia were dissolved as part of
the troop reductions ordered by the Allies, there would be no
effective force to counter future border violations by Russian
and Polish troops.   He demanded at least that the Reichswehr
units in East Prussia be left alone until the second part of
the army reduction, that from 150,000 to 100,000 men.[57]
     The German government informed the Allies of the decision
to form the border forces on 21 July, during the course of a
long meeting between the ambassador to France, Wilhelm Mayer,
and the French minister Alexandre Millerand.[58]   Predictably,
Millerand was unconvinced of the danger facing East Prussia.
Between the Reichswehr and the Security Police, he maintained,
East Prussia could find sufficient military protection from
border violations.   Mayer pointed out to him the difficulties
of maintaining Reichswehr formations through the Corridor and
warned that if the government did not form some self-defense
organization, the local inhabitants would form their own, with
unpredictable consequences.   Millerand answered that, if the
latter case proved true, no one could really object.   As to
Mayer's request for permission to move troops into the plebiscite areas of Allenstein and Marienwerder, Millerand promised that an Allied commission would visit the area in the
next week.   Mayer warned that the Russians were only eighty
kilometers away, in Grodno, and that they clearly intended to
set up soviets in any area they occupied.

Further developments on the battle front deepened German worries.   By 26 July, it was clear that the battles around Grodno had turned out favorably for the Red Army, and the Poles were still in headlong retreat.   Two Soviet cavalry regiments were as close to the East Prussian border as Augostowo.   Polish border posts only extended as far north as Raygrod.   North of this area, no forces protected the German frontier.   On that same day, the Germans denied the Polish request for use of the railway line Marggrabowa-Lyck-Prosthen for transportation of war materiel, a decision which the Interallied Control Commission approved.   In response to these developments, local German officials ordered, first of all, an increase in the number of border defense troops in the districts of Oletzko, Lyck, and Johannisburg by 150 infantry and 30 cavalry.   In addition, the commissioner for the East Prussian plebiscite ordered an increase of 400 men in the Security Police for the area.   The local German authorities requested that the Allied forces concentrate at Allenstein, with the Italian battalion at Lyck moving immediately.   For the Germans, asking Allied help to fight the Poles and Russians had potential disadvantages.   Justifiable concern existed that the Allies, and especially the French, would be more interested in saving Poland than in protecting German neutrality.   One German official expressed worry that the French would use East Prussia as a "deployment area" against the Russians.   Recognition of the inability of the Reichswehr to protect the borders and unwillingness to ask the Allied powers for help was the basis for the decision to form the new Grenzwehr.   "We must convince the Allies we have the strength, if only the Grenzwehr are permitted," wrote the commissioner on 26 July.[59] At the same time, he thought it might be better to wait until an emergency had arisen, then threaten to form defense forces whether or not the Allies approved.   For their part, the Allies were willing to let reinforcements of the German army intervene to preserve the integrity of the East Prussian borders, but not to sanction the formation of any kind of auxiliary force.[60] Two weeks later, the Germans were still waiting for an answer to their request to send more troops into the plebiscite area.

The claim of the German government that if the Allies refused to allow the establishment of a militia, the civilian population of the threatened areas would do so spontaneously was not merely a negotiating ploy.   On 17 July a letter from the chairman of the Masurian League to the authorities in Berlin declared that the population of those regions was very much disturbed by the prospects of a Russian invasion.   The resounding vote of confidence in the Reich which the people of the plebiscite areas had delivered must be repaid by military protection against the Red Army.   "The rest of the Reich can rely on the security police, but East Prussia is lost without adequate military protection," he wrote.[61] The director of the Foreign Office's Peace Commission, Göppert, cited the rising "anxiety and nervousness" of the local population and begged Allied permission to send troops into Allenstein and Marienwerder.

The situation on the battle front only increased the anxiety in East Prussia.   A military intelligence report of 1 August mentioned Russian advances toward Ostrolenka, with the front running west of Bialystok and Brest-Litovsk.   In the south, the two armies battled for possession of Tarnopol.[62]

To most German military observers, the fall of Warsaw appeared imminent, a prospect which filled most of them with joy. Seeckt stated in January 1920, "I renounce any aid to Poland, even if there be a danger that Poland will be swallowed up. On the contrary, I'm counting on it."[63] One month later he wrote:

> Only in a tight union with Great Russia does Germany have the possibility of regaining her position of power in the world. In Poland France seeks an eastern battlefield against Germany. Now France is shivering for Poland . . . and Germany is supposed to save its own mortal enemy. At this time no one should expect Germany to lift a finger to help even if the storm breaks over Poland.[64]

Even though he would greet Poland's demise "with thanks," he refrained from recommending military aid to Russia, since he knew that Germany's military capabilities were not sufficient to justify such a course, which would certainly lead to an attack by France against Germany. Later, however, Seeckt stated that the real danger in 1920 was the advance of the Bolshevik forces. Germany refused to enter into combat against the Red Army only because such a course would have played directly into Britain's strategy of recruiting continental armies to fight its battles. Germany would fight to defend its own borders, he stated, "and our enemies should arm us for this purpose out of their own self-interest."[65]

The views of General von Seeckt towards the Russo-Polish War were complex and reflect the nature of the man. In February 1920, before Pilsudski's invasion of the Ukraine, Seeckt had already proclaimed the Red Army to be a future danger for Germany. He estimated its numbers at 1,500,000 men and credited its leadership in the Civil War with understanding how to apply force at the decisive spot. Victory for the Bolsheviks in the Civil War meant a Soviet attack on Poland in the summer, he stated. Poland would succumb to such an attack, not only because the Polish forces were so much smaller, but because bolshevism had so infected the Polish army that the Poles would be unable to resist. Shortages of food and clothing also lowered Polish troop morale. In addition, there was a psychological factor at work. "Poland's will to fight on its western frontier is motivated by hatred of Germany," Seeckt declared, "but there is no comparable motive to resist in the East." This incredible statement shows that whatever Seeckt's merits as a soldier, he was ignorant of Polish historical development. In fact, his military analysis also proved to be wrong, although many shared his mistake. He judged the Polish army to be of inconsistent quality and underestimated its resilience. Poles trained in Prussian Poland he regarded as good soldiers. The Haller troops had lost much of their worth, due to the loss of most of their French elements. Those troops from Russian Poland he regarded as poor. He perceived parallel differences amongst the Polish officers. Staff positions tended to be the exclusive province of former Habsburg officers; Russian Poles tended to dominate the middle- and lower-ranking posts. In Seeckt's view, this officer cadre "of incompetent men" was unsuitable for modern warfare. Worse yet, the Poles lacked a proven higher leadership. Seeckt was merely echoing the thoughts of many who did not believe that Pilsudski was a capable leader. Apart from the leadership factor, simple arithmetic showed that the results of a Russo-Polish War would be a foregone conclusion, since Seeckt believed that the Poles would be unable to field more than 450,000 men. Even this relatively small army would have to disperse, for large forces would have to stay behind the front to garrison West Prussia, Poznan, and Galicia.

Belief in a Bolshevik victory in the summer did not lead Seeckt to suggest military support for Poland. Rather, he recommended that Germany bide its time, since the military and political situation permitted no other course of action:

> It should be established without a doubt that Germany denies any help to Poland. Poland is France's creation, and therefore our lasting enemy. Militarily, we find ourselves in a totally unbearable situation, with an open border, a separated East Prussia, and a threatened Berlin. So long as this situation does not improve, there can be no talk of even a relatively secure position for Germany to take in the East.[66]

With regard to the Soviet threat, Germany would only defend its own borders, he proclaimed, rather than come to the aid of Poland. At the same time, he recognized that the forces of the Reich were not sufficient to defeat a Russian attack. Successful defense had two preconditions: "The most important is the decisive will of the people or even a majority of them to take up the struggle once again. The second is the lifting of the restrictive military clauses of the Versailles Treaty." The latter point was the key to Seeckt's attitude in the Russo-Polish War. The small army permitted to the Germans by the treaty was insufficient to defeat a Russian attack. But the treaty specified that the German army was to be large enough to perform border guard duties. In addition, the Allies had tied the entire operation of German disarmament to the goal of universal disarmament and a future free from war. Seeckt therefore thought that the Russo-Polish War would force the Allies to alter the terms of the treaty, all the more so since France and England had an obvious interest in fighting bolshevism. If the Allies refused Germany the means to self-defense, he said, then Germany would have to break the treaty.

Besides being based on faulty political premises, Seeckt's policy was risky at best. He denied support to Poland, even if it appeared that Poland would collapse. Yet it is hard to see what good could have come to Germany from a Polish defeat. The consequences of a Polish defeat for Germany could have been catastrophic. Germany would have been alone, facing a victorious Red Army, with only 100,000 men between the Bolsheviks and Berlin. The only way out of this situation would have been Allied intervention on the side of Germany; Allied actions would thereby have become the crucial factor in German defense policy. While observers then and now have praised Seeckt for his neutrality policy, neutrality meant that Germany had surrendered its freedom of action in the military sphere. Admittedly, no alternative comes readily to mind, since it would have been impossible for any German government to suggest military aid to Poland. The fact

remains, though, that the decisive action which saved the
German eastern provinces was a Polish military victory.
Pilsudski, not Seeckt, saved East Prussia from the Bolsheviks.
Seeckt was well aware of his helpless position. In a
memorandum of 31 July, at a time when Tukhachevsky's offensive
was in full swing and the Red cavalry was approaching the East
Prussian border, Seeckt discussed the military and political
situation in the east.[67] At this time the right wing of the
Russian forces had reached Kolno, about one hundred kilometers
from Soldau in East Prussia. Seeckt predicted an attempt to
cut the Warsaw-Danzig line of communications on the Vistula,
as well as a drive for the railway connecting Warsaw and
Soldau via Mlawa. If this occurred, he stated, East Prussia
would be in grave danger. Yet in the memorandum, which was of
course for official use only, Seeckt offered no military
protection to the inhabitants of the area. Instead, to prevent
the war from engulfing East Prussia, he suggested that the
German government make a public appeal to the Russians to
spare the region. For someone who followed the precepts of
Clausewitz, this reliance on the good nature of an unruly
neighbor is surprising. Given the particular bases of his
strategy enumerated in February, however, he had left himself
no other choice. Seeckt defended his policy for political
reasons; he could scarcely do so for military ones. "Such a
step corresponds to the hopes of the German people and will
not fail to have a profound impact on the German and Polish
inhabitants of the separated areas," he wrote. What remained
to be seen was the impression such a public appeal would have
had on a Soviet government and army flushed with victory.
Even a lesser military figure such as Captain Georg
Escherich of the Bavarian Einwohnerwehr was aware of the
danger of Seeckt's plan of action.[68] In a letter to the
chancellor on 27 July 1920, Escherich warned of the proba-
bility that a Polish defeat would result in a Bolshevik government in Warsaw. "This would mean that the former German
districts, areas still inhabited predominantly by Germans,
would be at the mercy of Poland's red regiments, and that
Bolshevism would press in on East Prussia from all sides."
Escherich waxed apocalyptic. After the Bolshevik hordes conquered East Prussia, they would attack Germany and
Czechoslovakia, with good prospects of success against Prague.
Silesia would be the next domino to fall, "broken by a red
wave from three sides," which would create a "Bolshevik wedge"
into left-leaning Saxony. Bavaria would then stand alone.
Escherich complained that the Reich had done nothing to ward
off this peril and suggested the formation of border defense
forces for all the threatened territories, Pomerania,
Brandenburg, Silesia, and Bavaria, as well as East Prussia.
The Reichswehr, he suggested, was interested only in the
political aspects of the crisis, that is, the question of
whether to fight for or against the Entente. The possibility
existed of a split between "Red and White Reichswehr," he
claimed, which would have had the disastrous effect of making
Germany a theater of war for French and British forces fighting the Red Army. A strong border defense would keep Germany
at peace, he stated, and if the government did not take the
lead in organizing this force, the threatened population would
do so on its own. Escherich even offered to send his own
force to East Prussia, the Organization Escherich, or Orgesch.
These troops, "excellent, experienced men, loyal to the

constitution, from all parts of Germany," were ready to ward off the danger arising from the imminent Polish defeat. Escherich and his men did indeed travel to East Prussia, where they scared the civilian government as much as they scared the Poles and Russians. Still, Escherich had determined correctly the true strategic situation in the east. East Prussia needed guns and men, not smooth phrases, to protect itself from the horrors of a new war.

At first, the government in Berlin took few steps to protect East Prussia, which reflected a split between those who wanted to exploit the situation to weaken the Versailles treaty and those who wanted to help the Poles in order to curry favor with the Entente. In a cabinet meeting of 22 July, the government declared a state of emergency in East Prussia and entrusted General von Dassel, the commander of Defense District I, with defensive preparations in the beleaguered province. In addition, it ordered border defense preparations to proceed along the entire eastern border.[69]

Irregular defense forces had arisen in almost every section of Germany in the immediate aftermath of the war. On 23 November 1918 Hindenburg had ordered the formation of border guard units to preserve domestic order and protect the eastern borders.[70] In December, the High Command began to encourage former officers to recruit forces on their own.[71] In East Prussia, an appeal from Oberpräsident Batocki appeared in a Königsberg paper on 26 January 1919. "The fate of East Prussia depends upon honorable, patriotic, and capable men fulfilling their duty to defend province and fatherland, father and mother and child, through service in the East Prussian militia." The impetus for his appeal was the danger that the province faced from Bolshevik and Polish troops, although he stressed the former over the latter. "Whoever has experienced or heard about the Russian invasion of East Prussia in 1914, or the Bolshevik war in the Baltic lands, or the terror inside Russia, knows, despite all the talk of our own German Bolsheviks, what will happen to East Prussia, if we do not defend our homes immediately and with full force." Since East Prussia needed deeds more than words, Batocki declared himself ready, despite his fifty-one years, to return to service as a "simple soldier."[72] In Insterburg, a recruiting commission organized local infantry units, as well as an artillery battery formed from the remnants of the three batteries of the 1st Battalion of the 1st Artillery Regiment.[73] Developments in East Prussia were indicative of those elsewhere in the Reich. A law passed on 25 April 1919 had extended the system of Einwohnerwehr to all German towns.[74] These units were subordinate to the Reichswehr minister. Their officers were military men, their manpower civilian. Their mission was to maintain law and order in the villages and towns, and their light armament, pistols, rifles, carbines, and some machine guns, reflected this fact. The French historian Jacques Benoist-Mechin described their equipment as "a sash with a sword or baton, a steel helmet, a haversack and a bottle, two strips of bandages and a special brassard." The system of Einwohnerwehr grew quickly. General Georges Nollet of the Allied Control Commission estimated their number at over 1,000,000 men, equipped with rifles and 8,500 machine guns.[75]

Besides the regular and irregular military forces, there were available to the German authorities in East Prussia the

militarized police forces, the security police and the border
police. The government had taken steps in June to strengthen
these forces, especially those units serving near the border,
by reducing the size of the headquarters units. However, this
measure had little effect, since police units had smaller
headquarters units than the regular army. Other measures to
strengthen the border defenses included an increase in mounted
patrol activity on the border and improved cooperation between
the two police organizations. Still, there was one insur-
mountable difficulty in using the police as a defense force on
the border. This stemmed from the essential difference in
mission between police and army. The police policed--that is,
they regulated border traffic, checked papers, and defended
the state against espionage and smuggling. The mission of the
army was to defend the state from enemy attack and, once
joined in battle, to engage the enemy in a decisive battle and
defeat it. Despite the military aspects of police organi-
zation--weaponry, drills, uniforms, and the like--the police
were no more trained to perform army functions and defeat a
foreign invader than the army was trained to function as a
police force. Most notably, the police were deficient in
heavy weapons and training for maneuver warfare. The Allies
failed to realize that the police were insufficient protection
for Germany's borders. Throughout the summer crisis, two
ideas formed the basis of Allied strategy. First, they
believed that the German police would be able to defend the
border against the Red Army. Second, the Allies would condone
strengthening of the Reichswehr only if the police failed in
their mission.

The activity reports from the East Prussian police forces
indicate clearly the limits of police power in an armed conflict.[76] The director of the police in the region had his
hands full merely regulating the border traffic. Traffic
between East Prussia and Danzig was particularly heavy in both
directions, with over 6,000 persons and a large number of
vehicles in June alone. Of these the police turned back 78
because of unsatisfactory papers. On the border with Memel,
over 1,500 persons crossed the border in both directions, but
of 495 persons attempting to enter Germany, the border posts
had turned back 109. The border guards were kept most busy on
the Lithuanian frontier, where over 50,000 persons had
attempted to enter Germany in June. Apparently the guards had
to stop individual checks on those involved, since all but 181
entered Germany unchallenged. Counter-espionage also occupied
the attention of the police. In June, they arrested a German
officer who was found to be in the service of the Allied
Control Commission at Kowno. The police were also concerned
with an increase in Latvian and Estonian espionage activities
in Germany. It is clear that the workload of the police was
heavy enough without having to function as an ad hoc army.
Apart from their possible utility as a last-ditch force, the
police could not guarantee the inviolability of the East
Prussian frontier.

The realization that the province was in danger and could
not rely on its police forces for protection led Oberpräsident
Siehr to order the formation of a new defense force. To
remove the confusion of command which the presence of a large
number of private armies had created in the province, Siehr
wanted to enroll all irregular forces into a single defense
organization. This action would avoid the possibility of a

sharp conflict between the Right and the Left, a danger made more threatening by the formation of the right-wing East Prussian Orgesch (Preu) several weeks before. Indeed, Siehr had reservations about allowing the Orgesch (Preu) into his proposed defense force. He had found it easy to reach agreement with the leadership of the Social Democratic Party of Germany about the formation of the new defense forces. It was otherwise with the Orgesch leaders, who insisted on the right to elect their own district leaders and far-reaching military authority in civilian affairs. Siehr agreed that lower ranking officers should be elected by their men, but insisted that appointment of staff officers should be the responsibility of the civilian district councillor. In their disagreement, of course, Siehr and the Orgesch leaders were echoing the arguments about the role of the army in the German state which had been a regular feature of political discourse in Wilhelminian Germany. Siehr feared a putsch from the Right as much as he feared a Soviet invasion and the establishment of a Bolshevik regime in East Prussia. He accused the Orgesch of seeking to establish a state within the state and demanded that the new force be free from "partisan one-sidedness." He therefore reluctantly excluded the Orgesch from the new unified defense structure, even though he recognized its military ability. His position was that "a self-defense organization as a support for the normal security organs (army and police) may only be tolerated if it is controlled strictly by the state. Otherwise it does more harm than good and it is better to suppress it entirely."[77]

The decisive factor which led Siehr to form the new forces was the state of the Reichswehr in East Prussia. The Allies claimed that there were some 40,000 German troops in East Prussia, although in mid-August the number was actually closer to 15,000. The 1st Infantry Brigade was the principal German unit in the province.[78] This unit received reinforcements to deal with the emergency, but the reinforcements were very small, only about 2,000 men in all. They included four battalions: the II/6, with a strength of 755 men; the II/24, with 562 men; a coastal defense battalion of 446 men; and a formation scraped together from the reserves of Defense District II, which contained 446 men. The arrival of these forces raised the total number of the Reichswehr in East Prussia to 17,162.[79] The government in Berlin promised another four battalions by 9 September. These units were understrength, however, and included a weak detachment of 546 marines which would be of limited value for operations in the interior of the province.[80] Even with the arrival of these units, Reichswehr forces in East Prussia still numbered less than 20,000 men. The troops had the dual responsibility of guarding the border and carrying out the disarmament provisions of the Versailles treaty. While the latter was, for good reason, never an item of high priority with the Germans, the ability of the army to perform the former task was about to receive a severe test.

The military situation in July, when Siehr published his orders to form a new defense force, was grave. The new map of Europe had cut off East Prussia from the Reich and forced the province into the role of Germany's advance guard to the east. At the same time, the disarmament provisions of the treaty had rendered East Prussia practically indefensible. Strict neutrality in the Russo-Polish War was necessary, but should one of the hostile powers seek to violate this neutrality, there was little that the military forces in East Prussia could do to prevent it. To Siehr, only the mobilization of the entire population of the province would suffice to defend German neutrality. Siehr desired a broad-based movement, made up of farmers and workers, artisans and bourgeois, "a united front of all East Prussian men in the defense of their home-land," which would include all political elements from the extreme Right to the extreme Left.[81] As we have seen, the stubbornness of the Orgesch leadership prevented Siehr from realizing this goal. At the same time, he dissolved all armed bands not included in the new organization. He also ordered the formation of a provincial committee to coordinate defense measures. The committee included representatives of wealthy landowners, merchants, agricultural workers, and the Social Democratic party.

Siehr published his "Order for the Formation of Ortswehren in East Prussia" on 7 August 1920.[82] He stressed the provisional nature of these forces by stating that they would only be used if the regular security forces were no longer able to protect the province. The mission of the Ortswehren, he proclaimed, was the protection of Germandom in the east, the guarding of neutrality in the Russo-Polish War, and the maintenance of law and order at home. Admission was open to all classes of the population and all members of any party who renounced the use of force to change the constitu-tion. The new Ortswehren absorbed all existing self-defense organizations, and Siehr proscribed the formation of any such groups. The minimum age for membership in the Ortswehr was twenty years; that for the Grenzwehr was eighteen. Both organizations would consist of previously trained recruits. East Prussia, Siehr recognized, had no time in which to train its own force. Still, the order decreed that untrained or underage recruits could serve as "defense aides." These appointments included administrative and logistics personnel. Finally, entry into the Ortswehr bound the recruit to five promises: obedience to the constitutional regime; adherence to the mobilization notices; adherence to duty and to the orders of the leadership; careful maintenance of weapons and equipment; and participation in stipulated assemblies. For this last purpose a soldier would receive a statement of orders, which would also serve as an official receipt for his weaponry.

Siehr constructed an elaborate administrative mechanism for recruiting the defense forces. On the local level, local, district, or parish committees made up of seven members had the responsibility for admitting recruits. The committee had to represent all parties of the district. The Landrat, a representative of the Prussian government and therefore re-sponsible to Berlin, named the members of the local committee, with the mayor and the leading members of the community acting as advisors. In cities not belonging to any district, the mayor named the committee. All members had to sign a written declaration that "they accepted the constitution," and their basic task was to keep those who thought otherwise out of the Ortswehr.

The next step up the administrative ladder was the dis-trict committee. This body was made up of six men; its task was to handle complaints against the local committee. The Kreisrat, or district councillor, sat at the head. The order forming the district committees stipulated that of the six members, at least one had to be an agricultural worker and one a landowner. The purpose of this stipulation was to ensure that the cities in each district did not dominate the committee. To the district committee went the duty of controlling all forces in the district with regard to their formation and organization. The committee also received the right to recommend to the Landrat the dissolution of any defense forces if these forces no longer conformed to the regulations. Finally, the district committee requisitioned supplies for the defense forces from the civilian population.

The provincial committee confirmed the members of the district committee and was responsible for the overall administration of the Ortswehr. This committee included ten members of all classes and parties who were loyal to the constitution. The provincial committee chose its own chairman and had the responsibility of deciding protests against any decision of the district committee, as well as approving any organizational decisions made on the lower administrative levels. The chairman, in turn, exerted control over the administration and organization of the Ortswehr. Still, only Siehr himself could decide to dissolve a formation or to remove an officer.

Siehr's order said little about the actual organization of the Ortswehr, since he preferred to leave this matter up to the local committees. He did, however, make special mention of the Grenzwehr, or border defense force: "Members who pledge themselves to special duty on the border are to be designated specifically in the rolls as border defense. Border defense will be called in case of danger, to protect the province in cooperation with the army and the police." In order to free as many men as possible for such an eventuality, Siehr decreed that all independent (kreisfrei) cities should take only recruits for the Grenzwehr. This was possible since the Sicherheitspolizei were already active in those cities.

Leadership in the new militia lay in the hands of a commander called the Wehrführer. This military leader was chosen by the rank and file. Leaders received orders from and were responsible to the civilian leadership, especially the Landrat, or in the independent cities, the mayor. The border defense possessed a somewhat different chain of command, since it reported back to the district councillor and the district committee. This condition reflected the more general mission of the border defense to defend a larger area than its immediate surroundings. Likewise, although local officials confirmed the leaders nominated for the Ortswehr, Siehr himself confirmed those of the border defense. Leaders in both organizations served for one year. The length of the term actually depended, however, on the confidence of the soldiers, since a request by a simple majority of the soldiers in a unit was sufficient to call new elections. The election of leaders was not to be a mere popularity contest. Siehr stipulated that only those men who had actual military experience and who had served at least one year at the front were eligible to lead the new forces. This condition reflected his belief, shared by many in Germany, that there was a great hostility between "staff" and "front" soldiers in the German army.[83] Besides their tactical importance, the leaders of the Ortswehr possessed one important power. This was the ability to call

out sections of the militia if there were a threat to public
safety.

The creation of these new forces was a start toward
German military respectability, but no more than that. In
numbers, the new forces were impressive, particularly when
compared to the shrinking regular army. Still, large armies
do not win battles; good ones do. The East Prussian Ortswehr
was little more than a collection of the scraps of the once-
formidable German military machine. The First World War had
transformed the German army from a superbly trained regular
force to an ill-trained militia with a veteran cadre. In
Germany, the end of the war had also brought mass discharges
from the army in order to comply with the Allies' demands for
army reduction. The best soldiers, of course, stayed with the
regular army. A large pool of recently discharged veterans,
who often joined private armies, was created. Siehr's edict
tried to organize these unruly elements. Still, he was aware
of the low reliability of these freebooters, and considered
them suitable mainly to put down domestic insurrection. He
even thought it necessary to issue an edict describing exactly
when and where he would permit the forces to fire their
weapons. His order specifically forbade shooting into or over
the heads of a crowd, and called for greater fire discipline.[84] Siehr evidently had doubts about the usefulness and
loyalty of his new troops.

Siehr's new militia had one other glaring weakness. This
was a lack of heavy weapons. There were some carbines, heavy
guns, trench mortars, and machine guns from World War I stocks
scheduled for destruction, but the authorities had already
loaded most of these for shipment back to the Reich. The
commissioner of Allenstein ordered the retention of these
weapons in East Prussia, but there is no mention in the
records of their distribution to the militia, which remained a
light infantry force.[85] They lacked the careful training,
however, which in light infantry forces has historically com-
pensated for firepower deficiencies. If we judge the Ortswehr
by Napoleon's maxim that "the worse the troops, the more
artillery they require," then we see the essential weakness of
East Prussia's defenses in the summer of 1920.

It was at this moment that Pilsudski launched his
decisive offensive on the Wieprz south of Warsaw.[86] Advancing
against little opposition, the Polish forces caught units of
the Soviet West Front in the flank and put them to flight.
The lure of Warsaw had fixed Soviet attention in that
direction, ensuring that Pilsudski's maneuver achieved almost
total surprise. This caused the total rout of Russian forces
in the north, including those near the German border. While
the Polish victory appeared to have removed the justification
for the existence of the local defense forces, the sudden
change of fortune in the Russo-Polish War resulted in a new
danger for East Prussia. Whereas before, the main worry was
that the Red Army would attempt to conquer the province, the
concern now was how to handle those Russian troops who crossed
the German border to avoid the pursuing Poles. The numbers
involved here, compared to the numbers of Polish troops interned in July, were astronomical. By the end of August, some
fifty thousand Russian troops had entered East Prussia.[87] It
was necessary to round up these troops, disarm them, guard
them, and evacuate them. The militia, however, was clearly
insufficient for this task.

The government in Berlin received daily detailed reports on the military situation from its representative to the Allied commission in Königsberg, Major Schürmann.[88] On 21 July, he reported a conversation which he had had with Colonel Langlois of the French army. The Bolshevik forces had recently seized Bialystok, Baranowiczi, and Grodno, and were advancing along the axis Kowno-Suwalki-Lyck. Their goal, Langlois stated, was Warsaw, and they were assembling their main force with this objective in mind. It was possible that, after the destruction of Poland, the Soviet gaze would turn further to the west. Langlois believed the method of attack would be propaganda, not military force. In the immediate future, there was a clear danger to East Prussia should the Poles make a stand on the Bug. In this case, declared Langlois, there was a strong possibility that the Bolsheviks would attempt to outflank the Polish left wing by marching through the plebiscite areas. He promised Schürmann that the Entente forces would help with the protection of the border, but their weakness in numbers--only two battalions in all-- necessitated the use of the German army for this task. Interestingly enough, he did not believe Königsberg to be immediately threatened. If Warsaw were to fall into Bolshevik hands, Poznan would soon follow, which would represent a direct threat to Berlin. In any case, Langlois maintained that the threat to Berlin was more serious than the threat to Königsberg.

The military authorities in East Prussia--that is, Defense District I--were not idle during the Soviet advance. The first measure taken was the concentration and assembly of the available Reichswehr units in the area most threatened by the Red Army. A defense district order of 20 July ordered the 20th Infantry Brigade to the area Angerburg-Korschen- Rastenburg, the 1st Infantry Brigade to the area Insterburg- Gumbinnen, the 1st Cavalry Regiment to Mehlkuhnen-Eydtkuhnen- Stallupönen-Pillkallen, the 2nd Cavalry Regiment with two squadrons to Goldap, the 21st Armored Platoon to Rastenburg, and the 28th Armored Platoon to Goldap.[89] These deployments gave the eastern face of East Prussia no immediate military protection, but did place strong forces on the possible routes to Königsberg. The concentration of the 1st Brigade on the Pregel river was especially reminiscent of the deployment in 1914 of General von Francois's 1st Infantry Corps, which had defended Gumbinnen against the advance on the Russian 1st Army. From its position, the 1st Brigade controlled the Königsberg railway, as well as the rail nexus at Insterburg.

Schürmann informed the Allied representatives in Königsberg of the deployment on 22 July.[90] He included a plea for the maintenance of the German army at its current manpower level. This latter point met with a chilly reception from the Allies. The British representative, Lieutenant-Colonel MacKenzie, was especially hostile. He accused the Germans of helping the Bolsheviks and desiring the destruction of Poland. These sentiments were particularly noticeable amongst the civilian population of East Prussia. He attributed the recently improved performance of the Red Army to the many Germans serving in it. The Bolshevik forces, he stated, now appeared more disciplined and nationalistic.

Events in the war overtook the German deployment almost immediately. After the fall of Grodno on 23 July, the quick advance of the Russian forces threatened East Prussia from the south rather than the east.   Red Army cavalry spent the week following the fall of Grodno riding close reconnaissance on the East Prussian frontier through Grajevo, Szczucin, and Kolno.[91]

The district of Allenstein was the first area to make provisions for the security of its border, since the advance of the Bolsheviks most directly threatened the plebiscite areas.   On 28 July, German officials, including the commissioner, conferred with Colonel Hawker of the British army, inspector of the Plebiscite Police.   The meeting resulted in the nomination of Colonel Hawker as commander of all police forces in the district and the French Colonel Nuir as commander of all military forces.   This did not entail the placing of German soldiers under foreign command, however, since the plebiscite regulations still barred regular German troops from the area.   Should the Allies decide to declare martial law in Allenstein, Colonel Nuir would take command of all military and police forces.   Colonel Hawker would then relinquish his command.   The participants in the 28 July meeting also decided to strengthen the border defenses in the Oletzko, Lyck, and Johannisburg districts to protect German neutrality and to ward off streams of "unwanted refugees, bands, and deserters."   According to the latest intelligence, they believed that there was no immediate danger to Ortelsburg, Neidenburg, or Osterode.   In fact, Red Army cavalry would pass within miles of Neidenburg in the ensuing few weeks, which demonstrated the basic problem facing the German authorities throughout the summer. Virtually every attempt to create a defense force in a threatened district came too late to protect the border in that district.   If either the Poles or Russians had intended to violate East Prussian neutrality, they could certainly have done so.   In this case, by the time these measures came into effect, the danger facing Lyck and Johannisburg was secondary to that facing Neidenburg and Ortelsburg.

For the immediate strengthening of the border watch, the plebiscite police forces sent a small force of 30 cavalry from the mounted company at Arys and 150 infantry to the threatened areas.   In addition, Colonel Hawker promised to try to call back 450 men who had recently been discharged from the plebiscite police.   The German officer present at the meeting insisted that the police receive those heavy weapons which had been earmarked for transportation back to Germany, but Hawker stated that this was a matter for the Interallied Commission in Königsberg, headed by Colonel Langlois, and that the colonel was not likely to look with favor on the suggestion. Hawker did allow the newly expanded police to be outfitted with carbines, however.[92]

The rout of Tukhachevsky's forces, as well as the realization that the initial measures to provide for the security of the province had been inadequate, led Siehr to propose the formation of a larger and better-trained force, called the "volunteer   police,"   or   Freiwilliges   Polizeitruppe Ostpreussens.[93] Events had overtaken his first strategy of relying on the militia.   More than fifty thousand Russian and Polish troops stood on German soil, and there was a need to disarm and evacuate them.   Siehr decided to use the forces he had created in August as the basis for a new force; the volunteer   police force was formed from personnel previously enrolled in the militia.   This did not mean that the new force

was merely an extension of the old. There were essential differences between the volunteer police troop and the militia.
Whereas the latter was tied to a specific region and organized
for duty only in that region, the volunteer police had the
organizational structure of a regular army. While its size was
not great, it possessed the mobility to fight anywhere in the
province.   It also had the potential,   although there is   no
evidence that Siehr had this in mind, to act as the cadre for
an expanded organization; the militia had no such potential.
The new force, organized on 1 September 1920, cooperated
closely with the army, which provided some long-needed inte-
gration of the multifarious military forces in East Prussia.
The establishment of the volunteer police was a giant step
forward along the road to German military rebirth, a fact
which the Allies did not fail to notice.

        The volunteer police consisted of four battalions.   At
the head of the force was an organizational staff formed from
headquarters elements of Defense District I. The headquarters
was located at the Reichswehr camp at Arys.   Although Siehr
retained final control, in cooperation with the district coun-
cillors, over mobilization of the volunteer police, the
defense district retained tactical control over the force.

        Each district in the affected areas of East Prussia had
to provide a platoon (Zug) to the police troop.   The strength
of the platoon was at least forty enlisted men, one platoon
leader, one noncommissioned officer, and eight squad leaders.
Only former members of the militia were eligible for membership. This regulation meant that the police troop was a force
of infantry with only a few personnel capable of handling
artillery.   Siehr intended to form a cavalry arm, which would
have been more suitable for border patrol duties, at a later
date.   The journey from each district to the concentration
area was to begin on 7 September and end by 14 September.
Once in their concentration areas, the troops were to form up
into Hundertschaften, or companies.[94] The staff personnel for
the companies and battalions received orders to assemble by 6
September.   Chain of command was identical to the regular
army, with lieutenants commanding platoons, captains commanding companies, and majors commanding battalions.   The
orders stressed the desirability of filling officer positions
with veterans of the front, just as in the Ortswehr. The army
supported the battalion staff by providing two clerks and two
ordnance experts.   The army also provided wagons and a field
kitchen to each company.   The battalion received no horses,
since it could procure these from the Russian forces interned
in the area. The police troop, like its parent organizations,
was a territorial force.   It recruited in strictly defined
geographical regions.   Unlike the militia, though, it
possessed a chain of command which allowed it much greater
flexibility.   The 1st Battalion, for instance, had its headquarters at Heilsberg.   Any part of its three companies could
concentrate to meet an attack on that part of East Prussia.
Likewise, each of the three remaining battalions could concentrate four hundred to six hundred men in any part of their
assigned areas.   Each group of militia had been responsible
only for its own town or village.

        The deployment of the new force ensured that each threat-
ened part of East Prussia had some military protection,
although the battalions were too far apart for mutual support.
There were four battalions, headquartered at Heilsberg,

Angerburg, Elbing, and Bischofsburg. The 1st Battalion at
Heilsberg contained men from the Königsberg region and was
responsible for the defense of East Prussia's first city.   It
consisted of three companies, based at Braunsberg, Heilsberg,
and Bartenstein.   The first company, at Braunsberg, had four
platoons,   recruited from Braunsberg,   Heiligenbeil,   and
Königsberg city and environs.   Its operational area was the
area south and west of Königsberg. The second company had its
headquarters at Heilsberg, and consisted of three platoons
located at Heilsberg, Preussisch-Eylau, and Fischhausen. This
unit was responsible for the defense of the area south of
Königsberg.   The third company had its base at Bartenstein,
but it was actually responsible for the defense of the eastern
approaches to Königsberg.   Its platoons, four in all, were in
Friedland, Gerdanen, Wehlau, and Labiau. This company had a
much larger front to defend than the other two, even though
the military situation made unlikely a threat to Königsberg
from the east.
     As ordered by Siehr, each of these companies and head-
quarters units had a Reichswehr support unit.   The 1st
Battalion staff, as well as the first company, drew on the
logistical network of the 3rd Battalion/1st Infantry Regiment.
The second company used the army camp at Heilsberg, and the
third company drew on the noncommissioned officers barracks at
Bartenstein.   In addition, the 1st Battalion had at its
disposal the prewar fortifications around Königsberg and to
the south, the so-called "Heilsberg triangle."
     The 2nd Battalion, based at Angerburg, consisted of the
fourth, fifth, and sixth companies, based at Darkehmen,
Angerburg, and Goldap, respectively.   The responsibility of
this battalion was the defense of the eastern face of the
province, running roughly in a crescent from Angerburg out to
Goldap and Gumbinnen and finally through Raguet to Tilsit.
Again, the position of this battalion provided for the contingency of a sudden change in the military situation on the
Russo-Polish front.   As matters stood, East Prussia needed
defense to the south, not to the east.
     The placement of the 3rd Battalion at Elbing indicated
that the Germans also had their eyes on the Poles at this
critical time.   The smallest of the battalions, it had fewer
than four hundred men. Its three companies were located in
Elbing and Marienwerder, but it had platoons in Rosenberg,
Preussisch Holland, Osterode, Marienburg, and Mohrungen. The
entire force formed a triangle, with apices at Elbing, Marienwerder, and Osterode, which could concentrate to face a threat
from the west or from the south.
     The 4th Battalion, headquartered at Bischofsburg, had the
most important task of defending East Prussia's southern face.
It consisted of 541 men, organized into three companies. The
first company had platoons in Sensburg, Johannisburg, and
Ortelsburg, and stood in the center of the battalion.   The
second, on the western flank, had four platoons, which were
stationed in Bischofsburg, Allenstein, Neidenburg, and
Rastenburg.   The third guarded the eastern flank of the line
and was also responsible for maintaining contact with the 2nd
Battalion at Angerburg.   Its platoons were at Lötzen, which
guarded the gaps through the Masurian Lakes, Marggrabowa, and
Lyck.
     While these four battalions had only limited impact on
the military balance in the region, they did ensure that no

vital section of East Prussia would go without some military protection. In the event of a full-scale invasion by Polish or Soviet troops, the utility of a force of two thousand men was doubtful. In the crisis of 1920, however, the police troop was able to do several things: provide to the government a reliable military force to help disarm foreign troops in the province; calm the civilian population, which had appeared on the verge of panic earlier in the summer; and give flexibility to the civilian government by lessening its dependence on foreign troops.

The attitude of the Allies to the formation of the new force was consistent and negative. Since July, when the Allied ambassadors at Paris had first received notice of the German intentions, they had ordered repeatedly that such preparations be stopped. German ambassador Mayer reported that acceptance of the German plan was improbable, although military developments in the war could change Allied minds. The Allied position was that between the Reichswehr, security police, and the Allied forces in the plebiscite areas, East Prussia had sufficient protection. On 17 August, General Georges Nollet of the Military Control Commission complained of the "illicit movement of men and materiel in East Prussia," because of the formation of the militia.[95] Göppert responded, with some nerve, that the government had ordered no such movement. "You must be referring," he said, "to a change in the garrison areas of the police." As for the militia, "the people themselves had formed it."[96] This bit of play-acting was a result of the conversation between Mayer and Millerand on 20 July, when Millerand had suggested that if the people desired to form defense organizations, then the Allies would not object. Nollet was apparently unaware of this previous conversation and felt simply that Göppert was lying to him. On 31 August, Nollet accused Germany of mobilizing and ordered an immediate end to it.[97] Meanwhile, the Germans had submitted their proposition for the formation of the militia and border defense force to the Ambassadors Conference in Paris.[98] Most German authorities felt that the Allies would allow them a force in a one to ten ratio to the Russian troops in East Prussia, or about five thousand men.[99]

On 8 September, the Allies delivered their response. Germany possessed sufficient military forces, about 350,000 men, to protect East Prussia. The Allied governments would permit movement of troops within East Prussia in order to disarm the Russians "with all vigor" and to prevent more foreign troops from entering the province. They ordered the immediate dissolution of the Ortswehr and Grenzwehr.[100] As of that time they still had no knowledge of the existence of the police troop.

The German reaction to the Allied demands was a series of delaying actions. The Germans agreed in principle to the eventual dissolution of the militia, but suggested a series of reasons why the dissolution would have to wait. These ranged from the merely false, that East Prussia faced civil war without strong armed forces, to the comical, that the Allies had failed to provide the German government with legible written copies of their demands.[101] More seriously, the Germans thought that they needed the additional forces to search for and disarm the Russians. It was the task of the border defense, proclaimed army officials, to mop up the triangle Lötzen-Bialla-Lyck, then advance to the sectors around Fillipowo and Darkehmen. These were heavily wooded areas in which large numbers of Russians were hiding. Moreover, the Reichswehr needed auxiliary forces to help with guard duties at Arys, which was the main internment camp of the Russians.[102] For these reasons, Siehr requested that the Allies extend the deadline for dissolving the militia to 1 October.[103] The Ministry of the Interior desired that the auxiliary forces remain with the colors until the end of the Russo-Polish War.[104]

The Allies suspected that the Germans would retain these forces a good deal longer if permitted. The discovery on 16 September of the existence of the police troop seemed to confirm Allied suspicions that Germany was using the Russo-Polish War as an excuse to evade the military clauses of the Versailles treaty.[105] The Germans responded that the police troop was merely another name for the border defense, that it was not a new force.[106] However ingenious this reply may have been, it was not satisfying to the Allies. Even more upsetting was Siehr's use of the term "levee en masse" to describe the defensive preparations in East Prussia.[107]

The German claim that they needed additional troops to scour the woods for Russians fell on deaf ears in Paris. On 14 September, Siehr had stated to Nollet that the Grenzwehr had already evacuated seventeen thousand Russians and that the whole evacuation would be done by 21 September.[108] The Russians appeared to have lost their fighting spirit, and there were no untoward incidents, reported the Oberpräsident. As Nollet viewed it, the original German justification for the auxiliary forces was to aid with the evacuation. The Allies saw no reason why, with the evacuation almost finished, there should be any non-Reichswehr military forces in East Prussia.

By the end of September, it was clear that the military emergency was over. The Polish victory on the Niemen on 21 September pushed the Russian forces back, as the front moved away from East Prussia.[109] The Allies had tired of German equivocation and delay. On 10 October they informed the German Foreign Office that "they would view as duplicitous any further attempt to extend the deadline" for dissolution.[110] Siehr had announced the formal dissolution of the militia on 1 October and the border defense on 8 October.[111] On 12 October, he rescinded the order to create the police troop.[112] The Allies responded by declaring that, henceforth, they would not permit the German government to raise or train militia in East Prussia. In addition, in the future, the Germans would have to pose questions on this issue early enough so as not to present the Allies with a fait accompli.[113] The Germans, however, never intended to tear down the defense structure they had created in 1920.[114] Throughout the interwar period, the existence of self-defense forces in East Prussia was a well-known fact and the subject of repeated protests, but no concrete action, by the Allies.

The East Prussian crisis of 1920 ended quietly. It was an important affair since it pointed out the problems of national defense which Weimar Germany would have to face. Having a weak army was a new experience for this generation of Germans. When the armistice came into effect in 1918, the German army everywhere stood on foreign soil. At no time during the summer of 1920 was the army powerful enough to defend Germany's borders. Therefore, in 1920 and the following years, the Germans relied on a system of local, irregular

defense forces. The quality of these forces is hard to
determine, yet they came of necessity to play a key role in
German defense strategy.

Most importantly, the events of 1920 pointed out the need
for a coherent national strategy. Because of the lack of
direction from Berlin, East Prussian authorities had to impro-
vise their own defensive preparations. This devolution of
authority could have led to the development of a "provincial
strategy" whereby each province would tend to its own defense.
General von Seeckt had failed to provide a national strategy
in 1920. In the future, the major task of German strategists
would be to ensure, first, that events would not catch Germany
unawares as they had in 1920, and second, that military policy
fulfill national, rather than merely provincial, defense
needs.

There was one other aspect of the crisis of 1920 which
bears mentioning. This was the role played by the Interallied
Control Commission in regulating German military policy. In
1920 the Allied control had functioned poorly. While the
Germans asked Allied permission for even the smallest self-
defense measures, the Allies often found themselves unable to
enforce their decisions. The result was satisfying to neither
side. Allied violation of Germany's rights as a sovereign
state offended the Germans; repeated German attempts to evade
the treaty provisions angered the Allies. The East Prussian
crisis was, in the end, most important for its psychological
effects. The Germans never forgot how helpless they had been
in 1920, nor how the Allies had seemed more concerned with
maintaining the Versailles treaty than with the survival of
Germany as a nation. The Allies remembered the contempt which
the Germans had for their treaty obligations. The results
were a legacy of bitterness on both sides during the coming
years and a heightened anxiety on the part of Germany for the
safety of its eastern provinces.

During the immediate postwar period, Germany's military
leaders were unable to solve the problem of national defense.
Undoubtedly, this was in part a result of circumstances beyond
their control. The Treaty of Versailles determined German
military strength; the Russo-Polish War, likewise, was not an
event which German officers could influence. Even accounting
for the unfavorable situation in which Germany found itself,
the failure of German army leaders, primarily Seeckt, to
establish a national army was surprising. As we have seen,
Seeckt's geopolitical beliefs, especially his hostility to the
new Polish state, left him without a viable option during the
crisis of 1920. To be fair to Seeckt, his attention was on
the reorganization of the army, a process in which he succeeded admirably. Yet the fact remains that East Prussia
cried out for defense in 1920, and the army did nothing.

The real credit for establishing defenses in East Prussia
belonged to local officials, particularly Ernst Siehr.
Through his efforts in recognizing the regular army's limitations and in forming a cohesive militia and the volunteer
police troop, Siehr kept East Prussia at peace in 1920. The
impressiveness of his achievement was especially evident in
the disarming of the seventy to eighty thousand foreign troops
in East Prussia during the fall of 1920. German military aims
were limited in the crisis of 1920. They included the protection of the borders and the preservation of neutrality.
Within this limited context, Siehr did his duty.

The East Prussian crisis illustrated interwar Germany's fundamental military weakness. In the military restrictions of the treaty, France sought to render Germany indefensible and incapable of treaty revision. Most military men in Germany and elsewhere believed that France had succeeded. Some ninety thousand French troops occupied the provinces of Hesse and the Palatinate and the Rhine bridgehead at Mainz. At the same time, Germany lay open to invasion by the Polish army from the east. While some of Germany's problems, such as the search for allies and the revision of the treaty, would have to be solved by diplomacy, the problem of national defense under such unfavorable circumstances could only be solved by the military leadership. In the 1920s, German officers would have to formulate an operational and tactical doctrine to defend their state with the scanty resources at hand.

NOTES

1.   Friedrich von Rabenau, Seeckt: Aus seinem Leben, 1918-1936 (Leipzig: von Hase und Koehler Verlag, 1940), p. 176.

2.   Marshal Foch stated on 16 June 1919 that the forces ready for a further advance into Germany were twenty infantry divisions and three cavalry divisions. A further sixteen divisions were available for reserve and garrison duty to the rear of the assault force. Quoted in Jean Feller, Le Dossier de l'Armee Francaise (Paris: Perrin, 1966), p. 145.

3.   Letter from General von Hindenburg, Grosses Haupt-quartier, 17 June 1919, reprinted in Waldemar Erfurth, Die Geschichte des deutschen Generalstabes, 1918-1945 (Göttingen, Berlin, Frankfurt: Musterschmidt-Verlag, 1957), p. 42. Hindenburg concluded his letter by stating that, as a soldier, he preferred "an honorable downfall to a shameful peace."

4.   Wilhelm Groener, Lebenserinnerungen: Jugend, Generalstab, Weltkrieg (Osnabrück: Biblio Verlag, 1972), pp. 459-512; F. L. Carsten, The Reichswehr and Politics, 1918-1933 (Oxford: at the Clarendon Press, 1966), p. 41.

5.   Jacques Benoist-Mechin, Histoire de l'Armee Alle-mande, vol. 2 (Paris: Editions Albin Michel, 1938), pp. 11-58.

6.   Dorothea Groener-Geyer, General Groener: Soldat und Staatsmann (Frankfurt am Main: Societäts-Verlag, 1954), pp. 379-385.

7.   David Lloyd George, Memoirs of the Peace Conference (New Haven: Yale University Press, 1939), chapter 4, pp. 139-155.

8.   Gunther E. Rothenberg, The Army of Francis Joseph (West Lafayette: Purdue University Press, 1976), pp. 179-181.

9.   A. J. P. Taylor states that it was the two-front war which eventually led to Germany's defeat, but the "second front" he has in mind is that of Salonika. An Illustrated History of the First World War (New York: Capricorn, 1972), p. 236.

10.   Norman Stone, The Eastern Front, 1914-1917 (London: Hodder and Stoughton, 1975), pp. 40-42; Gerhard Ritter, Der Schlieffen Plan: Kritik eines Mythos (München: R. Oldenbourg, 1956).

11.   There are several adequate histories of the General Staff: Walter Görlitz, History of the German General Staff,

1657-1945 (New York: Praeger, 1959); Erfurth, Geschichte des deutschen Generalstabes; and Gordon A. Craig, The Politics of the Prussian Army, 1640-1945 (London: Oxford University Press, 1955).
12.   A. J. Ryder, Twentieth Century Germany: From Bismarck to Brandt (New York: Columbia University Press, 1973), pp. 201-208; John Hiden, Germany and Europe, 1919-1939 (London and New York: Longman, 1977), p. 19; Erich Koch-Weser, Deutschlands Aussenpolitik in der Nachkriegszeit, 1919-1929 (Berlin-Grunewald: Kurt Vowinckel Verlag, 1929), pp. 34-35.
13.   See Lloyd George, Memoirs, pp. 637-42, for the debate between Lloyd George, President Wilson, and the French delegation. For the debate over Upper Silesia, see Lloyd George, pp. 645-648. For a description of Anglo-French disagreements at Versailles, see Piotr S. Wandycz, France and Her Eastern Allies, 1919-1925 (Minneapolis: University of Minnesota Press, 1962), pp. 29-48.
14.   Harald van Riekhoff, German-Polish Relations, 1918-1933 (Baltimore: Johns Hopkins Press, 1971), pp. 39-51.
15.   Lloyd George, Memoirs, chapter 8, "The Rhine," pp. 252-286.
16.   Joint Proclamation by the Emperors of Germany and Austria-Hungary, quoted in Volkmar Kellermann, Schwarzer Adler-Weisser Adler: Die Polenpolitik der Weimarer Republik (Köln: Markus Verlag, 1970), p. 18.
17.   Kellermann, Schwarzer Adler, p. 43; Riekhoff, German-Polish Relations, p. 10.
18.   Erfurth, Geschichte des deutschen Generalstabes, pp. 33-34.
19.   Lloyd George, Memoirs, p. 201.
20.   Ibid., pp. 631-633.
21.   Memorandum from Dmowski to Wilson, 8 October 1918, printed in Kellermann, Schwarzer Adler, p. 26.
22.   Riekhoff, German-Polish Relations, p. 18.
23.   Wandycz, France and Her Eastern Allies, p. 47.
24.   The armistice had permitted troops to remain on Russian soil until the Allies thought it suitable to recall them "having regard to the internal situation of those territories." Ferdinand Foch, Memoirs (New York: Doubleday, Doran, and Co., 1931), p. 481.
25.   Georges Clemenceau, quoted in Gordon Wright, France in Modern Times (Chicago: Rand McNally, 1974), p. 317.
26.   Lloyd George, Memoirs, p. 203.
27.   Telegram, State Secretary Ago von Maltzan to Ambassador Brockdorff-Rantzau in Moscow, Berlin, 13 December 1924, reprinted in Riekhoff, German-Polish Relations, p. 79.
28.   See, for instance, Rabenau, Seeckt: Aus seinem Leben, pp. 316-317, for Seeckt's assessment of Russian-German cooperation in the Polish question.
29.   Quoted in Kellermann, Schwarzer Adler, pp. 32-34.
30.   Christian Meurer, Die Grundlage des Versailles Friedens und der Völkerbund (Würzburg: Kabbitsch & Mönnich, 1920), p. 43.
31.   Pamphlet, "Brauchen und dürfen wir auf unsere Ostmarken verzichten?" reprinted in Kellermann, Schwarzer Adler, p. 33.
32.   See Wandycz, France and Her Eastern Allies, pp. 44-46; Riekhoff, German-Polish Relations, pp. 17-19; Roman

Debicki, The Foreign Policy of Poland, 1919-1939 (New York: Praeger, 1962), pp. 23-25.
    33.   Hans Roos, Geschichte der polnischen Nation, 1916-1960 (Stuttgart: W. Kohlhammer, 1961), p. 56.
    34.   Alexander Skrzynski, Poland and Peace (London: G. Allen and Unwin ltd, 1923), p. 80.
    35.   The definitive work on the "eastern Locarno" question is Christian Höltje, Die Weimarer Republik und das Ostlocarno-Problem, 1919-1934 (Würzburg: Holzner-Verlag, 1958).
    36.   Henry L. Bretton, Stresemann and the Revision of Versailles (Stanford: Stanford University Press, 1953), chapter 11, "Territorial Revision in the East," pp. 116-125; Hans W. Gatzke, Stresemann and the Rearmament of Germany (Baltimore: Johns Hopkins Press, 1954).
    37.   Lloyd George, Memoirs, p. 393.
    38.   Groener, Lebenserinnerungen, p. 482.
    39.   Rabenau, Seeckt: Aus seinem Leben, p. 159.
    40.   Groener, Lebenserinnerungen, p. 492.
    41.   Speech of Brockdorff-Rantzau to the Representatives of the Allied and Associated Powers at Versailles, 7 May 1919, printed in Auswärtiges Amt, Materialien betreffend die Friedensverhandlungen, vols. 1 and 2 (Berlin), pp. 15-16. Brockdorff became a hero in Germany for reading his speech while seated, instead of rising as Clemenceau had done in the opening speech. Debate remains over whether Brockdorff was acting defiantly or whether he simply could not stop his knees from shaking enough to make standing up feasible.
    42.   Rabenau, Seeckt: Aus seinem Leben, pp. 170, 173, and 176.
    43.   David G. Chandler, The Campaigns of Napoleon (New York: Macmillan, 1966), pp. 159-160, 366; Gunther E. Rothenberg, The Art of Warfare in the Age of Napoleon (Bloomington: Indiana University Press, 1978), pp. 129-130.
    44.   Marc Ferro, La Grande Guerre (Paris: Gallimard, 1969), pp. 95-97.
    45.   Groener, Lebenserinnerungen, pp. 492-494.
    46.   Report No. 20, "Conditions on the Polish Front," in the microfilmed collection United States Military Intelligence Reports: Germany, 1919-1941 (Frederick, Md.: University Publications of America, 1983), reel 12, 0702-0705 (hereafter USMI, 12, 0702-0705).
    47.   Görlitz, History of the German General Staff, pp. 305-306.
    48.   Harold J. Gordon, The Reichswehr and the German Republic, 1919-1926 (Princeton, N.J.: Princeton University Press, 1957), pp. 53-56.
    49.   Georg Tessin, Deutsche Verbände und Truppen, 1918-1939 (Osnabrück: Biblio Verlag, 1974), Abschnitt 3, "Die Vorläufige Reichswehr," pp. 101-143.
    50.   Quoted in Heinz-Ludger Borgert, "Grundzüge der Landkriegführung von Schlieffen bis Guderian," in Handbuch zur deutschen Militärgeschichte, 1648-1939, vol. 9 (München: Bernard & Graefe Verlag für Wehrwesen, 1977), p. 530.
    51.   See Gordon, Reichswehr and the German Republic, pp. 113-143, for the most balanced and accurate depiction of the role of the regular army in the Kapp Putsch. There are many dissenters from Gordon's description of Seeckt's actions in 1920. See Alma Luckau, "Kapp Putsch: Success or Failure?" The Journal of Central European Affairs 7 (1948); Carsten,

Reichswehr and Politics; on the general question of civil-military relations in Weimar Germany, see Craig, Politics of the Prussian Army, pp. 342-467; John W. Wheeler-Bennett, The Nemesis of Power: The German Army in Politics, 1918-1945 (London: Macmillan & Co. ltd, 1964); Claus Guske, Das politische Denken des Generals von Seeckt (Lübeck and Hamburg: Matthiesen Verlag, 1971); Gaines Post, Jr., The Civil-Military Fabric of Weimar Foreign Policy (Princeton, N.J.: Princeton University Press, 1973).
    52. Report no. 10, "Report on Conditions Prevailing at Stettin," USMI, 4, 0007-0013.
    53. Rabenau, Seeckt: Aus seinem Leben, p. 252; Kellermann, Schwarzer Adler, pp. 58-59.
    54. The best work on the Russo-Polish War is Norman Davies, White Eagle--Red Star (London, Macdonald & Co., 1972). See also Adam Zamoyski, The Battle for the Marchlands (Boulder: East European Monographs, 1981); and Jozef Pilsudski, Year 1920 (London, Pilsudski Institute of London, 1972), which also contains Soviet Marshal Tukhachevsky's lectures to the Soviet Military Academy, entitled "The March Beyond the Vistula."
    55. Akten des Auswärtigen Amtes (Records of the German Foreign Office, Archiv des Auswärtigen Amtes, Bonn. A micro-filmed copy of these documents is deposited in the National Archives, Washington, D.C.), reel 3623, serial 9855H, frames H317 529-530. For the microfilmed records of the German Foreign Ministry, the following sequence will be used here-after: AA, standing for Auswärtiges Amt, to be followed by reel, serial, and frame numbers. Under this system of ab-breviation, the above document would be cited as AA/3623/9855H/H317 529-530. See also AA/3623/9855H/H317 571-572.
    56. Report from Allenstein to Foreign Office, AA/3623/9855H/H317 553-554, 3 July 1920.
    57. Reichskommissar of Allenstein to Foreign Office, AA/3623/9855H/H317 527-528, 17 July 1920.
    58. Telegram, Mayer to Foreign Office, AA/3623/9855H/H317 541-543, 21 July 1920.
    59. Reichs- und Staatskommissar für die ostpr. Abstim-mungsgebiete to Foreign Office, AA/3623/9855H/H317 549-552, 26 July 1920. See also, AA/3623/9855H/H317 579-581, 5 August 1920.
    60. Mayer to Foreign Office, AA/3623/9855H/H317 560-561, 31 July 1920. Mayer saw a possibility of convincing England to allow a new border defense force, but felt that French and Polish opposition made acceptance of Germany's wishes "improb-able."
    61. Max Worgitzki of the Masuren- und Ermländerbund, to Foreign Office, AA/3623/9855H/H317 529-530, 17 July 1920. See also, AA/3623/9855H/H317 565-566.
    62. AA/3623/9855H/H317 571-572.
    63. Kellermann, Schwarzer Adler, p. 58; Rabenau, Seeckt: Aus seinem Leben, p. 252.
    64. Kellermann, Schwarzer Adler, p. 58.
    65. Seeckt Papers, microfilmed copy, National Archives, Washington, D.C., reel 21, "Zur Eingabe der Landeskammer der Provinz Schlesien," 26 February, 1920.
    66. Ibid.
    67. Seeckt Papers, reel 21, "Die militär-politische Lage im Osten und Schlussfolgerungen," 31 July 1920.

    68.   Escherich to Foreign Office, AA/3623/9855H/H317 598-601.
    69.   Hans Meier-Welcker, Seeckt (Frankfurt am Main: Bernard & Graefe Verlag für Wehrwesen, 1967), p. 293.
    70.   Riekhoff, German-Polish Relations, pp. 14-17; Erfurth, Geschichte des deutschen Generalstabes, p. 32.
    71.   Craig, Politics of the Prussian Army, p. 354.
    72.   Seeckt Papers, reel 22, Preussischer Volksfreund, 26 January 1919, "Für den ostpreussischen Grenzschutz!"
    73.   Seeckt Papers, reel 22, Preussischer Volksfreund, 26 January 1919, "Die Insterburger."
    74.   Benoist-Mechin, Histoire de l'Armee Allemande, vol. 2, p. 147; Gordon, Reichswehr and the German Republic, p. 36.
    75.   General Nollet, Une Experience de Desarmament, p. 219. cited in Benoist-Mechin, Histoire de l'Armee Allemande, p.47.
    76.   Tätigkeitsbericht der Landesgrenzpolizei Ostpreussen, June 1920; Königsberg to Foreign Office, AA/3623/9855H/H 317 609-611, 26 July 1920.
    77.   Oberpräsident Siehr to Ministry of the Interior, AA/3623/9855H/H317 627, 16 August 1920.
    78.   Tessin, Deutsche Verbände und Truppen, pp. 150-151. The 1st Brigade was formed in October 1919 by merging the old 1st Brigade at Königsberg with the 33rd Brigade at Insterburg. In February 1920, the 43rd Brigade (Nordlitauen) was joined to the formation.   The 1st Brigade contained two regiments of three battalions each.   The 1st Regiment had its headquarters and two of its battalions at Königsberg.   The remaining battalion was stationed at Pillau.   The 2nd Regiment had its headquarters and one battalion at Insterburg, with the other two battalions stationed at Gumbinnen and Tilsit.   In addition, the brigade contained the 1st Artillery Regiment, stationed at Königsberg.
    79.   Reichswehrministerium to the Friedenskommission-Heer, AA/3623/9854H/H317 397-398, 15 August 1920.
    80.   Wehrkreiskommando I to Siehr, AA/3623/9854H/H317 382-384, 20 September 1920.
    81.   Proclamation from Siehr, "Ostpreussen Männer!" AA/3623/9854H/H317 285-286, written in longhand, n.d.
    82.   Siehr, "Erlass über Bildung von Ortswehren in Ostpreussen," AA/3623/9854H/H317 287-290, 17 August 1920.
    83.   See Gordon, Reichswehr and the German Republic, for Seeckt's dissenting opinion.
    84.   Siehr, "Vorschriften über den Waffengebrauch für die Orts- und Grenzwehren Ostpreussens," AA/3623/9854H/H317 283-284, 9 August 1920.
    85.   Foreign Office to Reichskommissar of Allenstein, AA/3623/9855H/ H317 545; Report, Reichs- und Staatskommissar für die ostpr. Abstimmungsgebiete, AA/3623/9855H/H317 549-552, 26 July 1920.
    86.   Davies, White Eagle, pp. 188-225.
    87.   Rabenau, Seeckt: Aus seinem Leben, p. 253, places the number at 45,000; the German delegation to Paris claimed 50,000, AA/3623/9854H/H317 304-305.
    88.   Major Schürmann to Foreign Office, AA/3623/9855H/H317 583-589.
    89.   Abschrift, Verbindungsstelle Friedenskommission, Königsberg, AA/3623/9855H/H317 587-589.
    90.   Major Schürmann, report, AA/3623/9855H/H317 587-589.
    91.   Davies, White Eagle, p. 149.

92.   Ministry of the Interior to Foreign Office, Abschrift, AA/3623/ 9855H/H317 594-595.
93.   Siehr, "Erlass über die Bildung," AA/3623/9854H/H317
345-347, 1 September 1920.
94.   Hundertschaft does not translate directly into "company," but the English word is used here for the sake of
convenience.
95.   General Nollet to Göppert, AA/3623/9854H/H317 293-
294, 17 August 1920.
96.   Göppert to Nollet, AA/3623/9854H/H317 295-302, 21
August 1920.
97.   Nollet to Göppert, AA/3623/9854H/H317 309-310, 31
August 1920.
98.   Foreign Office to Mutius, German representative to
the Ambassadors Conference in Paris, AA/3623/9854H/H317 312, 4
September 1920.   See also Mutius's report of his conversation
with the Italian ambassador Gorbasso, who stated that the
attitude of the French military was the main obstacle to
acceptance of the German position.
99.   Sthamer, German ambassador in London, to Foreign
Office, AA/3623/9854H/H317 326; Mayer to Foreign Office,
AA/3623/9854H/H317 327-328, 7 September 1920.
100.   Response of the Conference of Ambassadors, Mayer to
Foreign Office, AA/3623/9854H/H317 337-339, 10 September 1920.
101.   AA/3623/9854H/H317 509, 15 October 1920.
102.   Rabenau, Seeckt: Aus Seinem Leben, p. 253.
103.   Siehr to Foreign Minister, AA/3623/9854H/H317 377-
381, 20 September 1920.
104.   Ministry of Interior to Foreign Office, AA/3623/
9854H/H317 396, 21 September 1920.
105.   Nollet to Göppert, AA/3623/9854H/H317 359-360, 16
September 1920.
106.   Göppert to Nollet, AA/3623/9854H/H317 363, 19
September 1920.   Siehr's action in forming the Polizeitruppe
had evidently caught Göppert by surprise. In a rough draft of
a letter to Siehr, Göppert stated angrily that he "expected
the Polizeitruppe to vanish."
107.   Siehr to Reichswehr Minister, report of a conversation with Colonel Langlois, AA/3623/9854H/H317 374-375, 15
September 1920.
108.   Göppert, report of a conversation with Nollet,
AA/3623/9854H/H317 353, 14 September 1920.
109.   Davies, White Eagle, pp. 226-263.
110.   Sthamer to Foreign Office, Berlin, AA/3623/
9854H/H317 511-512, 10 October 1920.
111.   Verbalnote to Ambassadors' Conference, AA/3623/
9854H/H317 502, 8 October 1920.
112.   Verbalnote to Ambassadors' Conference, AA/3623/
9854H/H317 507, 12 October 1920.
113.   This had been a repeated complaint by the Allies.
Note, Allied Powers to German representative at the Ambassadors' Conference, AA/3623/9854H/H317 516, 8 October 1920.
114.   See, for instance, Ministry of Interior to Foreign
Office, AA/3623/9855H/H317 652, 26 January 1924, which makes
it clear that auxiliary defense forces still existed in East
Prussia at that time.

2
An Army Restored:
General Seeckt, the *Reichswehr*, and the East, 1921-1926

The post-1920 phase may be designated the true "Versailles period" in German-Polish military relations. In this era, the restrictions of the Versailles Treaty were applied with full force to the German army, while the Poles were free to construct their army in any way they saw fit. The size and shape of the postwar German army was more or less an Allied creation, and the Allies deployed military representatives on German soil to ensure that the Germans did not pursue an independent policy in the military sphere. After the end of the East Prussian crisis in 1920, the military situation on the German-Polish border moved from the postwar phase, involving heavy troop concentrations and occasional armed clashes between German and Polish troops, to a true peacetime deployment, characterized by the placement of troops in regular garrisons and lowered tensions between Germany and Poland. Skirmishes between German and Polish forces still occurred from time to time, but these usually involved irregular forces, border guards, or paramilitary groups on both sides.

This chapter will examine in detail the methods by which the Reichswehr attempted to fulfill its mission of defending Germany's borders. Along most of the border with Poland, there was no defensible terrain. The postwar territorial revisions had made frontier posts of some of Germany's major eastern cities, including Berlin, Stettin, and Breslau. Even worse, East Prussia was surrounded by Polish territory; most military observers, as we have seen, considered it indefensible.

The deployment of German forces in the east was therefore critical, due to Germany's poor geographical situation. Seeckt, the German commander, had two choices with regard to the placement of his small army. The first choice was to concentrate his forces so that they would be prepared to counterattack any Polish invading force. According to most military doctrine, this decision would have been the correct one. The second choice was to disperse the small force throughout the countryside. Dispersion of the army had the advantage of reassuring the nervous civilian population of the border areas. As we shall see, Seeckt chose the second option. His idea was to prevent a Polish coup de main, a

limited-objective attack against an undefended German border
province.

The dispersion of German forces offered the Polish army
an opportunity of defeating the Reichswehr in detail in the
first days of a war. The question arises, then, as to whether
Seeckt risked Germany's security by his deployment strategy.
Of crucial importance here is the question of Polish military
strategy.   This   chapter will also analyze the deployment of
the Polish army to see if its intentions toward Germany were
aggressive or defensive.

The story of the Reichswehr in the early 1920s revolves
around one man, General Hans von Seeckt. He alone formulated
German tactical and operational doctrine during this period.
He had two options for the training of the army. The first
was to instill a purely passive, defensive attitude in his
forces, which would rely upon fixed fortifications and heavy
firepower.   The second was to create a highly mobile force,
which stressed maneuver and aggressive defense.   For various
reasons which this chapter will examine, Seeckt chose the
second strategy.   He borrowed the tradition of the old imperial army and combined it with his own ideas about the character of modern mobile warfare.   In so doing, Seeckt attempted
to create the finest army in Europe, an army whose high
quality would make up for its small size. The fate of Germany
would rest on his success or failure.

The German-Polish border area during the interwar period
was one with few distinguishing characteristics.   It crossed
the eastern part of the North European plain, a region which
has been a proving ground for the generals of many nations.
The location of the German and Polish nations in this region
has meant that, historically, both have been vulnerable to
invasion; indeed, of all the European nations, Germany and
Poland together probably hold the dubious distinction of
playing host to the greatest number of hostile armies. German
lands had functioned as the battleground for the Thirty Years
War and those of the Emperor Napoleon, Polish lands for a
whole series of conquerors from Ghenghis Khan through Charles
XII of Sweden.   Most recently, the advance of the Bolshevik
army into the heart of Poland in the summer of 1920 had
threatened the security not only of Poland, but of Germany as
well.

Poland itself is a land bridge between the plains of
northern Germany and the marshlands of Belorussia.   It
possesses defensible terrain in only two places: in the
Carpathian Mountains in the south, along the Czechoslovakian
border; and along the line of the Narew, Vistula, and San
rivers.   The Carpathians, of course, would be of little value
against an invasion from Germany. The river line roughly
bisected the country in the interwar period.   Hence, it was
also less than ideal as a defensive position. To defend along
the Vistula would mean the sacrifice of half the country,
including the industrial center of Lodz, and would place
Warsaw in the front line.   The central sector of Poland, that
is, the lands within the quadrilateral formed by Bydgoszcz
(Bromberg), Lodz, Bialystok, and Lublin was at once the most
important region of Poland and the most vulnerable to attack,
as the terrain within this area is particularly featureless.
Since it was the heart of Polish economic life, the central
region boasted the best rail and road network in the country.[1]

Poland's climate has a "transitional character between oceanic and continental types,"[2] and is influenced by the collision of warm oceanic air masses with colder air from the polar region. Weather conditions are highly variable, with hot summers and cold snowy winters. There is usually ample precipitation throughout the year. During the spring, melted snow causes many of the rivers in the lowland regions to flood. Heavy rains in the fall have a similar effect. During both the spring and fall, flooding can be a serious hindrance to the conduct of military operations.

The Vistula is the major river of Poland, a fact which has remained unchanged wherever Poland's borders have happened to be.[3] The source of the Vistula is in the Carpathians, near Krakow. From there it makes a wide arc and flows through Warsaw, then through Plock and Torun, and finally past Danzig into the Baltic Sea. As already mentioned, its central location in Poland, which has made it so important to Polish commerce, makes the Vistula an unsuitable defensive position. Other large rivers include the Warta (Warthe), which descends from the mountains near Czestochowa, flows north and then west through Poznan, crosses the German border, and empties into the Oder at Küstrin; the San and the Bug, both of which originate in the southern mountains and flow north into the Vistula; and the Narew, which originates near Bialystok and flows west into the Vistula. With their bridges destroyed, all of these rivers would serve as major obstacles to an army on the march, particularly during the rain and thaw seasons.

Except for East Prussia, those provinces of Germany bordering Poland, that is, Pomerania, Brandenburg, and Silesia, have the same geographic characteristics as the Polish areas they face. East Prussia, with its thick forests and multitudinous lakes, has a far different geography than that which we normally associate with the North German Plain. Outside of East Prussia, there was no defensible terrain along the border save for the line of the Oder River. If German forces defended on the Oder, however, three important industrial and commercial centers--Stettin, Frankfurt on the Oder, and Breslau--would be placed in jeopardy. Silesia, the industrial heartland of eastern Germany, would face severe danger in such a case, since an invading Polish force would be able to interdict the main rail line of the province, that running from Oppeln on the Oder through Brieg, Ohlau, and Breslau, and finally through Liegnitz to Saxony. Silesia, of course, boasted a highly developed road and rail network; the other German border provinces had less well developed communications. Pomerania, for instance, had one major rail line, that linking Stettin, Stargard, Köslin, and Lauenburg. The central region, which included the Grenzmark, the German name for that small part of Poznan still left to Germany, and Brandenburg, like the Polish central region, was both highly valuable and highly vulnerable. This area marks the farthest eastward extension of the North German Plain, where the general flatness of the land is broken only occasionally by gentle rises in elevation. The triangle formed by Breslau, Berlin, and Stettin is an especially alluring target for any invading army. It is important to realize that Berlin in 1920 was a much more important strategic center than it is today. With a population of over 4,000,000, it was the largest city in Germany and the third largest in the world.[4]

There are two main types of climate in Germany: the coastal or oceanic and the interior or continental. The North German Plain has a basically oceanic climate, although the farther east one travels from the Elbe, the more continental become the weather patterns. The German geographer Wegener has divided Germany into eight "climactic provinces," of which three concern us here: the East German region (cold winters, warm short summers, summer rains), which includes East Prussia except for the coast, and extends westward to fifteen degrees longitude, or about sixty miles east of Berlin; the Baltic area (cool summers, mild winters, becoming more continental toward the east), which includes the Baltic coast and hinterland; and the Central region, a zone of transition from coast to interior climate, which includes all of the North German Plain east of eleven degrees longitude. In each of these regions, the rainfall decreases with the distance from the ocean, but heavy rains--usually in the early summer and winter--can be a serious obstacle to the conduct of military operations.[5]

Navigation on all German rivers except the Rhine is sometimes hindered by low water, but the floods caused by heavy rains often do vast damage, as well as make the rivers impenetrable to an armed force. In 1926, for instance, large stretches of the Oder and the Elbe overflowed their banks, broke through dikes and other hastily erected works, and devastated much valuable farm land. There were four major rivers in interwar Germany, the Rhine, Weser, Elbe, and Oder. They flow roughly one hundred miles apart from each other in a parallel direction from the south to the north. Of the two major rivers in the German-Polish theater of operations, the Elbe is the larger, with a length of 1,160 kilometers. In 1927, it carried approximately one-quarter of all the merchandise transported on German waterways. The Elbe crosses the middle of Germany, has its mouth within German territory, and contains Berlin within its basin. Because of its central location, the Elbe was not suitable as a line of defense. Allowing an enemy force to reach the Elbe from either the west or the east would have meant surrendering half of the country. The second of the major rivers in eastern Germany, the Oder, has a length of 940 kilometers and is navigable for ocean-going ships to Stettin and for riverboats to Ratibor on the Czech border, a distance of 770 kilometers. Its volume and depth are variable, since its tributaries often swell it appreciably. This circumstance and the fact that the river is frozen for an average of seventy days a year reduce its value as a waterway. The military value of the Oder depends on the season. While flooded, it is a serious obstacle to an invader from the east, but during the winter it could be traversed by crossing the ice. The Oder is the principal river of Silesia; it bisects the province length-wise, through Glogau, Breslau, Oppeln, and Ratibor. Its principal tributary is the Warta, which flows through Poznan, crosses the border near Schwerin, and joins the Oder at Küstrin. During the rainy season, with their bridges destroyed, any of these rivers can seriously hinder military operations.[6]

Of the seven largest cities in Germany at the time, only two concern this study. The first, of course, is Berlin. Besides its immense size and importance as the national capital, Berlin occupied an important geostrategic position in the center of the North German Plain, equidistant from the

Baltic and the southern mountains, and from the Ems and Vistula rivers. Since the early Hohenzollern era, it has been an important post on the overland trade routes of eastern Germany; from the middle of the nineteenth century, it was Germany's main railroad nexus. The main European traffic routes from London and Paris to Moscow and Leningrad passed through Berlin, as did those from Scandinavia to Mediterranean Europe. Berlin, truly, was the crossroads of Europe in the 1920s.

In addition to its significance as an administrative and population center, Berlin was an industrial center of great importance. An American military intelligence report from this period stated:

> 69% of the inhabitants are engaged in industry, since the capital of the Reich is the foremost industrial city not only of Germany but of the entire European continent. 5200 factories, employing 1,600,000 workers, represent every branch of industry, notably machinery (Borsig), electric articles (Siemens & Halske, General Electric Co.), chemicals, furniture, clothing, books, lace, and porcelain. 20% more of the population are engaged in commerce, which consists not only of the industrial products of the city but also of the agricultural products of Northern Germany.[7]

The second major German city in the area is Breslau. With a population of over one-half million, it was the seventh largest city in Germany and the largest in Silesia. Breslau lies at the confluence of the Ohlau with the Oder in a fertile, well-cultivated region, and controls the approaches to the Moravian Gate, which leads down to Vienna and the Adriatic. Besides being the main assembly point for Silesian products, it is an important industrial center in its own right.

One manual on German geography published in the 1920s claimed that Germany's geographic situation "imposed a high, but also a bitterly difficult mission" upon the German nation:

> No other among the larger European countries has such unfavorable frontiers as Germany. In the northeast, East Prussia, almost entirely severed from the rest of the German language territory, projects into Slavic land; on the other hand, the Czechs thrust themselves, like a beam in the flesh, deep into the German racial territory, and the boundary with Poland follows a quite indefinite course; Polish language islands are totally surrounded by German territory and still more German language islands by Polish language territory. Only the Balkan peninsula shows similar conditions.[8]

The Versailles treaty had done little to erase the fears of either the Polish or German peoples for the security of their common frontier. Viewed objectively, though, it is clear that the treaty made German security much more problematic, both in terms of the new geography and the military restrictions placed on the Reich. Germany, more than any other European country, was hemmed in on all sides. Its

boundary touched ten different countries: Lithuania to the
north; Poland to the east; Czechoslovakia to the southeast;
Austria and Switzerland to the south;   France, Belgium,
Luxemburg, and the Netherlands to the west; and Denmark to the
north.   The Baltic Sea was open to Germany, but access to the
North Sea and the Atlantic Ocean could be denied easily in
wartime by either France or Britain.[9]

The encirclement of Germany by hostile powers marked a
great deterioration of Germany's geographical position from
what it had been in 1914.   Before the war, Germany and its
ally Austria-Hungary occupied a solid block of territory no
less than five hundred miles wide at its narrowest point,
which extended from the North Sea to the Adriatic Sea.   The
treaty split up Austria-Hungary and forced Germany to cede
Alsace-Lorraine in the west, parts of Schleswig in the north,
and Poznan and West Prussia in the east.   As the American
military attache Colonel A. L. Conger recognized, this redis-
tribution of territory created two huge salients, Alsace-
Lorraine and Poznan, which protruded into German territory,
and whose tips were barely more than four hundred miles
apart.[10] Germany's position in the east, particularly, had
deteriorated as a result of Versailles.   Before 1914,
Germany's eastern provinces were protected by the fortified
line of the Vistula, and Austria-Hungary had the protection of
the easily defended Carpathian Mountains.   Poznan had been
vulnerable to invasion from the east, but still acted as a
buffer between the Russian army and Berlin.   East Prussia, as
a salient, offered to the Germans the advantages and disadvantages peculiar to every salient.   On the negative side, East
Prussia was threatened by concentric attack; the main city in
the province, Königsberg, had been fortified against such an
eventuality, as had the approaches to the city.   On the
positive side, East Prussia could be used as an advanced post
from which to descend on the right flank of any Russian army
attacking Poznan.   Hence, East Prussia served as a sort of
"sentinel to the east," whose presence protected the important
agricultural areas of West Prussia as well as the capital,
Berlin.

Germany's geographical situation after the war was far
worse than that which had existed in 1914. In Conger's words:

Since the War the creation of the independent states
of Poland, Lithuania, Latvia, and Estonia now separate Germany from Russia.   Poland, as a threat to
Germany on the east, is very favorably located geo-
graphically for an offensive against Berlin, while
the Polish Corridor cuts off direct communication
between Germany proper and East Prussia, which, from
a geographical point of view, would be as powerless
to defend itself alone against its neighbors as if
it were located on the continent of Africa--i.e.
unless Germany came to her rescue by herself taking
the offensive against Poland. The Prussian province
of Silesia on the other hand which, before the War,
was only exposed in part on the Russian front, is
now, by the detaching of the province of Posen from
Germany and the creation of the hostile state of
Czechoslovakia on the south, a narrow strip of territory 80 miles wide, roughly speaking, and
extending 200 miles between the hostile Poland on

one side and Czechoslovakia on the other. The importance of this threat against Silesia is all the more important to Germany in view of the important mineral and other resources there--although part of the principal mining region in Upper Silesia has been detached by the League of Nations and given to Poland.[11]

Conger's assessment was accurate. The German East lacked depth on all sectors; a quick thrust through Pomerania by an enemy force could seize Stettin, one through Brandenburg could seize Berlin. In the south, Breslau was a mere fifty kilometers from Poland, or about a single day's march for a Polish army marching out of southern Poznan. "What a monstrous military and economic threat faces the island of East Prussia and the two peninsulas of Pomerania and Silesia! What a threat to Berlin!" wrote Karl Werner, a Breslauer.[12]

Although Werner was not a military official, he identified correctly the strategic threat to eastern Germany which had arisen from the Versailles treaty. The real injury which the postwar settlement dealt to Germany was not the loss of West Prussia and Poznan, per se. These were rather sparsely populated areas of little significance as industrial or commercial centers. Rather, cession of these territories harmed Germany by separating East Prussia from the rest of the Reich and turning several valuable areas of eastern Germany into frontier zones. Berlin was now only a little over 100 miles from the Polish border, Stettin about 120 miles, Frankfurt on the Oder only 59.

The treaty had also drastically weakened the position of East Prussia. It was no longer a salient into hostile territory. Instead, it had now become an island, with all of its former disadvantages and none of its advantages. On the one hand, East Prussia was no longer suitable as a base from which to threaten the flank of an army advancing from the east, since it would now be difficult to supply even a small force within the separated province. On the other hand, the province was more vulnerable than ever to a concentric attack from the Polish districts of Pomorze, Warsaw, Bialystok, and Wilno. Indeed, one military observer at the time commented that the treaty had reduced East Prussia to "a sort of colony" of Poland.[13]

The removal of German buffer zones on the border, as well as the encirclement of East Prussia, posed a great danger to the eastern German districts in case of a new war. This was particularly true in light of the new possibilities which aerial warfare had created. Although still in its infancy, air warfare had attracted the interest of military strategists since its debut in the First World War. Had the war not ended when it did, it is likely that Berlin would have experienced the first hundred-plane air raids in the spring of 1919. A report by American military intelligence recognized the possibility of an air offensive against Germany: "The War has left Germany defenseless as far as an air force is concerned, and also exposed on her eastern, western, and southern frontiers by the salients created by Poland, Czechoslovakia, Alsace-Lorraine and the temporary salient created by the Mainz-Koblenz bridgeheads.[14] No section of Germany was safe from an enemy air attack, since not only Berlin but all of the major industrial areas of the east were within range of Polish

and Czech airplanes. The French could reach all the cities of
the western and northwestern parts of Germany.   In addition,
there was the possibility that French warplanes would redeploy
to bases in Czechoslovakia and Poland to reinforce the air
forces of those countries.   Germany, of course, could do
nothing to oppose enemy air attacks, since the Versailles
treaty had abolished the German air force.   The Germans were
permitted only flak guns, and these only in small numbers.
Throughout the interwar period, the lack of air power was
Germany's gravest strategic weakness, and one felt acutely by
the border provinces of the east.
     The   treaty restrictions extended not only to German air
power, but to land forces as well.   The Versailles treaty set
the size of the German army at 100,000 men, to be organized
into seven infantry and three cavalry divisions.   The number
of officers was limited to 4,000 men.   These restrictions were
confirmed by the Allies at the Spa Conference in the summer of
1920. Despite their great anger at these treaty stipulations,
which they saw as making Germany a slave state to the victorious powers, German military leaders obeyed them.   By the
end of 1920, the 100,000-man army had come into existence. In
the words of General von Seeckt, "A new chapter in German
military history had begun."[15] Seeckt and many of his colleagues did not consider the 100,000-man army a permanent
institution and looked forward to the day when they could
reform a truly national army.   For the time being, however,
Seeckt realized that there was no alternative to bowing to the
wishes of the Allies.[16]
     The army established by the Defense Law of 23 March 1921
conformed to the dictates of the Versailles treaty.   Its seven
infantry divisions, corresponding to the seven Wehrkreise, or
defense districts, were divided into two Gruppenkommandos, or
group commands.   The 1st Infantry Division was located at
Königsberg, the 2nd at Stettin, the 3rd at Berlin, and the 4th
at Dresden.   Together, these four divisions formed Group Command I; the headquarters of Group Command I was located in
Berlin.   The 5th, 6th, and 7th Infantry Divisions, located at
Stuttgart, Münster, and Munich, respectively, formed Group
Command II.   The three cavalry divisions, theoretically not
assigned to any defense district, were located at Frankfurt on
the Oder (1st Cavalry Division), Breslau (2nd Cavalry Division), and Weimar (3rd Cavalry Division).   As stipulated in
the treaty, the army contained 4,000 officers but no General
Staff.
     The troops immediately concerned with the defense of the
eastern border were the 1st Infantry Division, which was
responsible for the defense of East Prussia; the 2nd Infantry
Division, which was responsible for the defense of Pomerania;
and the 3rd Infantry Division, whose tasks included the
defense of the Oder bridges at Frankfurt, the protection of
the capital, Berlin, and the defense of Silesia.   Two of the
cavalry divisions, the 1st and 2nd, were also responsible for
sectors of the eastern border.   Both had as their primary
mission support for the 3rd Infantry Division; the 1st Cavalry
Division at Frankfurt could help to defend the approaches to
Berlin and the Oder crossings, and the 3rd Cavalry Division at
Breslau could help to protect the important industrial province of Silesia.   All in all, one-half of Germany's forces,
five out of its ten divisions and two out of its three cavalry
divisions, were stationed on the Polish front.   Component

infantry regiments and battalions were well dispersed throughout the eastern areas (table 2.1).[17] Each cavalry division
consisted of six Reiter regiments. Each regiment consisted of
four squadrons and a fifth training squadron. In addition,
seven regiments possessed a sixth squadron; these were par-
celled out among the infantry divisions as divisional cavalry.
Again, the component regiments and squadrons were dispersed
throughout the region (table 2.2).

Of the seven artillery regiments in the army, three were
part of the forces facing the Poles. These included the 1st
Artillery Regiment (Königsberg), with battalions at
Insterburg, Königsberg, and Allenstein; the 2nd Artillery
Regiment (Schwerin), with battalions at Stettin, Güstrow, and
Itzehoe; and the 3rd Artillery Regiment, with battalions at
Schweidnitz, Frankfurt on the Oder, Jüterbog, Potsdam, and
Sprottau. The Potsdam and Sprottau battalions were actually
horse artillery, designed to act in tandem with the cavalry.
In keeping with the provisions of the Versailles treaty, the
artillery batteries were made up of light pieces. Of the nine
batteries in each regiment, six were armed with four 77mm
field guns and three with 105mm light field howitzers. The
96mm/16 field cannon of the third battery and the automobile-
mounted cannon of the ninth battery were included in the 77mm
field cannon. The mounted cavalry sections of the cavalry
divisions each possessed three batteries, which were equipped
with four 77mm field cannon.[18] Finally, there were three
pioneer battalions on the Polish front: the 1st (Königsberg),
2nd (Stettin), and 3rd (Küstrin).

Altogether, then, the German "army of the East" consisted
of three infantry divisions, two cavalry divisions, three
artillery regiments, and three pioneer battalions; in all,
some twenty-seven battalions of infantry and forty-eight
squadrons of cavalry. Several units included in this total,
however, did not have as their main mission defense of the
Reich against Poland. The task of the 6th Infantry Regiment
(Lübeck), for instance, was to defend the coast from amphibious landing. Although it could turn to the east to meet a
threat from that direction, its main opponents in any future
conflict figured to be British marines, not Polish infantry
units. Likewise, the 10th Cavalry Regiment was located in
Saxony, facing the Czechs, as was the 12th Cavalry Regiment.
There were other regiments whose individual battalions had
primary missions directed against threats from the coastal
region and from the Czechs. Adjusting for these facts, the
army had only twenty-three battalions of infantry and forty-
three squadrons of cavalry, about thirty-five thousand men in
all, to defend Germany's long and vulnerable eastern frontier.
Since one division of infantry was capable of defending about
three miles of front, the Germans possessed enough strength to
defend about ten miles of their border.

The German High Command had two basic options with regard
to the deployment of these meager forces. It could concentrate them along the approaches to Germany's major population
and industrial centers, or it could disperse them throughout
the country to try and defend everywhere. The correct military solution would have been to attempt to protect only the
vital areas, according to the maxim "He who would defend
everything defends nothing." In this scenario, the Germans
should have placed at least two infantry divisions and at
least one cavalry division along the routes to their most

Table 2.1
German Infantry Formations in the East

===

1st Infantry Division
(Königsberg, Defense District I)

1st Infantry Regiment--Königsberg
    I Battalion   --   Königsberg
    II Battalion   --   Tilsit
    III Battalion --   Insterburg, Gumbinnen

2nd Infantry Regiment--Allenstein
    I Battalion   --   Allenstein
    II Battalion   --   Rastenburg
    III Battalion --   Lötzen

3rd Infantry Regiment--Deutsch-Eylau
    I Battalion   --   Marienwerder, Marienburg
    II Battalion   --   Deutsch-Eylau
    III Battalion --   Osterode

2nd Infantry Division
(Stettin, Defense District II)

4th Infantry Regiment--Kolberg
    I Battalion   --   Stargard
    II Battalion   --   Kolberg
    III Battalion --   Deutsch-Krone, Scheidemühl

5th Infantry Regiment--Stettin
    I Battalion   --   Stettin
    II Battalion   --   Prenzlau, Angermünde
    III Battalion --   Rostock

6th Infantry Regiment--Lübeck
    I Battalion   --   Schwerin
    II Battalion   --   Lübeck, Eutin
    III Battalion --   Flensburg

3rd Infantry Division
(Berlin, Defense District III)

7th Infantry Regiment--Schweidnitz
    I Battalion   --   Brieg, Neisse
    II Battalion   --   Hirschberg, Glatz
    III Battalion --   Breslau

8th Infantry Regiment--Frankfurt on the Oder
    I Battalion   --   Frankfurt on the Oder
    II Battalion   --   Liegnitz, Glogau
    III Battalion --   Görlitz

9th Infantry Regiment--Potsdam
    I Battalion   --   Potsdam
    II Battalion   --   Lichterfelde, Wünsdorf
    III Battalion --   Spandau

Table 2.2
German Cavalry Formations in the East

1st Cavalry Division
(Frankfurt on the Oder)

1st Cavalry Regiment--Tilsit
1st Squadron	--	Tilsit
2nd Squadron	--	Insterburg
3rd Squadron	--	Insterburg
4th Squadron	--	Tilsit
5th Squadron	--	Insterburg
(Training)		

2nd Cavalry Regiment--Angerburg, Königsberg
1st Squadron	--	Lyck
2nd Squadron	--	Lyck
3rd Squadron	--	Allenstein
4th Squadron	--	Allenstein
5th Squadron	--	Allenstein
(Training)		
6th Squadron	--	Königsberg
(Divisional Cavalry, 1st Infantry Division)		

3rd Cavalry Regiment--Rathenow
1st Squadron	--	Rathenow
2nd Squadron	--	Rathenow
3rd Squadron	--	Stendal
4th Squadron	--	Stendal
5th Squadron	--	Rathenow
(Training)		

4th Cavalry Regiment--Potsdam
1st Squadron	--	Potsdam
2nd Squadron	--	Potsdam
3rd Squadron	--	Potsdam
4th Squadron	--	Potsdam
5th Squadron	--	Potsdam
(Training)		
6th Squadron	--	Potsdam
(Divisional Cavalry, 3rd Infantry Division)		

5th Cavalry Regiment--Stolp
1st Squadron	--	Belgard
2nd Squadron	--	Belgard
3rd Squadron	--	Stolp
4th Squadron	--	Stolp
5th Squadron	--	Stolp
(Training)		

6th Cavalry Regiment--Pasewalk
1st Squadron	--	Pasewalk
2nd Squadron	--	Pasewalk
3rd Squadron	--	Demmin
4th Squadron	--	Schwedt
5th Squadron	--	Pasewalk
(Training)		
6th Squadron	--	Demmin
(Divisional Cavalry, 2nd Infantry Division)		

```
              2nd Cavalry Division
                   (Breslau)

    7th Cavalry Regiment--Breslau
         1st Squadron    --    Breslau
         2nd Squadron    --    Breslau
         3rd Squadron    --    Ohlau
         4th Squadron    --    Ohlau
         5th Squadron    --    Breslau
         (Training)

     8th Cavalry Regiment--Oels
         1st Squadron    --    Militsch
         2nd Squadron    --    Oels
         3rd Squadron    --    Militsch
         4th Squadron    --    Namslau
         5th Squadron    --    Bernstadt
         (Training)

 9th Cavalry Regiment--Fürstenwalde
         1st Squadron    --    Fürstenwalde
         2nd Squadron    --    Fürstenwalde
         3rd Squadron    --    Beeskow
         4th Squadron    --    Beeskow
         5th Squadron    --    Fürstenwalde
         (Training)

    10th Cavalry Regiment--Züllichau
         1st Squadron    --    Torgau
         2nd Squadron    --    Torgau
         3rd Squadron    --    Züllichau
         4th Squadron    --    Züllichau
         5th Squadron    --    Züllichau
         (Training)

     11th Cavalry Regiment--Lüben
         1st Squadron    --    Lüben
         2nd Squadron    --    Lüben
         3rd Squadron    --    Sprottau
         4th Squadron    --    Sprottau
         5th Squadron    --    Lüben
         (Training)

    12th Cavalry Regiment--Dresden
         1st Squadron    --    Grimma
         2nd Squadron    --    Grossenhain
         3rd Squadron    --    Grimma
         4th Squadron    --    Grossenhain
         5th Squadron    --    Dresden
         (Training)
         6th Squadron    --    Dresden
         (Divisional Cavalry, 4th Infantry Division)
```

important city, Berlin. Other strong forces, at least a full
infantry division, should have been placed in Breslau to act
as a "fire brigade" should the Poles or Czechs threaten any
part of Silesia. East Prussia, indefensible in any case,
should have received only token forces, perhaps a battalion in
Königsberg, to reassure the local civilian population. The
approaches to Stettin and the rest of Pomerania required a
certain amount of protection should the Poles attempt to reach
the Elbe and link up with a French force approaching from the
west. In our scenario, one cavalry division should have been
placed in this province. This force would have been sufficiently mobile for a delaying action and a retreat toward the
Elbe. These forces placed in the east would have been capable
of a strong defense of the capital and Silesia, surely the two
most valuable military targets within reach of the Polish
army. These deployments would still have left four infantry
divisions and one cavalry division to guard against the
French.

Given the treaty limitations placed on the German army,
the actual positioning of forces on the Polish frontier was a
credible attempt by the Truppenamt to ensure that no part of
the German East went without at least the appearance of military protection. While the number of troops in any given area
was quite small, the presence of army units in the border
provinces did serve to calm the civilian population, whose
jittery nerves were responsible for most of the war scares
with Poland during this period. In the eyes of the military
leadership, a strategy of dispersion rather than concentration
served to deter the Poles from any armed coups such as those
against Poznan in 1919, Wilno in 1920, or Upper Silesia in
1919, 1920, or 1921. The German generals viewed the coup as
very much a part of the Polish national character and feared
for the safety of East Prussia and Silesia against this type
of attack. Of secondary, but nonetheless real, concern was
the safety of Pomerania. Oddly enough, despite the exposed
position of Berlin, there was never a great worry that the
Poles would make a sudden move in the direction of the
capital. Rather, the security of Berlin was only viewed as a
problem in case of a formal two-front war with France and
Poland.

The deployment of the 1st Infantry Division in Königsberg
demonstrates the decision of the High Command to spread its
forces the length and breadth of the country rather than
concentrate around several key objectives. First, placing an
entire infantry division in encircled East Prussia was tantamount to sacrificing it in any future conflict. Second, the
actual deployment of the division within East Prussia was not
a concentration of force in any real sense. The logical way
to defend East Prussia with a single infantry division was to
use it to defend Königsberg, the political, commercial, and
cultural center of the province, as well as an important
fortress in its own right. The fortified works around
Königsberg, built in the 1860s and regarded by the Germans as
semi-obsolete, were of doubtful value in modern war, so the
correct course would have been to defend the approaches to
Königsberg. While the 1st Division, with its three regiments
drawn up in an arc around Königsberg, might have been equal to
this task, the actual deployment of the division raises doubts
about whether its main purpose was military or political. In
fact, one regiment, the 1st, was stationed along the routes to

Königsberg.   The   placement   of its battalions at Königsberg,
Tilsit,   and   the axis Insterburg-Gumbinnen provided only the
thinnest of screens should Polish forces strike at Königsberg
from the Grodno region.   The placement of the other two battalions in the Allenstein-Rastenburg-Lötzen and Marienwerder-
Eylau-Osterode regions provided East Prussia with a token area
defense which would have been easily brushed aside by a concerted Polish attack.   While the government had established
border guard forces to fill in the gaps between regular army
units and to provide a screen behind which the regular army
could concentrate and deploy,   the efficiency of these
irregular units was highly questionable.
     The deployment of parts of the 3rd Infantry Division and
the 2nd Cavalry Division in Silesia had many of the same
weaknesses as the East Prussian deployment.   There were five
battalions of infantry and twelve squadrons of cavalry in
Silesia.   This relatively large force, however, was stationed
in one of the most vulnerable of all the border provinces.
Hostile territory, in the form of Poland and Czechoslovakia,
encircled the province.   Silesia protruded like a narrow limb
into the territories of these two states and had an uncomfortably slim waist a little more than fifty miles wide at its
narrowest point.   It was necessary for the German army to
guard both the Czech and Polish frontiers, and this split the
forces available for the defense of Silesia into two groups
facing in opposite directions.   In the worst-case scenario, a
combined Polish-Czech offensive towards Breslau, the German
position in Silesia was hopeless, while an attack by even one
of the enemy states posed grave danger to the province.
Breslau, the provincial capital, was the highest-priority
target for any hostile force entering Silesia and required at
least an infantry division for its defense.   The single battalion stationed at Breslau was a weak substitute.   Its task
was actually to function as a reserve for the 7th Infantry
Regiment, which was deployed at Neisse, Glatz, and Hirschberg.
This regiment was directed only against the Czechs.   The two
battalions of the 8th Infantry Regiment in Silesia, split up
among Liegnitz, Glogau, and Görlitz, functioned as a reserve
in the west-central part of the province, and was capable of
responding to an attack from either Poland or Czechoslovakia.
Faced with the necessity to guard both the northern and southern faces of the province, but lacking the necessary manpower
to do so in an effective manner, the Germans opted to leave
the northern face without any infantry protection whatsoever.
Instead, cavalry and border guard units performed the mission
of defending the approaches to Breslau from the north.   It was
known that the Poles relied to a large degree on the mobility
of their cavalry in warfare, and this may have been an attempt
to meet the Polish cavalry with a similar force.   The 8th
Cavalry Regiment performed border duty, with squadrons at
Militsch, Oels, and Namslau, while squadrons of the 7th and
11th Cavalry Regiments functioned as reserve units in the
center of the province.   Two squadrons were stationed in
Breslau itself to aid the one infantry battalion there.   In
all, Breslau, which was a crucial strategic center, possessed
a defense force of about one thousand men.   At the same time,
the screening force in front of Breslau was so weak--the
distance between Oels and Militsch was about thirty-six
kilometers, covered by one squadron of cavalry, or about five
horsemen per kilometer--that any competent invader could have

overrun it easily. The Reichswehr was simply incapable of defending either Silesia or East Prussia during these years, it is true, but the dispersion of troops along the border of the two provinces made a bad situation even worse.

The threat to Pomerania was no less than that to the other eastern territories, although this region was clearly viewed by the German High Command as of less strategic importance than either East Prussia or Silesia. Hence there were only five battalions of infantry and four squadrons of cavalry in the province, although several battalions of both arms were stationed in Brandenburg to guard the southern approaches to Stettin. The four battalions at Stargard, Kolberg, Deutsch-Krone and Schneidemühl, and Stettin formed a quadrilateral guarding the heart of the province. The III Battalion of the 4th Infantry Regiment, which was deployed in Schneidemühl and Deutsch-Krone, also performed the duties of a border guard, since these two towns were located almost directly on the German-Polish border. Schneidemühl was also particularly important since it sat astride the Berlin-Danzig railway. Parts of the 5th Cavalry Regiment were also stationed in Pomerania. Its squadrons, stationed at Belgard and Stolp, were to guard against Polish troops in the Corridor. Although the position of Pomerania, whose northern flank rested on the sea, would appear to be stronger than encircled Silesia, this was not the case. The Versailles treaty prevented Germany from fortifying any part of its coast. Therefore, the Pomeranian beaches were entirely devoid of any defensive works. Except for the small naval base at Swinemünde, Pomerania lay open to the mighty sea power of Britain and France in the event of war. Although Stettin was the command center of Defense District II, as well as the headquarters of the 2nd Infantry Division, much of that division was assigned the task of guarding the Baltic ports and seacoast rather than protecting Stettin. Troops in Lübeck and Rostock could not be of much help in a German-Polish war.

Finally, along the historic invasion route of the North German Plain lay the most tempting target for a force invading Germany from the east, Berlin. Besides being the capital, Berlin was the center of Defense District III and the site of Group Command I. Two divisions, the 3rd Infantry and the 1st Cavalry, were stationed in the area, as were elements of the 2nd Cavalry Division. Because of the inclusion of Silesia in Defense District III, however, and the subsequent diversion of forces necessary to defend Breslau, Berlin's defense force amounted to only four battalions of infantry and eight squadrons of cavalry. This left the sector Berlin-Frankfurt on the Oder, surely a prime invasion route should Warsaw decide to take the plunge, relatively less well guarded than any of the regions discussed so far, and is further evidence that the deployment of the Reichsheer was dominated by political rather than military considerations. The city of Berlin itself had a relatively large force of two complete regiments, one infantry and one cavalry, but Frankfurt on the Oder, whose bridges were the real gateway to the capital, was protected by a single infantry battalion. The Oder River, the principal--indeed, the only--defensive position in the entire theater, was garrisoned by two infantry battalions and eight squadrons of cavalry. Throughout this period, to be sure, the German army paid close attention to the problem of defending the Oder; defense of the river against a hostile force attempting to

cross was the centerpiece of at least one great maneuver.   As
matters stood, however, the Oder River region and Berlin were
sorely undermanned.   Should the international situation have
convinced the Poles to go to war with Germany, a Polish force
advancing along the axis Poznan-Frankfurt on the Oder-Berlin
would have encountered no more than five thousand German
regulars.

Unconstrained by any treaty restrictions and possessing
the confidence of a victorious war, Poland could field a
powerful army on its western border with Germany, at least in
terms of size.   In the early 1920s, Poland's armed forces
included ten army corps of three infantry divisions each, plus
ten cavalry brigades.   In addition, there were large numbers
of independent corps and army formations, including border
defense battalions, armored platoons, and even a chemical battalion.   Not all of these forces, of course, were active on
the German front; Poland's geostrategic position was scarcely
better than Germany's.   The Red Army, which Poland's forces
had defeated so decisively in 1920, stood menacingly to the
east, and Poland's borders on every sector save the the
Romanian had to be guarded closely.   Still, the Polish army
could muster five corps (the I, IV, V, VII, and VIII), around
250,000 men, for service in the German theater.   Each of these
corps was based at one of Poland's major cities (table 2.3).[19]
On every sector of its border with Germany, Poland had what
has to be considered decisive numerical superiority.   On the
Silesian front, for example, the Polish forces amounted to no
less than five full divisions, plus a brigade of cavalry, over
seventy thousand men in all, to face four German battalions.
This amounted to more than a ten to to one Polish superiority
in this crucial region.   The situation was virtually identical
on all the other fronts.   The surrounded province of East
Prussia also faced a severe numerical disadvantage to add to
its hopeless geographical situation.

While the deployment of Polish forces along the border at
first appears aggressive and threatening toward Germany,
closer examination reveals that, just as the German forces
were deployed defensively and in positions not well suited
toward offensive action, so too were the Poles. If the Poles
had been of a mind to obtain further territory to the west,
their deployments should have been near the border.   From
these jumping-off points it was only a short march to the
German heartland. In reality, though, the deployment of large
parts of the Polish army in the interior of the country shows
that the Poles probably feared the Germans just as much as the
Germans feared the Poles.

The deployment of I Corps around Warsaw, Lomza, and
Ostroleka served to screen the capital city from any German
force advancing out of East Prussia.   The 8th Cavalry Brigade
at Ostroleka was especially well suited for this purpose, and
at the same time ill equipped to advance into the tangled
terrain of East Prussia.   In addition, the dispersal of the
8th Cavalry Brigade's regiments along the east-west axis at
Ostroleka and Przasnysz was evidence of its defensive posture.
The horse artillery battalion belonging to the brigade was
actually deployed some miles to the east, at Zambrow, rather
than at Ostroleka with the rest of the brigade.   There is
little doubt that the mission of the 8th Cavalry Brigade was
not to advance into Germany, but merely to act as a screen
against German forces marching on Warsaw from the north.   In

Table 2.3
Polish Forces Facing Germany

I Corps

8th Infantry Division--Warsaw
    21st Infantry Regiment--Warsaw
    13th Infantry Regiment--Pultusk
    32nd Infantry Regiment--Modlin

18th Infantry Division--Lomza
    42nd Infantry Regiment--Bialystok
    33rd Infantry Regiment--Lomza
    71st Infantry Regiment--Ostrow

28th Infantry Division--Warsaw
    36th Infantry Regiment--Warsaw
    15th Infantry Regiment--Demblin
    72nd Infantry Regiment--Radom

1st Cavalry Brigade--Warsaw
    1st Cavalry Regiment--Warsaw
    7th Uhlan Regiment--Minsk-Mazowiecki

8th Cavalry Brigade--Ostroleka
    5th Uhlan Regiment--Ostroleka
    11th Uhlan Regiment--Przasnysz

IV Corps

7th Infantry Division--Czestochowa
    11th Infantry Regiment--Tarnowitz
    25th Infantry Regiment--Piotrkow
    27th Infantry Regiment--Czestochowa

10th Infantry Division--Lodz
    28th Infantry Regiment--Lodz
    30th Infantry Regiment--Warsaw
    31st Infantry Regiment--Lodz

26th Infantry Division--Skiernowice
    10th Infantry Regiment--Lowicz
    37th Infantry Regiment--Leczyca-Kolo

V Corps

6th Infantry Division--Krakow
    12th Infantry Regiment--Wadowice
    16th Infantry Regiment--Tarnow
    20th Infantry Regiment--Krakow

21st Infantry Division--Bielsko-Biala
    1st Infantry Regiment--Zakopane
    3rd Infantry Regiment--Bielsko-Biala
    4th Infantry Regiment--Cieszyn

```
    23rd Infantry Division--Katowice
       74th Infantry Regiment--Lubliniec
       73rd Infantry Regiment--Rybnik, Königshütte
       75th Infantry Regiment--Rybnik, Königshütte

     5th Cavalry Brigade--Krakow
       3rd Uhlan Regiment--Tarnowitz
       8th Uhlan Regiment--Katowice, Krolewska Huta
       2nd Cavalry Regiment--Bielitz


                    VII Corps

    14th Infantry Division--Poznan
       55th Infantry Regiment--Leszno
       57th Infantry Regiment--Poznan
       58th Infantry Regiment--Poznan

  17th Infantry Division--Gniezno
       68th Infantry Regiment--Srem
       69th Infantry Regiment--Gniezno
       70th Infantry Regiment--Jarocin

    25th Infantry Division--Kalisz
       29th Infantry Regiment--Kalisz
       56th Infantry Regiment--Krotoszyn
       60th Infantry Regiment--Pleszew, Ostrow

     7th Cavalry Brigade--Poznan
       15th Uhlan Regiment--Poznan
       16th Uhlan Regiment--Bydgoszcz
       17th Uhlan Regiment--Leszno


                   VIII Corps

     4th Infantry Division--Torun
       14th Infantry Regiment--Wloclawek
       63rd Infantry Regiment--Torun
       67th Infantry Regiment--Torun, Brodnica

  15th Infantry Division--Bydgoszcz
       59th Infantry Regiment--Inowroclaw
       61st Infantry Regiment--Bydgoszcz
       62nd Infantry Regiment--Bydgoszcz

  16th Infantry Division--Grudziadz
       64th Infantry Regiment--Grudziadz
       65th Infantry Regiment--Starogard
       66th Infantry Regiment--Chojnice, Chelmno

     1st Cavalry Brigade--Torun
       18th Uhlan Regiment--Torun
```

the same vein, the 1st Cavalry Brigade was deployed entirely in Warsaw and environs, not in an advanced position near the East Prussian frontier. From this assembly area, it was capable of acting as a reserve should a foreign army threaten the capital from any direction. Both the 1st and 8th Cavalry Brigades had the advantage of superior mobility, so that their garrison areas could be rapidly changed. In their current locations, these units represented a potential rather than a real threat to the security of the German borders. In fact, the placement of the entire I Corps was overwhelmingly defensive in character; the Poles would have been hard-pressed to launch any sort of surprise offensive against Germany with this corps, at least without changing its garrison areas. This precluded any sort of surprise coup de main, which was of course precisely the sort of offensive move the Germans feared most from the Poles.

The placement of IV Corps had the same defensive characteristics as that of I Corps, although it, too, must have seemed threatening to the Germans. Although it contained the 7th Infantry Division at Czestochowa, less than forty kilometers from the Silesian border, the other two divisions were located well to the rear at Lodz and Skiernowice. The division stationed in the latter city, the 26th Infantry, was obviously part of the Warsaw defensive system, while the 10th Infantry Division at Lodz had a primary mission of defending that important industrial and commercial city. The corps contained no cavalry, which was indeed odd if the Poles were planning aggressive war with these troops. The deployment of IV Corps, all in all, was entirely in keeping with the right of national self-defense, and not evidence of a Polish desire for expansion to the west.

Likewise, the deployment of V Corps, which was the unit adjacent to IV Corps, was intended to protect Poland's newly acquired industrial province of Upper Silesia, as well as the region of Cieszyn, which was the object of bitter dispute between Poland and Czechoslovakia. No less than two divisions of infantry, or two-thirds of the entire complement of V Corps, faced south towards the Czechs. The 6th Infantry Division had its regiments strung out west to east, guarding against the Czechs, at Wadowice, Tarnow, and Krakow. From these positions, the division could protect the crucial railway which ran from Przemysl in the east through Rzeszow, Krakow, and finally to Katowice. The west-east orientation of this division meant that it could present no real threat to German Silesia. Even against the Czechs, this division could only function defensively, given the dispersion of its regiments. Likewise, the placement of the 21st Infantry Division, with regiments at Nowy-Sacz, Zakopane, Bielsko-Biala, and Cieszyn, was directed entirely against the Czechs. From these positions the division could protect Krakow, the city of the old Polish kings. The presence of a mountain artillery regiment in this division is further evidence that the Polish General Staff was thinking more in terms of a campaign in the High Tatras than in the relatively flat terrain of Silesia. Only one division, the 23rd Infantry, was directed against the Germans, with one regiment at Lubliniec and two at Rybnik. The divisional staff and artillery were in the center of the division at Katowice. This division was less dispersed than some others in the Polish army, and appeared capable of rapid concentration against Silesia. Still, the Polish deployment

of forces in Upper Silesia was basically defensive, to protect
the new industrial heartland of Poland from expected future
German depredations.   After all, Upper Silesia was the scene
of the only real "German-Polish War" of the period, in 1921.
Throughout the 1920s, the Silesian sector of the border
remained a powderkeg, with constant border violations and very
active irregular forces on both sides.   Both the Poles and
Germans were aware of the importance of Silesia, and both
labored as best they could to amass sufficient strength in
this region.   The deployment of V Corps, then, was certainly
not evidence that the Poles planned to march on Breslau, but a
guarantee that a future rearmed Germany could not march easily
on Czestochowa or Krakow.

     The placement of VII and VIII Corps was similar to that
of the Upper Silesian deployments, but due to their geographic
location, these corps were wholly devoted to the German front.
VII Corps contained divisions at Poznan, Gniezno, and Kalisz,
plus a cavalry brigade at Poznan, and from these positions
this corps was definitely capable of a direct march to
Frankfurt on the Oder and thence to Berlin.   The 14th Infantry
Division had two infantry regiments, plus a light artillery
regiment, concentrated in the city of Poznan.   Its third
infantry regiment was also located in a forward position, at
Leszno.   The 17th Infantry Division had infantry regiments at
Srem, Gniezno, and Jarocin, all within easy marching distance
of the German border.   The 25th Infantry Division had its
regiments particularly close to the border, at Kalisz,
Krotoszyn, Pleszew, and Ostrow, plus a light artillery regiment at Kalisz.   At first glance, these deployments all appear
provocative and threatening.   But Poznan had only joined
Poland as a result of a popular uprising at the end of 1919
and was a region for which the Polish High Command, as well as
popular opinion throughout Poland, feared greatly.   Should a
revived and powerful Germany seek to overturn the verdict of
the past war, it would be very difficult for Poland to hold
this region, given the lack of any defensible terrain in the
area.   The placement of troops within the Poznan region, then,
was to defend the region, not to attack out of it.   From its
garrison areas, VII Corps was best situated to protect the
southern face of the Poznan salient, that is, the sector
bordering on Silesia.

     The task of protecting the northern face of the Poznan
salient went to VIII Corps.   In addition, however, this unit
was ready to face a threat from East Prussia, should the
Germans attack from the north.   The dual mission of VIII Corps
was evident in its divisional deployments.   The 4th Infantry
Division had its headquarters and two infantry regiments at
Torun, where they could move quickly down the Vistula to
reinforce Bydgoszcz against any threat from the west.   At the
same time, however, the division's 14th Infantry Regiment was
placed upriver at Wloclawek, which would enable the division
to deploy facing north in the event of a German invasion from
the Eylau district of East Prussia.   The 15th Infantry had the
same two up-one back deployment.   Two of its regiments, plus
the headquarters and divisional artillery, were placed at
Bydgoszcz, where they could protect the northern sector of
Poznan from a German invasion emanating from the Schneidemühl-
Deutsch Krone region.   Bydgoszcz was also an important river,
rail, and road center, and commanded the routes of communication between Danzig and the Polish heartland.   In addition,

the division's 59th Infantry Regiment was at Inowroclaw, so that the division was capable, as was the 4th Division, of turning to face East Prussia if a threat should develop from the Marienwerder district. Finally, the deployment of the 16th Infantry Division was even more obviously defensive than the rest of VIII Corps. The Versailles treaty had created a defensive nightmare for Poland in the so-called "Polish Corridor." Uncomfortably squeezed between the German provinces of Pomerania and East Prussia and no more than thirty kilometers wide at its narrowest point, the Corridor was a thorny defensive problem for the Poles. The Corridor could not be abandoned in case of war, since the region represented Poland's access to the Baltic Sea and contained the primary port city of Gdynia. The creation of the Corridor is often portrayed, and indeed was considered by the Germans at the time, as a grave strategic blow to Germany, since it cut off East Prussia from the Reich and the mouth of the Vistula from German territory. Yet Poland's acquisition of the territory gave Poland a great stake in defending the region for both offensive reasons, since the Corridor kept Germany weak and divided, and defensive reasons, since it guaranteed Polish communications with Gdynia and the Baltic. At the same time, political considerations and the sometimes jittery nerves of the inhabitants of the region forced the Polish government to provide the area with a strong defensive force. It was the task of the 16th Infantry Division to guard the Corridor, but, given the peculiar geography of the region, it would have been potentially disastrous to deploy the entire division in the Corridor itself. The solution of the Polish High Command was to deploy the division at the base of the Corridor, with its regiments at Grudziadz, Starogard, and the Chojnice-Chelmno region. This arrangement served several purposes. The Polish forces in Starogard and Chojnice were within marching distance of Danzig and Gdynia; the regiment at Chojnice also guarded the border with Pomerania, while those at Grudziadz and Starogard watched over the Marienwerder district of East Prussia. The last unit of VIII Corps was the understrength 1st Cavalry Brigade, which contained only a single uhlan regiment. It was stationed at Torun, where it assisted the 4th Infantry Division in defense of the Torun-Inowroclaw-Wloclawek region. While the Germans complained repeatedly of threatening Polish troop concentrations in the Corridor throughout this period, the fact is that, given the particularly difficult mission of VIII Corps, its deployment was in no way a strategic threat to Germany.

Despite the defensive character of the deployment of the Polish army, however, the Poles did hold a potentially decisive numerical superiority over the Reichsheer in the probable theater of war. The political and military leadership of Germany, as well as the German population at large, feared for the safety of their eastern provinces and felt especially threatened by the possibility of a Polish fait accompli somewhere along the border. The events of the immediate postwar period, particularly the Polish seizure of Poznan and Wilno, had convinced the German leadership, especially General Seeckt, that Poland would likely turn again to arms to gain its national objectives. For this reason, the German military found it necessary to search for ways to redress the numerical imbalance. One such method was the recruitment of irregular border guard forces, often made up of violent, poorly disciplined, anti-Republican freebooters. The border guards were distributed all along the eastern border, but they were particularly active in Silesia, Pomerania, and East Prussia. Although they were large in number, their military effectiveness should not be overestimated. Seeckt himself had only distrust for these irregular forces, whose lack of discipline and true military bearing was the antithesis of Seeckt's concept of soldiering. It would not be extreme to say that he viewed the paramilitary formations as a hindrance rather than a help in solving Germany's defense problems.

Another method by which the German army attempted to make up for its small size was the preservation, and in some cases the expansion, of Germany's extensive system of fortifications on its eastern and southern borders. Article 180 of the Versailles treaty stipulated that the fortifications on the south and east frontiers of Germany were to remain in the state they were in at the time of the coming into effect of the treaty, that is, 10 January 1920, while Article 167 stated that, on the ratification of the treaty, the German government had to communicate to the Allied governments the number and caliber of guns in the fortresses, fortress works, and fortified places. These figures were to represent maximums not to be exceeded by Germany.[20]

The question of the fortifications was a major issue throughout the 1920s. The civilian population of the border provinces came to see in the fortifications their last line of defense against the Poles. Likewise, the German government thought that the fortifications were indispensable for Germany's frontiers and based their arguments in the fortress controversy on Articles 180 and 167 of the Versailles treaty. "These two articles," wrote the chief of German coastal artillery, "undoubtedly purposed to give Germany which had been denuded of fortresses in the west, a certain degree of security in the east."[21] The Poles, for their part, came to see the fortifications as places d'armes, behind which the Germans were assembling a powerful army of revenge. The Allies, who actually exercised jurisdiction over the entire matter through their Commission of Control, viewed the fortifications as yet another symptom of German obstinacy toward fulfilling the provisions of the Versailles treaty. Ironically, while the fortifications held the attention of the military officials of all the concerned countries, it was felt by many contemporary military thinkers that the fortifications themselves were obsolete and of doubtful utility to the conduct of modern war.

A memorandum on the fortifications question, drawn up by the German War Office in 1920, argued that the forts were necessary for Germany.[22] The new German boundaries, the War Office argued, were much more unfavorable than the old ones from the standpoint of national defense. In the west, the Rhine boundary was protection much inferior to the Vosges Mountains; in the south and east, Germany now had restless, unreliable, and highly nationalistic states from which it was separated only partly by an historical and natural boundary (the Erzgebirge in Bohemia). To compensate for its lack of defensible borders, Germany required effective fortifications. Even before the war, the Reich had exceedingly small and weak boundary forts, considering the dangers to which its boundaries were exposed. In addition, the War Office claimed, the peace treaty had specified that Germany raze or abandon its best works.   The new borders, therefore, had only the minimum level of protection.

The memorandum listed four groups of fortifications: the East Prussian and West Prussian forts (Königsberg, Pillau, Lötzen with the lake fortifications, and Marienburg); fortifications on the Czech border and the Oder fortifications (Königstein, Glatz, Neisse, Breslau, Glogau, Küstrin, and Swinemünde); western and inland German fortresses (Ulm, Ingolstadt, and Spandau); and the coast and island defenses.   Of these four groups, only two were of significance to the eastern front.   The East and West Prussian forts were the most important group, given the exposed nature of East Prussia. Königsberg and Pillau together formed the main fortification system.   Lötzen and the extensive Masurian Lakes fortifications provided cover for Königsberg on the southeast. Marienburg was an important crossing point for road and rail communications on the German right flank.

Königsberg, the War Office declared, was the central point of the administrative, economic, and spiritual life of the parts of East and West Prussia remaining to Germany.   The most important East Prussian railway lines passed through the city.   As a Baltic harbor and as an outlet city for the navigable Pregel River, Königsberg is also connected with numerous waterways.   Whoever occupied Königsberg was therefore in control of the province, and that is why the fortifications around the city were so important in German eyes.

The operational mission of the fortress of Königsberg was twofold in nature: to cut off access to the Samland from the land side, in connection with the line of communication provided by the Kurisches Haff and the Pregel-Deime line (Königsberg-Tapiau-Labiau); and in case the resources for the first task were insufficient, to serve as an independent system of outlying forts and secure the possession of the city of Königsberg and block the lines of communication.

The fortress of Pillau acted as a naval strongpoint, as well as protecting the entrance to the Frisches Haff and the approaches to the Kurisches Haff.   The fortress also served as a rear protection for Königsberg.   The seaward front was therefore its main front.   Where Pillau faced the interior of the province, the fort was only minimally secure, for the fortress Königsberg formed its land cover.   Together with Königsberg, Pillau had to protect the greater part of the Samland coast.

Boyen, an independent little fortress, blocked the most important narrow passes through the East Prussian lake chain at Lötzen and the lines of communication there.   It was also the main point of the Masurian Lakes fortifications, a fortified line of simple form which stretched from Ortelsburg almost up to Angerburg.   The purpose of this line was to prevent a penetration of the front by the enemy, but it consisted of relatively small concrete dugouts and some artillery emplacements.

The fortress of Marienburg centered around the old walled city.   It was originally the bridgehead of the important Vistula and Nogat river crossings at Dirschau and Marienburg. According to the new geo-political situation, the fortress now served as a protection for the railway lines and waterways which unite at Marienburg.   Its main front faced to the south. It could interdict important approaches in the direction of Königsberg and Elbing as well as Danzig.   The newly created

Free State of Danzig protected the northern flank of the fortress.   As long as Danzig remained neutral, the possibilities
for attack against Marienburg were limited.
     The Czech border was covered by only three relatively
small and old forts, Königstein, Glatz, and Neisse.   These
were of local importance since they could block the roads
which pass through and near them, and Königstein had the added
significance of blocking the Elbe some twenty kilometers up-
stream of Dresden.   Although it was not difficult, the War
Office argued, to bypass these forts, they were so equipped as
to be able, independently--in this case as a ring fort--to
resist for a long time any attacking force which was not
equipped with heavy siege guns.   The attacker, should he
decide to merely bypass the forts, would find his lines of
communication and reinforcement to any bypassing force
hindered.
     According to the War Office, the Polish border was lack-
ing in almost every sort of protection by fortification.   On
the Oder, there were only three separate fortresses, all of
which were primarily bridgeheads on the right bank of the
river.   They also had to be able, in case of necessity, to
hold out independently as long as possible.   The three Oder
forts were the following:

     1. Breslau.   The Königsberg of Silesia, Breslau was
     the economic and administrative center of the prov-
     ince.   The most important Silesian lines of communi-
     cation joined here, and there were, of course, a
     large number of Oder bridges in the city.   The
     fortress protected both the important city and the
     Oder crossings.
     2.   Glogau.   Almost 100 kilometers downstream along
     the Oder from Breslau, Glogau was of significance as
     an Oder bridgehead, and for protecting other impor-
     tant Oder crossings in its vicinity.
     3.   Küstrin.   Another 150 kilometers down the Oder
     from Glogau, Küstrin was a more extensive fortified
     area because of its advanced forts.   Of great stra-
     tegic importance, it guarded the confluence of the
     Warta and Oder rivers.   It was only 70 kilometers
     from Berlin, and sat astride the Berlin-Poznan axis.
     In addition, many Oder bridges were within its
     reach.

Finally, the Oder group of forts included the Baltic port of
Swinemünde, because this fort protected the Oder mouth and
Stettin against attacks from the sea.   Like Pillau, the main
front of this fortress faced the sea; the land front was only
secure against sudden attacks. The War Office considered this
sufficient, since a landward siege of Swinemünde hardly
appeared probable in the near future.   Should Swinemünde be
threatened from its landward side, it was quite likely that
the German High Command, if one was left, would have more
pressing worries than defense of the Baltic coast.
     According to the War Office, the permanent structures of
most of these forts were few in number and old.   In many
cases, they did not even lie within the defensive line of the
fortresses.   In spite of this, the Germans considered the
permanent structures to be of considerable value as local supporting points.   They did at least offer safe shelter against

light fire and storms, and required heavy fire for their destruction. "They serve the most important function of every fortification--the gaining of time." To speak of a German "system of fortifications," however, was to exaggerate the degree to which the forts protected the frontier. Individual spots, such as Königsberg and Pillau, were strongly protected, but the greater part of the Polish-German border was what nature had created in the area--an open plain.

In conclusion, the War Office argued that the number of forts left to Germany was exceedingly small in proportion to German territory. However, in proportion to the number of troops permitted to Germany, it was too large. While this might seem illogical, it was not. The Germans did not feel that it would be necessary to reckon with a simultaneous defense of all the forts. The garrison troops could, in case of necessity, be transferred to the threatened fortifications. The level of equipment which Germany was demanding for these fortresses, about 4,100 pieces of artillery in all, was more than the small number the troops could operate. The Germans argued that, in case of emergency, the equipment of a fort had to be so arranged that garrison troops thrown into the fort would find everything already there and would not have to come fully equipped.

The Allies did not accept the German arguments regarding the arming of the fortresses. On 20 March 1920, the head of the Interallied Control Commission, the French General Nollet, declared that, in his opinion, the armament levels which the Germans had requested were excessive. In a note to the German government, he stated that "only those guns could be retained which actually belonged to the barbettes on the ratification date of the Treaty."[23] In layman's terms, only those guns which were permanently emplaced could be kept by the Germans. This decision meant that Breslau, Glogau, Glatz, Neisse, Spandau, Boyen, Marienburg, Ingolstadt, and Königstein could not retain any artillery, since "they possessed no fortifications worthy of the name to permit of battery emplacement, or do not at present possess such battery armament."[24] Nollet and the commission permitted Pillau and Swinemünde to retain their heavy guns, 25 at Pillau and 28 at Swinemünde, which formed the coastal batteries of these two naval strongpoints.

On 16 April, the German government protested against what it called "this narrow and partial interpretation of the Peace Treaty."[25] Modern fortresses, it claimed, no longer possessed permanent battery emplacements. The French did not contemplate the defense of their fortresses by emplaced guns, since in modern warfare the artillery was for the most part placed outside of the permanent works. It was further pointed out that the treaty contained no justification for such a limitation of the German fortress artillery. On 23 May, the Allies received another German protest, plus an armament scheme by which the fortresses of Königsberg, Swinemünde, Pillau, Küstrin, and Ulm would have been allowed a total of 836 cannon.[26]

Nollet rejected totally these German demands. In response to the German note of 23 May, he reduced even further the amount of artillery permitted to the Germans by stating that Küstrin and Ulm would be allowed no artillery at all, because of a lack of suitable battery positions. Also, on 18 October, Nollet rendered his decision with regard to Königsberg, which he granted the grand total of 22 artillery

pieces.   Needless to say,   allowing 22 artillery pieces to   a
city   the size of Königsberg was tantamount to   disarming   it
totally.[27]
    Though   the German government protested against this   ex-
tension of the treaty provisions,   it ordered on 20 December
that all fortress guns be surrendered to the Allies.   At the
same time,   on account of the menace from Poland,   the government requested that the disarmament of Königsberg, Küstrin,
and Boyen be postponed.   The Allies were informed that the
three fortresses required 578 guns to be defended adequately;
390 guns,   including 298 of heavy caliber,   were to be left in
Königsberg.   On 25 January 1921,   the Allies   informed   the
German   government   that   its   request   had   been   denied.
Consequently,   the guns at Königsberg, Küstrin, and Boyen were
handed over to the Allies.
    The German High Command considered East Prussia to be the
region most in need of supporting fortifications.   The number
of guns permitted to the province's major city, however, was
so small   that it virtually precluded a successful   artillery
defense of the fortress.   In June 1921,   the Germans reported
that they had the following artillery pieces in Königsberg:
12 150mm howitzers (range, 8,500 meters); 2 long 210mm mortars
(range, 10,200 meters); 6 100mm cannon (range, 11,900 meters);
and 2 150mm cannon (range,   22,000 meters).   Besides these 22
guns,   there were 16 flak guns in Königsberg and 10 in Pillau.
The Allies permitted this small number so that the Germans
could protect the artillery in the two forts.[28]
    Nollet's demand that fixed carriages be provided to all
the fortress guns,   besides serving as a pretext for reducing
the number of artillery pieces allowed to the Germans,   also
created severe tactical constraints on the use of Königsberg
as a fort.   Once mounted,   the guns could neither be stripped
for use by troops in the field nor moved tactically for a more
flexible   defense   of Königsberg.   The Germans protested
vigorously against Nollet's demand by arguing that it stepped
beyond   the   bounds of the Versailles treaty and also that
mounting the guns permanently would make them useless, since
it would   not be possible for the guns   to change position,
making   them vulnerable to enemy counter-battery fire.[29]   The
question of fixed mounts for the fortress artillery pieces was
a constant source of friction between the Allies   and   the
Germans.   At an inspection which the Interallied Control
Commission carried out between 8 September 1924 and 25 January
1925,   it was found that only 4 of Königsberg's 38 guns were
permanently mounted,   while 22 had no fixed bases.   Of the 22
artillery pieces,   only 12 were mounted.   Twelve of the 16 flak
guns were even used in the maneuvers of 1924.[30]
    The best description we have of fortress Königsberg is
that of the American military attache during the 1920s,
Colonel A. L. Conger.   During a trip to East Prussia, Conger
was invited by the German High Command to see the fortress   of
Königsberg and the coast fort of Pillau.   Conger accepted, and
the commandant of Königsberg received orders to show the
American any part of the works he cared to see.   Conger sent
this   description,   in a confidential report,   back   to
Washington:

        The ancient fortress dating back several centuries
        comprises works on the Vauban system immediately
        surrounding the town. . . including the moat on the

south side, which is fed by the Pregel. The present
modern fortress dates back to the period between '60
and '70, when most of the forts of the middle
circle, about 64 in number, were constructed. As
the valley of the Pregel in which this circle lies
is, particularly on the south side, low and marshy,
these forts for the most part are raised above
ground and were built before the days of modern
heavy artillery, so that they are not of sufficient
strength to withstand modern heavy calibers. In
fact, the Germans regard them as semi-obsolete. At
the time of the construction of this line of forts
the circular road was constructed both to facilitate
the construction and to serve as a line of communications between the forts, some of which are inside
and some outside the fortified line. This road is
flanked by a double row of trees on the outer side
and a single row on the inner side and the
Commandant with a passing remark laughed about the
simplicity of the constructors of that period who
thus advertised their line of communications between
the forts.

Shortly after 1900 it became recognized that
the line of forts was too near the town to afford
safety from long-range artillery and that a line
farther out must be adopted to furnish adequate
protection, and work on the construction of a new
line was begun. This line consists of a zone
several kilometers in depth, which was never really
completed until after the outbreak of the World War.
During the World War this line of outer works was
further extended along the north bank of the Pregel
and from the Pregel northward to the Baltic.

This wartime construction was mostly of wood
and earth and consisted for the most part of shelters for the personnel and a few emplacements for
guns, Minenwerfer, etc. Since the War, many of
these have been replaced with concrete.

The Commandant remarked rather bitterly:
"There is now no reason why you or anyone else
should not be shown the plans of this fort and every
part of it, since the British and the French both
have these plans and they are no longer a secret."

Conger also visited and described several small forts and
shelters around Königsberg:

The fort which we visited on the first line was a
brick construction on its inner face and consisted
of a long arched tunnel with transversal arms
covered overhead with six feet of earth. There were
several flanking tunnels and the whole work, which
was about 200 meters east and west by about 150
north and south, was planned to furnish quarters for
an infantry battalion. It had various iron turrets
on the outer wall to serve as command and observation posts. On the walls stood two anti-aircraft
guns, which the Commandant remarked were perfectly
useless, since they had been required to adopt
definite locations for all their anti-aircraft guns,

which rendered them useless as the locations were of
course made known promptly to the Poles. The total
height of the fort above ground level is about 30
feet. The Commandant remarked that it was perfectly
useless, since it would not stand modern artillery
fire and was merely a historical relic. The date of
its construction, as I remember, was 1879.   There
were no guns in this fort (except the anti-aircraft)
but to the right rear on the other side of the
fortified line was an artillery fort which housed a
number of 6 and 8 inch guns.
     We then went to see some of the more modern
concrete shelters. Most of these are located in the
woods but some of them are concealed within farm
buildings or outbuildings.   One of these had just
been destroyed and I saw that the concrete walls
were about a meter thick and that the foundations
extended about 4 feet below the surface. The floors
of the shelters were about 3 feet below the ground
surface, which was as far down as they dared to put
them on account of the ground water.
     I was then shown a second shelter, which con-
sisted of a lateral passage-way with two entrances
and two rooms, separated by a concrete wall, each
capable of housing a squad. These rooms were closed
with quarter-inch iron doors leading from the
passage-way, which was on the rear side of the
shelter and protected against a shell burst in the
rear of the shelter by an outer wall of concrete
faced with earth.   The whole was covered with about
6 feet of earth, which was grass-covered, so that
the only thing that showed from the outside was a
grass-grown mound with the two entrances on the rear
side by the passage-way. . . .
     It is quite evident to me from this inspection
and from what was told me that the defense of
Königsberg is not planned to be made from any fixed
positions but it is to be an elastic machine gun
defense with the position of the machine guns and
the artillery constantly changing, not only from day
to day but from hour to hour, and the shelters are
only to protect the machine gun and artillery
personnel in the event of a heavy bombardment.
These shelters can be constructed in a few days time
at the outside and it is safe to say that the wires
to furnish telephone connection in the places
selected for the additional works desired are
already in place.
     The works which connect the fortified line
with the Baltic Sea to the north do not appear to
have been kept up since the War, as since that date
a Russian advance has no longer been feared, but the
works on the south of the Pregel are much more
modern and much more closely spaced than those north
of the Pregel.[31]

Conger's last observation reflects the fact that German
anxiety for Königsberg was now directed to the south of the
city, to a possible Polish advance into East Prussia.

It is clear, then, that Königsberg was not much of a fortress. As a defensive position, it left much to be desired, especially with regard to its vulnerability to fire and lack of artillery support. Traditionally, however, fortified areas had an important function besides their purely defensive one. They could also act as a screen behind which armies might concentrate for offensive action and as important supply centers in their own right. In 1805, Napoleon concentrated his corps behind the line of fortresses on the Rhine River before swooping down on the unfortunate Austrian General Karl Mack at Ulm. Likewise, it was the skillful defense of the fortified Vosges Mountains which had enabled the German army to assemble so many corps for the march of its right wing through Belgium in 1914. Not surprisingly, it was the offensive potential of the German fortresses which the Poles and their French sponsors preferred to stress. The American military attache to Poland during this period, Colonel R. McKenney, reported that the Poles questioned the defensive character of the German fortifications, particularly in light of the Regulations on Field Fortification which the Germans had published in 1922. These regulations stated that "a position is of no value unless it creates favorable conditions for an attack. Fortified positions must be so chosen that they may not only permit a defense, but offer also favorable conditions for a subsequent attack."[32] McKenney agreed with the Polish view that, for the Germans, there were no other fortifications but offensive.

The discovery in 1926 that the Germans had been constructing new concrete Unterstände, or bunkers, around Königsberg, Küstrin, and Glogau further worried the Poles and angered the Interallied Control Commission, under whose collective nose the construction had proceeded. Again, what the Germans considered to be clearly defensive works, the Poles feared as a potential base for a future offensive. Although the Germans agreed, under Allied pressure, to destroy these bunkers, the affair heightened tension between the Germans on the one hand and the French and the Poles on the other.

The question of the fortifications and the bunkers received wide attention in popular journals and newspapers in Paris and Warsaw. An article in Le Temps of 20 January 1927 accused the Germans of creating in East Prussia "an offensive and defensive base against Poland" with one hand while signing the Locarno pact with the other:

> We now know that 88 concrete shelters have been constructed since 1922 on the German-Polish frontier, and there are undoubtedly others. These fortified bases, which form part of the fortifications of Königsberg, Lötzen, Küstrin, and Glogau, menace and surround Poland. Thus, Königsberg becomes a great base, both maritime and military, and constitutes with Lötzen, in the Mazurian lakes, a direct menace to Warsaw, which is some 200 km to the south. The fortified position of Königsberg is 20 kilometers long, at 20 kilometers south of the town, and includes 54 new concrete constructions--known--which are no less than 1m.50 in height and which lend themselves to many different uses. Lötzen is the second great base in eastern Prussia. Partly covered by the Mazurian lakes, it commands

the roads to Bialystok and Suwalki, and consequently
is capable of cutting the communications between
Warsaw and Wilno.   Such is the northern part of the
German pincers erected against Poland.[33]

It is hard to find a suitable place to begin criticizing this
characterization of the German defense system. It suffices to
say only that any military analyst who believed that the
fortress of Lötzen was "capable of cutting the communications
between Warsaw and Wilno" was in desperate need of a geography
lesson. The article is interesting, however, in that it is an
example of the kind of popular journalistic account to which
the populations of France, Germany, and Poland were so often
subjected.

An article in the Polish newspaper Rzeczpospolita from
the same period stated that the German fortresses could act as
strongpoints for a field army. The author failed to point
out, however, that the Germans had no field army at the time,
but insisted that the existence of the fortifications showed
that the Germans were preparing for a climactic final struggle
with Poland.[34] Simultaneously, the Paris journal
Intransigeant carried two lengthy articles describing an
"extensive zone of fortifications," which, unfortunately for
the Germans, existed only in the writer's imagination:

> The most extensive zone of fortifications is that of
> the Mazurian Lakes, which commands all routes of
> access toward Königsberg and Danzig. It has a
> frontage of 120 kilometers and a depth of 40 kilo-
> meters; it includes the wooded areas and extremely
> difficult roads and presents an impenetrable front.
> Boyen is the center of this zone. To the north of
> the Mazurian Lakes around 50 kilometers east of
> Königsberg is another region, that of the Deime
> River, which blocks access from the east. Finally,
> to the north and south of Königsberg, forming a sort
> of secondary line in case the first has been
> breached, are two other fortified positions. It is
> clear that the city of Königsberg has become the
> center of a vast fortified region.[35]

In fact, there was no such extensive system of fortresses
in East Prussia or anywhere on the German-Polish frontier. In
a report to Washington in February 1927, Colonel Conger gave
his assessment of Königsberg fortress, stating that it "has
never been and is not now a fortress comparable to Metz or
Verdun as the latter stood in the World War."[36] Later, he
responded to McKenney's description of Königsberg, Marienburg,
and Küstrin as "three great fortresses" by noting that the
three were

> antiquated fortified towns according to the system
> of Vauban, constructed in the time of Frederick the
> Great and already obsolete and incapable of defense
> in the time of Napoleon. The defenses of Marienburg
> consist chiefly in a bridge with tessellated brick
> piers over the Vistula, provided with fancy sentry
> boxes unoccupied on the six occasions I have passed
> over it.[37]

We should give Conger, who had access to the fortresses and probably knew as much about them as any non-German, the final word on the matter. He called the fortresses "merely relics of curiosity," not important factors in the balance of military power between Germany and Poland.[38]

Despite the attention given by the Allies to the question of the fortifications, the German High Command knew that semi-obsolete and weakly armed fortifications could not guarantee the security of Germany's borders. Still less could Germany rely on the power of its army, due to its small size. Army expansion, however, was forbidden by the Versailles treaty, and an Interallied Control Commission operated on German soil to ensure German compliance. The only logical solution to Germany's military dilemma was to improve the quality of the German army, to substitute increased mobility, striking power, and tactical savvy for the mass on which Germany had relied during the First World War. This solution was, of course, more easily recognized than achieved. Fortunately for the Germans, however, the leader of the Reichswehr was precisely the right sort of man for the job of creating a small elite force. This man was General Hans von Seeckt.

For Hans von Seeckt, leadership of the Reichswehr marked "the last and most brilliant phase of an illustrious career."[39] Seeckt was born on 22 April 1868 in Schleswig, the son of a Prussian general. His own military career was characterized by quick progress up the ladder of promotion. He received his commission in 1887 with the Guard Grenadier Regiment. In 1899, while still a lieutenant, he received a post with the Great General Staff in Berlin. By 1902, he was a captain, by 1909 a major. He became chief of the General Staff of the IIIrd Army Corps in 1913 and he held this post when war broke out in 1914.

Seeckt's laurels in the war were won exclusively on the eastern front. As chief of staff to the armies under the command of General August von Mackensen, he directed the decisive breakthrough of the Russian front between Gorlice and Tarnow in 1915, an achievement which won him great acclaim in the military circles of all the warring nations. In 1916, still playing Ludendorff to Mackensen's Hindenburg, he led the German armies in their lightning conquest of the Romanian army. As the war's main theater shifted to the west, Seeckt was transferred to Constantinople as chief of operations for the German military mission in Turkey.

Seeckt's experiences on the eastern front indelibly stamped his own military doctrine. Although the victories over which he presided were certainly hard-fought, the very vastness and lack of covering terrain in the east prevented the development of the same kind of Stellungskrieg, or war of position, which had occurred in northern France. In an important sense, Seeckt was unimpressed with the so-called "lessons of the First World War," or at least those lessons which he saw as nothing more than the lessons of the western front: the invulnerability of entrenched infantry, the futility of infantry assault, the omnipotence of the machine gun, the utter dominance of the defense. Of course, Seeckt was aware of the developments in military technology during the previous few decades and understood their significance to contemporary warfare. At the same time, however, he refused to bow to the inevitability of machines dominating men on the battlefield of the future and continued to think of modern war as a war of movement. During the 1915 Gorlice campaign, Seeckt had personally observed the 2nd Guards Division take no fewer than fifty-three strongly fortified Russian positions by a skillful combination of fire and movement. With proper direction, he thought, the army of the future would participate in decisive battles of maneuver and annihilation, rather than sterile and indecisive contests of position and attrition.

Seeckt viewed the existence of mass armies as an anachronism. During the war, these huge masses had been totally incapable, in his opinion, of forcing a decision. Seeckt considered their lack of mobility as the root cause of their inability to win decisive victories. In an article which he wrote in 1928, "Modernes Heer," Seeckt stated, "The mass cannot maneuver; therefore it cannot win." The development of military technology had transformed these immovable masses into "cannon fodder for a small number of technicians on the opposite side."[40] The army of the future would be large enough only to fight off an enemy surprise attack, and would have three main characteristics: high mobility, aided by a large contingent of cavalry, well-conditioned infantry, and motorization and/or mechanization; effective weaponry, including light machine guns and mobile artillery; and small size, since Seeckt thought that quality and quantity were not compatible in his modern army. The last point is particularly relevant to Seeckt's position as Reichswehr commander, since he had been called upon to lead one of Europe's smallest armies. The First World War had been an era of increasing size and decreasing effectiveness for all of Europe's armies. Universal conscription meant nothing more than poorly trained recruits, increased casualties, and discipline problems. The limitations imposed by these forces had, in his view, led to the war of position in the west. In the future, armies should consist of long-term volunteers. The use of volunteers would ensure that the force had good morale and a high degree of self-motivation; the increased length of service would enable the soldiers to develop a sense of discipline, comradeship, and patriotism, as well as provide the necessary time for the enlisted personnel to become well versed in the handling and performance of the new military technology.

One facet of Seeckt's military thought which deserves special mention was his idea that cavalry still retained usefulness in modern war. Seeckt considered the phrase "cavalry is superfluous" to be a mere slogan which stemmed from a basic misreading of the events of the war.[41] While he recognized the limitations of cavalry in the face of heavy firepower, he did not consider it to be obsolete. In particular, he felt that the development of air power and mechanization of ground forces, far from replacing cavalry, could augment it and make it even more effective. Air power could aid the cavalry in one of its traditional tasks, long-range reconnaissance; motorization of infantry would allow the foot soldiers to accompany and support the cavalry.[42] Other tasks delegated to the cavalry in Seeckt's doctrine included taking a foe in his flank or rear, protection of the borders while the main army mobilized, disruption of an enemy's mobilization, and protecting the flank of friendly armies on the march. In short, Seeckt viewed the future of cavalry as an extension of its past, once the conduct of war had been freed from the shackles of positional warfare. The true effective-

ness of cavalry, Seeckt believed, lay in its superior
mobility. Seeckt's study of the American Civil War, the
Russian Civil War, and the Turkish-Greek War had convinced him
that cavalry was still capable of effective maneuver on the
battlefield. Tactically, cavalry could use its mobility to
seize favorable terrain, engage the enemy in short firefights
using light machine guns and carbines, break off the engagement, then reappear elsewhere, all with an eye to discomfiting
the enemy force. Of course, it was axiomatic by this time
that cavalry must engage the enemy dismounted and operate
mounted only to change its location. Seeckt urged that
cavalrymen remain in the saddle as long as possible so as to
exploit more fully their advantage in maneuver and thought
that where the enemy was weak or disrupted, mounted attack was
still possible.

What was perhaps most interesting about Seeckt was his
stress on offensive action as the only suitable strategy for a
modern army. At a time when the French army was thinking of a
future war in terms of static positions and overwhelming
firepower, Seeckt emphasized the superiority of offensive to
defensive strategy. In "Modernes Heer," he wrote that "destruction of the opposing army . . . is still the highest law
of war." The method which he preferred, and which had been a
favored strategy of all the great German strategists, was the
encirclement of the enemy.[43] Total victory, he wrote in a
later article, was still possible through exploitation of
superior mobility: "The goal of modern strategy will be to
achieve a decision with highly mobile, highly capable forces,
before the masses have begun to move.[44] While the mobility he
had in mind was basically the mobility of the horse rather
than the internal combustion engine, Seeckt did give considerable encouragement to those within the army who argued for the
motorization of the armed forces. As early as October 1921,
the Reichswehr conducted maneuvers of motorized units in the
Harz mountains; in the winter of 1923-24, the army used
maneuvers to investigate the possibilities of cooperation
between motorized ground forces and air forces.[45] The latter
arm, of course, was still forbidden to Germany at the time.
Throughout Seeckt's career as head of the Reichswehr, he made
sure, through strenuous field and classroom training for each
officer and enlisted man, that the army was imbued with his
own offensive spirit. In his stress on quick maneuver to
crush the enemy before he had fully mobilized was the seed
which later German military strategists would transform into
Blitzkrieg, or lightning war. One of Seeckt's earliest operational plans for a campaign against Poland, drawn up in 1920,
illustrated his predilection for aggressive, offensive
maneuver and also demonstrated his preference for the great
encirclement. The plan called for a vast pincers movement
against the Polish heartland. One German army would invade
Poland from the districts of Bentschen and Glogau in Silesia;
the other, northern wing would concentrate on the Polish
border around Schneidemühl and move south towards an eventual
link-up with the southern arm. Although Seeckt never got a
chance to try out this plan, a later group of German military
leaders did attempt a quite similar one--in 1939.[46]

If we compare Seeckt's concept of an ideal army--a small,
highly trained, highly maneuverable force, consisting of
volunteers and schooled in the art of offensive warfare--with
the army he actually commanded, we see that the Reichswehr was

very much a force to his liking.   He was not merely making a
virtue out of Germany's adversity; he truly felt that his
Reichswehr was the army of the future.   Even the gravest
organizational weakness of the army, that 30 percent of its
effectives were enlisted in cavalry divisions, did not dis-
tress him.   In 1927, he stated that "he never regretted" the
decision of the Allies to include so much cavalry in the
Reichswehr.[47]

Actually, the army was only about half as large as Seeckt
would have liked.   He was not so much disturbed by its small
size as about its size relative to the armies of Poland and
France.   At the Spa Conference of 1920, where the Allies
decided to enforce a 100,000-man limit on the Reichswehr,
Seeckt had argued unsuccessfully for a 200,000-man army.   Even
this figure was actually far less than what Seeckt felt was
necessary for Germany's defense.   Without a general disarmament, though, Seeckt considered the 100,000-man limit a ridic-
ulously small figure.   The Allies, of course, did not agree,
and ordered the German army to reduce its effectives to
100,000 men by January 1921.   Seeckt placed the blame for
Allied intransigence on the army issue at the door of the
French, who in his opinion had finally achieved their primary
war aim of a militarily powerless Germany.[48]

Seeckt took the same view toward the reestablishment of
the Polish state, in which he saw nothing more than a French
attempt to perpetuate German weakness by providing itself with
a permanent eastern front against Germany.   Although Seeckt
has become known to history as "the Sphinx" for his reserve
and inscrutability, he was quite outspoken on the Polish
question.   Poland's existence, he wrote, was unbearable to
Germany, and irreconcilable with Germany's national
existence.[49]

Seeckt's views toward Poland, which were shared by much
of the rest of the German Officer Corps, were a result of his
Prussian background as well as his personal participation in
many of the events which led to Poland's reappearance on the
European map.   During the war, of course, he had campaigned on
Polish soil.   Immediately after the war, he was attached to
the High Command Liaison Office in Königsberg.   In this post,
he was involved in the retreat of the German armies from the
east, an incredibly complex task made more difficult by the
advance of the Bolshevik forces and the chaotic conditions
prevailing on the rail lines running through central Poland.
In January 1919, he was named chief of the General Staff of
the newly formed Border Guard North (Oberkommando Grenzschutz
Nord), whose mission was to establish a viable defense of the
German border between the Vistula and the Baltic Sea against
the Bolsheviks.   He participated in the reorganization of the
army in March 1919, and in April was named to the German
delegation to Versailles as military advisor.

It was his humiliating treatment by the Allies at
Versailles and the terms of the treaty itself which did the
most to shape Seeckt's views toward Poland.   The provisions
which disarmed Germany and forced it to surrender so much
territory to Poland, he stated, had made the Reich "defenseless and dishonored" (wehrlos und ehrlos).[50] The establishment of an independent Poland, which in his view could be
nothing more than a French satellite, especially disturbed
him.   There was only one path to a brighter future for
Germany, and that was, first, to reestablish Germany's

military power.   Once Germany had rejoined the ranks of great
powers and become "capable of forming an alliance" (bündnisfähig), it would have to find an ally.   Ideally,   this ally
would have to have a large army and be well suited geograph-
ically to aid Germany in revising the treaty.
     Naturally,   Seeckt looked to Russia as a state with which
Germany   shared a community of interests regarding   the
Versailles treaty in general and Poland in particular.   Russia
and Germany,   the two outcast states of the postwar world,
encircled Poland just as France and Poland encircled Germany.
With Russian aid, Germany was reasonably secure against a
joint Franco-Polish invasion.   In the future, the two great
powers could cooperate for the destruction of Poland, since
"Poland's existence was more unbearable for Russia than for
Germany." In a long promemoria which Seeckt wrote in 1922, he
maintained that

>   Russia cannot reach a settlement with Poland.   With
>   Poland falls one of the strongest pillars of the
>   Versailles Peace, the powerful outpost of France.
>   To achieve this goal must be one of the most
>   fundamental drives of German policy, since it is
>   achievable.   But it can be achieved only through
>   Russia or with Russia's help.   Poland can never
>   offer any advantage to Germany; not economic, since
>   it is incapable of development, nor political, as
>   she is France's vassal. . . . Russia and Germany in
>   the borders of 1914 should be the foundation of
>   understanding between the two states.   Germany's
>   attitude towards Poland need not be a secret.   Its
>   proclamation can awaken only trust in Russia.
>   Poland's hostility towards Germany could not be
>   greater.   The threat from both sides will, in the
>   long run, shake Poland's foundations ever more.
>   Above all, it would be of inestimable advantage to
>   Germany if Poland was sure that in case it partici-
>   pated in a war of sanctions with France against
>   Germany, it would have Russia on its neck.[51]

     The Treaty of Rapallo, signed by Germany and Russia in
April 1922, came as a surprise to Seeckt.   Although it was
more a statement of common interests than a military arrangement, it nevertheless set the stage for greater German-Russian
cooperation in the military sphere.   In Seeckt's opinion, the
real value of the Rapallo treaty was not the establishment of
research and production facilities in the Soviet Union for
weapons forbidden to Germany, although these were certainly
valuable by-products of the pact.   Rather, Rapallo provided
Germany with the appearance of greatly expanded power, without
actually binding the Reich to any commitments vis a vis the
Soviet Union. In the same promemoria of 1922, he wrote, "Even
though the Treaty of Rapallo only has the appearance of a
military pact, it suffices to influence Polish policy for the
good."[52]
     Seeckt's belief that the Rapallo arrangement was advan-
tageous to Germany since it gave the Reich the appearance of
vastly increased military power was   correct.   General
Degoutte, commanding general of the Allied Force of Occupation
in Germany, wrote that Rapallo raised the possibility that
Germany would attempt to revise the Versailles treaty and

someday   seek revenge for the war which it had lost   in   1918.
He saw particular danger for Poland:

> The Russian alliance is, in fact, the door opened
> wide to ideas of revenge, the right that has been
> acquired to utilize Russia's unlimited reserves of
> men at will and, at the same time, to reorganize a
> formidable arsenal in that country.   In a word, it
> is the prospect of someday recommencing the war of
> conquest.   Poland is the first and most proximate
> obstacle in the way of the new allies in their
> realization of this alluring program.   The solution
> which the Russo-German bloc would make of the Polish
> problem is obvious.   It is the duty of the   Entente
> to render this solution impossible.[53]

Degoutte's mention of the military balance between Germany and
Poland   is   interesting since it illustrates the way in   which
Germany's adversaries viewed the Rapallo pact.   Whatever the
merits of German-Soviet military cooperation, however, little
was done during the Seeckt era to expand on this cooperation.
No joint planning, for instance, took place.
      One other   event of the immediate postwar period had a
great effect upon Seeckt's military policy toward Poland.   The
original provisions of the Versailles treaty had awarded
almost all of Upper Silesia to Poland.   After vigorous protests by the Germans, who based their arguments on President
Woodrow Wilson's Fourteen Points, the Allies agreed to hold a
plebiscite in Upper Silesia to determine the wishes of the
inhabitants.   As Poland had expected to receive the entire
territory, the announcement that a plebiscite would be held
caused great dissatisfaction, both among the Poles living in
Upper Silesia and in Poland proper. The fear that the Germans
would rig the plebiscite in their own favor, as well as the
tension between the Poles and Germans living in Upper Silesia,
led eventually to three armed uprisings of the Polish population in the province.   The first, in August 1919, was put down
by German regular forces; the second, one year later, by
German Freikorps, Security Police, and the 117th Infantry
Division of the regular army.
      By far the most serious of these insurrections was the
third, which occurred in May 1921, immediately after the
plebiscite. The voting had not gone at all in Poland's favor;
by a 60 to 40 percent majority, the population had declared
its desire to remain with Germany.   The result of the voting
meant that the province would be partitioned between Germany
and Poland.   The Polish government, while disappointed with
the result, did not order the insurrection, although it did
support Polish forces in the province with money, food, and
arms. Rather, the uprising appears to have been the result of
two circumstances: spontaneous nationalist outrage amongst
the indigenous Polish population and the machinations of
Wojciech Korfanty, the Polish plebiscite commissioner.[54] The
uprising broke out on 3 May, and by 6 May most of the plebiscite area was in Polish hands.   So well prepared were the
leaders of the insurgency that within the first twelve hours
of the uprising, the insurgents were masters of the districts
of Pless, Rybnik, Katowice, Beuthen, Tarnowitz, Gliwice,
Hindenburg, Ratibor, and Cosel.   In the initial battles,
Italian forces in Silesia to oversee the plebiscite suffered

casualties of forty dead and two hundred wounded, while the
French forces stood aside and offered no resistance to the
Poles.
     The plan of Korfanty's forces in Upper Silesia had three
objectives: to seize all the centers of the industrial zone;
to advance to the line Landsberg-Oberwitz, the so-called
"Korfanty Line"; and to destroy the Oder bridges and cut off
Upper Silesia's communications with the north.[55]   By the
evening of 5 May, all of these objectives had been achieved by
the Poles.   Only several small bridgeheads on the right bank
of the Oder, near Ratibor, Cosel, and Krappitz, remained in
German hands.
     Opposing the Polish forces in Upper Silesia was a motley
collection of German irregulars, known as the Selbstschutz, or
Self-Defense.   This militia-style force had come into being
soon after the war in response to Hindenburg's call for volunteer forces to protect Germany's borders from the Czechs,
Poles, and Bolsheviks.   In 1921, immediately after the outbreak of the insurrection, a central committee of the Self-
Defense was established.   The committee divided the Polish-
German front into three sectors: the southern sector, parallel to the Oder Valley and including all the territory
situated between the Czech frontier and the line Friedland-
Brezina (headquarters at Ratibor);   the central sector,
situated to the east of Oppeln, bordering on the southern
sector and extending up to the line Michelwitz-Friedrichsgrätz
(headquarters at first in the chateau of Schurgast, near
Oppeln, then at Löwen); and the northern sector, running
northeasterly to the Polish frontier, along the railroad
between Landsberg and Rosenberg (headquarters at Namslau).
Assisting the Silesian militia was a large-scale influx of
paramilitary formations and Freikorps from all over Germany.
These reinforcements included the Stahlhelm, the Jungdeutscher
Orden, the Orgesch, and many other formations.   Like its
Polish counterpart, the German government offered no direct
military support to the German forces, but did provide
transportation and supplies to those groups traveling to Upper
Silesia.
     Seeckt's attitude toward aiding the German groups
battling the Poles was particularly disappointing to many of
his fire-breathing colleagues.   As his biographer, Friedrich
von Rabenau, wrote, this crisis was a "hard test."[56] He knew
that any help for the Self-Defense had to be camouflaged, and
that the entry of regular German troops into the province
would mean war with the Entente.   To Seeckt, the question was
not merely Upper Silesia, but losing the Ruhr and Upper
Silesia simultaneously by the rash use of regular forces
against the insurgency.   He was confident that the areas
assigned to Germany by the plebiscite would sooner or later
become German through England's influence.   Therefore, there
was no reason to shed German blood in a situation which
neither Germany nor Poland could change.   In Seeckt's mind the
Entente forces in the plebiscite area had the responsibility
to fight against the Polish insurgency; let them die, he
seemed to suggest, to free Upper Silesia.   So it was that he
gave orders to the forces in Upper Silesia to hold their
ground, but not to attack.   Rabenau described with clarity
Seeckt's position in 1921:   "Never had he so clearly shown
that he was not about to try and achieve great things with
small means."[57] Seeckt's actions during the Upper Silesian

uprising show that he was able to separate his fiery rhetoric
from the possibilities of a real-life situation.   While the
destruction of the Polish state lay at the heart of Seeckt's
long-range strategic plans, the current tactical situation, as
embodied in the Franco-Polish alliance, meant that he had to
put off his ultimate goal and adopt a more defensive attitude.

The refusal of either the Polish or German government to
intervene directly in the Upper Silesian uprising left matters
in the hands of the irregular forces on the scene. The German
forces, although outnumbered, soon seized the initiative.
This was not surprising, given the fact that the German groups
involved in the fighting were the paramilitary groups of
veterans mentioned above, while the Polish forces consisted
mainly of the civilian population of Upper Silesia.   The
arrival of powerful German reinforcements in the province
sealed the fate of the insurrection.   On 9 May, the Poles
seized Cosel and crossed the left bank of the Oder; on 12 May,
further Polish attacks in the northern sector drove the
Germans out of Rosenberg.   German counterattacks, however,
began as early as 15 May, when Cosel was retaken. On 20 May,
in what was the high-water mark of their success, the Poles
attacked along the rail line leading from Kreuzburg to
Zembowitz.   The attack, interestingly enough, was spearheaded
by an armored train and two 105mm cannon. After a preliminary
bombardment, the Poles attempted to storm the German
positions. The well-trained German force allowed the Poles to
close to within one hundred yards, then opened fire with
machine guns, "sowing death in the ranks of the insurgents,"
to use Benoist-Mechin's phrase.[58] By 22 May, Rosenberg was
back in German hands.

The major geographical feature in Upper Silesia is a
chain of hills which dominates the right bank of the Oder.
The most important of these hills is the Annaberg, about ten
kilometers to the east of Krappitz.   The master of this hill,
which is three hundred meters high, would be master of Upper
Silesia.   For the Germans, seizure of the Annaberg meant
splitting the Polish line into two sections, defusing the
Polish threat to Cosel, as well as opening the route to
Gleiwitz and the industrial zone.   The Annaberg therefore
became the primary objective of the Germans, once they had
gone over to the offensive. Seven new battalions of Freikorps
were brought up and concentrated in front of the hill.
Indeed, the Germans seemed to have stripped the rest of the
front to gather sufficient numbers of troops for the storming
of the Annaberg.   On 21 May, the attack began, and by 22 May
the Annaberg was once again in German hands.

After the successful assault on the Annaberg, the major
fighting in Upper Silesia was over. Although both Germany and
Poland had provided arms, supplies, and advisors to the
combatants, neither desired to go to war over the issue of
Upper Silesia.   In Poland, the government disowned the
insurgency movement, partly because of the negative reaction
of the Allies, in particular Britain, and partly because the
insurrection's chances of success did not appear favorable.
To the Germans, the matter was much as Seeckt had described
it.   The final demarcation line would be determined not by
German-Polish negotiation but by Allied decree.   At the same
time, any attempt by the Germans to exploit their victory at
the Annaberg and destroy the Polish forces in Upper Silesia
would likely result in French intervention, probably in the

form of an occupation of the Ruhr. Neither Germany nor Poland ever seriously considered the use of regular troops in Upper Silesia, even though popular opinion in both states would have supported such a move and considerable sentiment existed among the officer corps of both countries for an armed showdown. The responsible leadership in both Berlin and Warsaw realized, however, that the Allies held the power of decision with regard to the future disposition of Upper Silesia. Seeckt himself was not as timid about lending aid to the German forces as was the Socialist government in Berlin, whose mili- tary policy he characterized as "Hände hoch im Westen und Osten," but he, too, recognized Germany's inability to inter- vene directly.[59] Years after the crisis, Seeckt discussed the strategic situation during the spring of 1921:

> The German defense of Upper Silesia had to be conducted by volunteers whose organization and equipment could not be prepared openly. I rejected any use of the Reichswehr. This would have led to a clash with the regular Polish troops that were standing by and would have thereby have provided the casus foederis which the French General [LeRond] desired. I could not accept the responsibility for the consequences thereof.[60]

In addition Seeckt characteristically lacked confidence in the irregular forces which were carrying the German banner in Upper Silesia:

> A resumption of the offensive was hopeless; it would have led either to a defeat or to the use of the Reichswehr with the above-mentioned consequences. That the irregulars in Upper Silesia did not under- stand this was understandable. It was possible to judge the situation differently and to condemn our decision. I believe that it was the correct decision and that the reproaches against the govern- ment were unjust.[61]

Seeckt, the Polish General Staff, and the governments of both countries did indeed choose the correct path in not intervening. On 20 October, the Allies, acting through the Conference of Ambassadors, announced their decision to partition the area under dispute. Thus, German and Polish blood was shed over a matter that could only be decided by outside forces. But for the cool heads in Warsaw and Berlin, however, many more lives could have been lost.

Seeckt's actions during the Upper Silesian insurrection were indicative of his military concepts in general. As discussed above, Seeckt was a firm believer in the power of the offensive. However, the reality of Germany's military situation was such that the nation had no possibility of resorting to force to revise the Versailles treaty. On the contrary, from the German point of view, a much more likely scenario for a future war involved an invasion of Germany by the Polish army, either acting alone or in concert with a French invasion from the west. The military problem placed before Germany was how to defend itself from such an invasion. Its forces were small, but they were carefully trained, highly motivated, and, for an infantry-cavalry force, were highly

mobile. In part, this last attribute was a result of the fact
that the Reichswehr was allowed no heavy artillery, which cut
down greatly on the traditional impedimenta of an army on the
march.   The main problem for the Germans was that while their
army was of admirable quality, it was not really suited to a
purely defensive role.   While military analysts, both at the
time and today, make much of the so-called "superiority of the
defensive," that superiority is attainable only when there is
a sufficient number of troops. The Reichswehr did not possess
the requisite numbers of soldiers to establish a firm defense
anywhere along the border with Poland.   In addition, the
careful training in open, mobile warfare to which Seeckt
subjected his troops would have been wasted if the Reichswehr
was merely going to dig trenches for itself at the outbreak of
the future war.
      Rather than commit his army to a purely defensive
strategy, Seeckt favored what can be called an "offensive-
defensive strategy." This method of warfare seeks to protect
the home country by counterattacking aggressively any enemy
penetration.   Thus, local attacks are undertaken, but only
within the general framework of a defensive strategy.   Only
when the invader's forces have been crushed does the
opportunity arise for carrying the war onto enemy soil.   In
the case of an invasion by the Polish army, Seeckt thought
that attention would have to be given to encircling and
destroying it by quick and aggressive maneuvering.[62]
      In discussing peacetime military strategy, it is usually
difficult to determine an army's exact plans and the methods
by which it intends to execute those plans.   War bares all
military secrets, while an army at peace can be a highly
mysterious organization.   The testing ground for military
ideas is the maneuver, but maneuvers are often secretive and
little publicized.   Therefore, to analyze the German strategy
of aggressive defense, particularly in the context of a war
with Poland, has been almost impossible.   Fortunately,
detailed descriptions of army maneuvers during Seeckt's tenure
as Reichswehr chief have recently been uncovered. These offer
fascinating insights into actual German plans to defend the
country against a Polish attack.[63]
      On 6 September 1922, the 1st Infantry Division (East
Prussia) took part in the first maneuver held since 1913.   It
was no accident that Seeckt chose the 1st Division to lead off
the maneuvers.   Seeckt felt, as did most of the German
generals, that East Prussia was the likely site of the next
war's first battle.   The maneuvers took place at Czychen, in
the Oletzko district of East Prussia, but little is known of
their actual execution.[64]
      The first maneuver for which we have a detailed descrip-
tion is the fall maneuver of 1923.[65] Upon invitation of the
Reichswehr minister, the American military attache, Colonel
Conger, traveled to East Prussia for the purpose of observing
field exercises involving elements of the 1st Division during
the week of 8 September.   The exercises took place on 10-11
September in the area between Johannisburg and Sensburg, thus
almost directly on the Polish frontier.   The detachments
taking part in the exercise were the 2nd Infantry Regiment,
one battalion of artillery, one Minenwerfer, and one regiment
of cavalry.
      The exercise of 1923 consisted of a campaign maneuver
based on the historical situation of 1914, a continuous

operation extending over a period of six days.   The German forces took the part of a detachment pushed out from a northern Red army invading East Prussia from the east (Rennenkampf's 1st Army).   The mission of the detachment was to move around the southern end of Lake Spirding and to establish communications with another Red army (Samsonov's 2nd Army), which was advancing from the south along the axis Ortelsburg-Bischofsburg.   The detached force was to move from the 1st Division Training Ground at Arys via Johannisburg, to the south of Lake Spirding, and then to advance on Sensburg and drive out any hostile detachments in that area.   At the same time, it was ordered to establish communications between the left wing of the northern Red army through Nikolaiken and the right wing of the southern Red army which was passing through Willenberg, Ortelsburg, and Bischofsburg.   The establishment of this communication was made by the chief umpire of the maneuver.

The use of the Tannenberg campaign as a training tool is interesting, since it was representative of overall German strategy.   The battle of Tannenberg, in which East Prussia was saved by crushing one invading army in an encirclement battle and then turning to maul the other, was perhaps the ultimate example of an offensive-defensive strategy.   The great German victory had been largely the result of the Russian failure to coordinate or even establish communications between the two invading armies.   The Germans were thus able to deal with one army at a time.   The exercise of 1923 attempted to show that it was possible for two armies, one from the south and one from the east, to cooperate in an invasion of East Prussia. In 1923, however, the territories from which these armies would invade was Polish.   One may therefore view the 1923 maneuver as a test of the feasibility of a Polish invasion of Germany's isolated eastern province.

Colonel Conger was quite impressed with what he saw of the German army in 1923.   In a report sent to Washington, he remarked that all the equipment seemed well cared for, the animals were in excellent condition and well groomed, and the men were alert at their work and looked fit.   The officers, he noted, were thorough and conscientious.   The officer who was directing the exercise remarked to him, "We feel that we can depend on the troops of this division."   Conger's general estimate as to morale and efficiency was "far above average."

Specifically, the attache was impressed with the mobility of the German forces and the march discipline of the troops he observed:

> The troops carried what is called the light field pack weighing about 60 pounds.   No rations or ball ammunition are carried with this pack.   During Monday the 10th of September the troops marched an average of about 28 kilometers; the mounted troops very much farther due to the nature of their work. One of the battery commanders told me that he had ridden his horse at nightfall full 75 kilometers. In spite of this distance, however, there were no signs of undue fatigue on the part of the infantry or any of the animals I observed.   At the end of the day I came to the conclusion that both men and animals were in good hardened condition.

As if to underscore their belief in offensive, maneuver-oriented warfare, and their view of trench warfare as "degenerate," the German officers present repeatedly pointed out to the American the limitations of the Minenwerfer:

A very frequent remark made by the umpires was: "I am no friend of the Minenwerfer." On account of their very short range the difficulties of keeping them near enough to the front to be effectively used in an attack was apparent even in the maneuvers.

The exercise also demonstrated that the German army had not neglected to train its troops in the technique of infantry assault, which was the lynchpin of the offensive-defensive strategy. Conger described the following method by which German infantry advanced over dangerous ground:

The infantry continues its advance to the front. Heavy machine guns are placed in position and advanced by echelons so that there are always a number in position to fire in case the enemy should show himself. The light machine guns move forward with their units until opposition is actually encountered.
    It is a fixed principle that the machine guns must furnish the small arms firepower and that the infantry must close to the assault. The firing is of secondary importance and he is not permitted to use his rifle except at good targets at very close range.

It is clear, then, that at the tactical level, the German army remained faithful to the Clausewitzian goal of destruction of the enemy force. The infantry assault remained the logical culmination of battle, even if the army was committed to a defensive posture on the strategic level.
    The choice of the Johannisburg district as the site of the maneuver was not accidental, and it had more to do with the realities of 1923 than the historical situation of 1914. The colonel was perhaps closer to the truth than he realized when he wrote the following:

The advantages of maneuvers near the frontier of a country cannot be overestimated because both strategy and tactics can always be introduced in a normal role from which valuable lessons can be learned. Situations that are sure to repeat themselves in case of war can be worked over and the principles thoroughly fixed in the minds of officers and men. In 1914 the 1st German Division, with its training ground at Arys, had just completed its maneuvers when the war broke out, and the problem it had to work out against the Russians was identical with the maneuvers of a few days before. It was stated by one of the officers there that the infantry repeated the identical marches that it had made only a few days before in peace maneuvers.[66]

In other words, the 1923 maneuver was good training for the troops should Germany go to war with Poland in the near

future.   The question raised in the maneuver, however, and
which remained unanswered at the end of the exercise, was
whether German forces were capable of containing a Polish
advance into East Prussia.
A much larger maneuver of the 1st Infantry Division in
1925 attempted to answer the question raised in 1923.[67]   The
maneuver, which took place in the Marienwerder district of
East Prussia, actually consisted of three distinct problems.
The first, which took place on 3-4 September, postulated a
Blue (Polish) invading force, consisting of the I Army Corps,
advancing from the south about five kilometers west of Deutsch
Eylau.   By 2 September, I Corps had reached the general line
Buchwalde-Alt Christburg-Gross Teschendorf, some twenty kilo-
meters south of Elbing.   At the same time, the reinforced 3rd
Infantry Regiment, consisting of three infantry battalions and
six artillery batteries, was advancing from the south through
Garnsee. After a forced march, the regiment was quartered for
the night of 2 September at Oschen-Littschen-Krebsfelde, just
east of Marienwerder.
To counter the Blue invasion, Red (Germany) fielded its
III Army Corps, including the 7th, 8th, and 9th Infantry
Divisions.   These units advanced southward via Elbing-
Preussisch Holland.   By 2 September, III Corps occupied the
general line Lake Baalauer-Alt Christburg-Preussisch Mark, and
had made contact with the Blue forces advancing from the
south.   In addition, the reinforced 1st Infantry Brigade,
consisting of five infantry battalions, a reconnaissance
detachment, six batteries, and a pioneer battalion, moved up
from Dirschau and Marienburg.   By the night of 2 September,
after a strenuous march, its advanced guard had reached Stuhm.
The main body spent the night at Konradswalde, just south of
Marienburg.
The situation was thus one of relatively equal strength.
The opposing corps occupied a front stretching roughly from
Lake Baalauer to Preussisch Mark, with the Red forces
echeloned slightly to the left of Blue.   To the far west, it
was likely that the Red detachment advancing from the north
would attempt to march toward the flank or rear of the Blue
force.   To do this, however, it would first have to dispose of
the Blue detachment posted between Marienwerder and Riesenburg
for the purpose of protecting the main body of Blue's I Corps.
On the night of 2 September, Blue received the following
orders for the next day's operations:

1.   Hostile west wing of enemy facing I Corps rests
on Lake Baalauer.   From airplane reports a hostile
column of all arms, strength unknown, crossed the
Nogat at Marienburg at 6:00 p.m., 2 September, and
marched on Stuhm.
2.   The I Corps attacks 3 September, its left wing
along Lake Baalauer, on Morainen (four kilometers
southeast of Gross Waplitz).
3.   The reinforced 3rd Infantry Regiment protects
the left flank of the corps from the enemy advancing
on Stuhm.
4.   The 1st Cavalry Regiment at Riesenburg will
suppport the 3rd Infantry Regiment.
5.   I Battalion, 2nd Infantry Regiment, will reach
Freystadt at 8:30 a.m. by trucks coming from
Bischofswerder.   The battalion will support the 3rd

Infantry Regiment and is available upon its   arrival
at Freystadt.

Blue was thus informed of the threat to its flank from the Red
detachment, and its own detached regiment was given orders to
protect the flank of I Corps.   In addition, the 1st Cavalry
Regiment was detached from the corps to aid with flank support
in the west.   A reinforcing motorized infantry battalion,
moving up from Freystadt, was also ordered to support the 3rd
Regiment on the flank.   Finally, with both of its flanks
secured, the main body of the corps was ordered to attack in a
northerly direction.
     Red's orders for 3 September attempted to defeat Blue's
invasion by encircling and destroying the enemy force:

     1.   Enemy west wing in front of III Corps holding
     line at Gross Teschendorf-Mothalen. No enemy troops
     observed west of Lake Baalauer-Lake Sorgen except
     patrols.
     2. III Corps makes an enveloping attack against the
     enemy's east wing on 3 September with the 7th and
     8th Divisions in the front and the 9th Division
     advancing via Saalfeld-Gerswalde. General direction
     of attack: Rosenberg.
     3.   The reinforced 1st Infantry Brigade advances on
     3 September via Paleschken and south of Lake Sorgen
     against the rear of the enemy in front of III Corps.

The main attack, involving all three divisions of III Corps,
had two components.   The attack by the 7th and 8th Divisions
had the objective of fixing Blue's attention to the north.   In
the meantime, the 9th Division would attempt a wide flanking
maneuver through Saalfeld and Gerswalde with the mission of
caving in Blue's open right flank.   The geographical objective
of the attack was a deep penetration of the Blue front as far
as Rosenberg, but the primary mission of Red's forces was the
destruction of the Blue invader.   To help achieve decisive
results, the Red 1st Brigade was to continue its advance and
to come up behind Blue's main body from the left. If this was
achieved, and the main assault toward Rosenberg was successful, then Blue would be well and truly trapped.
     Red's attack commenced on the morning of 3 September, and
at first developed favorably.   By 11:00 a.m., the threatened
envelopment of its east wing had compelled Blue to withdraw to
the line Riesenburg-Rosenberg.   On the positive side for Blue,
reinforcements in the form of the 3rd Infantry Division had
arrived at Deutsch Eylau after marching through Libawa.
Blue's corps now occupied a line from Riesenburg to Eylau,
angled sharply to the right, and with its now vulnerable left
guarded only by a single infantry regiment.   Meanwhile, Red's
III Corps continued the attack.   The 7th and 8th Divisions
continued to hammer Blue's center at Riesenwalde and Gross
Brunau, and the 9th continued its enveloping advance toward
Peterkau.   The 1st Brigade received orders to advance via
Littschen, on the Marienwerder-Riesenburg road, toward the
rear of the enemy's main force at Riesenburg.
     By 7:30 p.m., the front had basically stabilized. Blue's
line stood from Littschen through Riesenburg and Rosenberg and
thence to Peterkau, where the newly arrived Blue 3rd Infantry
Division stood locked in combat with the Red 9th Division

advancing from Gerswalde. Both Red and Blue planned attacks for early the next morning. Of special importance would be the combat between the two detachments, Blue's 3rd Infantry Regiment and Red's 1st Brigade, who had so far only skirmished lightly north of Marienwerder. The victor in this struggle would be able to march unhindered on the flank of the enemy's main body.

In its strategic context, the first maneuver demonstrated that, given a roughly equal balance of forces, the Germans thought they could arrest and even repel a Polish advance into East Prussia. The qualifier was a large one. On the one hand, the Poles were certainly capable of assembling an army corps for a march into the province. The Germans, on the other hand, were capable of fielding only a single infantry division, so that the well-conceived and elegantly executed maneuver carried out by the Red III Corps in this exercise was not within the realm of possibility. Red's performance, however, did demonstrate rather conclusively the potential for offensive action even within a defensive framework. At the same time, the maneuver showed how fully the German army had recovered from its defeat in the war. Once again, as before 1914, the army had adopted encirclement and destruction of the enemy as its primary strategic tenet.

Tactically, the exercise was a fascinating display of the primitive level of motorization achieved by the German army, both in terms of equipment and doctrine. The American military attache present described one encounter between Red and Blue forces just north of Marienwerder:

> Each side had two armored cars armed with heavy machine guns. The Red commander had, however, placed an artillery 77mm field gun mounted apparently on a naval mount in a motor wagon between his two armored cars. In the engagement between the opposing cars the umpire's decision was given to the side having the 3-inch gun which was promptly brought into action in the engagement, which occurred as the Red wagons rounded the bend north of Tiefenau. Each armored car detachment was preceded by three motorcycle scouts in the bend of the road, but they were unable to get word back in time of the approach of the hostile motor wagons. Each of the hostile wagons moved up promptly to the support of its motorcyclists and thus came together at the bend. Thereafter the Red armored motor wagons roamed about in rear of the Blue lines but played no special role in the main operations.[68]

Another encounter illustrates the trouble which the troops had in assimilating the new technology:

> The Blue commander had posted his reserve of two battalions and a detachment of twelve camouflaged tanks in the wood for a counterattack which was delivered upon when the enemy's attacking lines had reached the open field between the two lines of woods. This counterattack was entirely successful in driving back the enemy's main attack and in forcing him back north of the Liebe. The tanks were employed in three lines about 100 yards apart,

consisting of 5, 4, and 3 tanks respectively. This
was the first maneuver in which the Germans had used
these camouflaged tanks and the infantry did not
seem to know what to do with them. In one company
the platoons were formed up in platoon columns in
rear of the tanks. In another they marched parallel
with the tank and in another company they preceded
it. These difficulties were ironed out evidently in
the umpires' critiques because on subsequent days
the infantry kept clear of the tanks so as neither
to obstruct their fire nor to come under the hostile
artillery fire directed at the tanks.[69]

It was from the improvised solutions to such comical situations that the Germans developed their later, fearsome armored
expertise.
 The situation postulated in the second exercise of the
maneuvers of 1925 was more pessimistic than the first. In
this exercise, the East Prussian-Polish border was designated
as the border between a Blue northeast nation (Germany) and a
Red southwest nation (Poland). War had broken out between the
two nations. Red's main forces had concentrated by 4
September along the general line Brodnica-Jablonowo and
intended to attack the Blue force concentrating at Gilgenburg
and Deutsch Eylau. Blue's initial plan of advance was to
move toward Jablonowo and Brodnica on 5 September, with its
right wing advancing from Deutsch Eylau via the rail line
through Bischofswerder. Blue was assigned no Grenzschutz, or
border protection units, so the combat was between regular
forces only. In order to heighten the realism, Red was given
strong air forces, but these appear to have engaged in reconnaissance activity only.[70]
 As in the first exercise, the real centerpiece of the
maneuver occurred to the west of the main forces. Here, a
Blue section consisting of three battalions of infantry, four
squadrons of cavalry, six batteries, and a pioneer battalion
was deployed at Riesenburg. Its general mission was to
observe the border between Rehhof, east of Gniew, and
Freystadt. Eventually, it was to use the support of the local
population to establish communication with the main body. The
section had orders to drive back any local advances of enemy
troops across the border and also to occupy the major Vistula
crossing at Münsterwalde. It was deployed in the sector
Riesenburg-Riesenwalde and received orders to make reconnaissance westward toward the border.
 The adversary of the Blue section was the reinforced Red
1st Infantry Brigade, consisting of six battalions of infantry, one reconnaissance detachment, and six batteries. The
brigade was split into two detachments: the Grudziadz detachment, consisting of three battalions of infantry, the reconnaissance detachment, and three batteries; and the Starogard
detachment of three battalions and three batteries. On the
evening of 4 September, the brigade received orders to advance
quickly to Riesenburg, where aviators had observed the concentration of the Blue section. The brigade commenced its
advance at once. By midnight on 4-5 September the Grudziadz
detachment had reached the sector Seuberdorf-Gross Ottlau-
Garnsee, almost directly on the Polish border. The Starogard
detachment stood at Lindenberg, twelve kilometers southwest of
Gniew. Two companies were ordered to cross the Münsterwalde

Bridge by truck and advance as far as the Sedlinen-Marienwerder rail line.

The situation at the opening of the maneuver was therefore one in which the Blue section at Riesenburg had the mission of holding off two opposing Red detachments advancing respectively from the southwest and northwest. On the side of the Red forces, the Grudziadz detachment was the nearer to the Blue force and its commander was also the senior, so that he had the option of bringing in the Starogard detachment either in his rear or his flank, according to the situation. The Grudziadz detachment's line of march was from Garnsee through Kröxen and Wandau on Riesenburg, and the commander consequently ordered the Starogard detachment to advance by Marienwerder-Grosse Krebs directly on Riesenburg, with the idea that it would come in on the flank of the Grudziadz detachment in case of need.

The Blue commander, kept informed of Red's movement by the friendly population and local officials,[71] resolved to march on Wandau and confront the Grudziadz detachment, while sending most of his cavalry against the force advancing from Starogard. The cavalry had a dual mission: keeping the Blue commander informed of the Starogard detachment's movements and delaying its arrival on the field of battle until the Grudziadz detachment could be defeated.

At first, however, Blue's plan appeared to be failing. The small amount of cavalry which Blue had kept with its main force encountered stiff resistance from the Red Reconnaissance Detachment (part of the Grudziadz force) and found itself thrown back on Neudorfchen. The Red Grudziadz detachment was therefore the first to reach Wandau, where the Red commander was informed of the approach of the Blue force. He decided to halt his advance and take up a defensive position east of Wandau. The arrival of the Blue section was followed by an assault against the Red force around Wandau. Conger described the situation around Wandau:

> This attack was favored both by the folds of the rolling terrain, which afforded good opportunity for cover of the advancing troops, and particularly for the advance of supports and reserves, and by the exposure to view of the enemy's positions on the heights east of Wandau, which enabled the supporting Blue artillery to give very effective support to the infantry attack.[72]

At first, Blue had great success in driving Red out of Wandau and occupying the hills and woods west of the town. South of the Wandau-Neudorfchen road, however, the Blue attack was held up by the presence of a lake and also by the timely arrival of Red's reserve, which the Red commander had posted at Rosainen with a view to counterattacking Blue's left flank. This counterattack was, in turn, held off by one of Blue's reserve battalions.

The situation in the early afternoon looked grim for the Grudziadz detachment, which had lost over a battalion of prisoners during the initial Blue advance. Hastening to the rescue, however, was the Starogard detachment, which was advancing from the north. Blue, instead of following up its victory at Wandau, had to go over to the defensive. After detailing four companies to hold off the remnants of the

Grudziadz detachment, the Blue commander was able to assemble
two infantry battalions, one pioneer battalion, and a hitherto
unused section of twelve tanks to face the Starogard force.
The Blue forces were deployed so as to attack the right of the
advancing Red force.   After allowing the Starogard detachment
to advance to the outskirts of Wandau, the Blue infantry and
armor counterattacked from the west, supported by the Blue
cavalry from the east. By 3:00 p.m., when recall was sounded,
both Red detachments had been dealt tactical defeats, although
both still remained on the field.

On one level, the exercise seemed to prove that, with
superior leadership, mobility, and coordination, a smaller
German force was capable of holding off a larger Polish
invading force.   Most significant in this context was the
excellent performance of Blue's cavalry, which held up the
advance of Red's Starogard detachment just long enough to
prevent it from participating in a simultaneous, concentric
attack on Wandau.   The similarities to the battle of
Tannenberg, where Rennenkampf's army was delayed long enough
for Samsonov's to be destroyed, and which seems to have become
a paradigm for Germany's military planners, is obvious.

Yet the basic premise of the maneuver was that the main
body of German forces, that assembling on the border at
Deutsch Eylau and Gilgenburg, would be able to hold off the
Poles concentrating at Brodnica and Jablonowo.   Indeed, the
initial corps orders even referred to a possible German
advance on Brodnica.   Without a greatly expanded army,
however, one which permitted the Germans to deploy at least a
corps in East Prussia, any thought of an advance out of East
Prussia was a pipe dream. Like the first exercise, the second
did indeed provide Germany with an entire corps.   With only
one division for defense, though, it was very questionable
whether the German army would be able to stand firm against a
Polish invasion.

On the tactical level, too, matters were not as favorable
as they might appear.   The American observer at the maneuver
wrote:

> Superficially the maneuver had gone very well for
> the Blue troops, but had bullets been used instead
> of blanks, the Blue troops would not have advanced
> so rapidly in the first attack against the Detach-
> ment Grudziadz, and further in actual warfare the
> battalion   could not so readily have been re-
> assembled after one engagement to meet a fresh
> attack of fresh troops coming from another
> direction.[73]

Hence, even in a maneuver with an artificially favorable
strategic basis, the Germans were not entirely successful in
defending East Prussia on the tactical level.   But the exercise, especially the final flanking attack by the Blue
section, did demonstrate clearly that Germany intended to rely
upon an aggressive, counterattacking defense in any future
conflict with Poland.

The third exercise of the maneuvers of 1925 again
postulated a Polish invasion of East Prussia.   A strong Red
(Polish) enemy, consisting of I Corps (three infantry
divisions), forced a crossing over the Vistula at Münsterwalde
on 6 September, after throwing back weak Blue (German) forces

in the vicinity of the bridge.   Red's 2nd Division, the first
to   cross the Vistula,   pursued the enemy via Marienwerder   as
far   as Hanswalde-Grosse Krebs-Brakau and rested on this line.
On the evening of 6 September,   Red's aviators,   who ruled the
skies against minimal Blue opposition,   reported the   presence
of   enemy   forces at Riesenburg and Littschen.   The   3rd   Red
Division was to cross the Vistula at Gniew on a pontoon bridge
during the night of 6-7 September.   The bridge,   however, had
not   been completed by 5:00 a.m.,   7 September.   The 1st   Red
Division   crossed   the   bridge   at   Münsterwalde during   the
evening,   after the 2nd Division.   After reaching the Garnsee-
Marienwerder road,   the division rested for the evening on and
west of the road.

To oppose this Red force,   a Blue force consisting of III
Corps (three infantry divisions) advanced from the   northeast.
After   a strenuous march,   the corps had reached the following
locations: 7th Infantry Division at Hirschfeld,   eight kilometers southwest of Preussisch Holland; 6th Infantry Division,
Draulitten;   Corps Headquarters,   Preussisch Holland.   The 5th
Infantry   Division,   hurriedly pushing forward via   Preussisch
Mark toward the Vistula,   reached Riesenburg on the evening of
6 September.   The Border Protection Unit Deutsch Eylau,   consisting   of   five   infantry   regiments,   four   battalions   of
cavalry,   and   six batteries,   was not confronted   immediately
with an enemy,   and was consequently placed under the   command
of the 5th Division.   This unit was brought up and deployed on
6 September at Gross Bellschwitz-Freiwalde.   Rounding out the
Blue   force   was the 1st Cavalry Regiment,   which   arrived   at
Freystadt by the evening of 6 September.

The   initial orders for both sides called for attacks   on
7-8 September.   The Red I Corps received orders to attack the
enemy at Riesenburg,   with the 2nd Division advancing directly
on   Riesenburg from the southwest and the 1st Division to   its
right advancing via Zigahnen-Kröxen-Hanswalde in the direction
of   Klein   Tromnau.   The mission of the 1st Division   was   to
envelop   the Blue force at Riesenburg.   Blue's III Corps   was
ordered   to advance with the 6th and 7th Divisions via Altmark
and   Nikolaiken   and   attack the enemy from   the   north   on   8
September.   While   the divisions executed this wide   flanking
maneuver,   the 5th Division and the Border Protection Unit were
ordered   to   delay the advance of Red's forces to the west   of
Riesenburg.   The   Border   Protection Unit also   received   the
specific task of guarding the left flank of the 5th   Division,
and   was   ordered to the crossroads at Klein Tromnau for   this
purpose.   In short,   then,   the situation on 7 September   was
that   a   single German infantry division,   plus   some   attached
irregular units,   was attempting to hold off the advance of two
Polish divisions.   The canons of encirclement which the German
army never ceased preaching in this period were not abandoned,
however.   The   two   Blue divisions advancing on Altmark   and
Nikolaiken would be in a perfect position to swoop down on the
Red 1st and 2nd Divisions,   if only the Blue 5th Division could
hold out against Red's assault against Riesenburg.

Red's attack on the Blue 5th Division at first went quite
well,   with the Red 2nd Division reaching Wachsmuth,   threatening   Riesenburg   from   the   south,   and   the   1st   Division
advancing   far to the east toward Faulen.   If this town   were
taken,   Red   forces   would control the road from Rosenberg   to
Deutsch   Eylau   and cut off the Border   Protection   Unit   from
Blue's   5th Division.   But Blue resistance stiffened,   and by

evening the Blue commander could report that he had repulsed
Red's attack and was still in possession of Riesenburg.
Blue's encircling force drew ever nearer, but a new Red force
appeared in the west to challenge it.   This was the Red 3rd
Division, which had finally crossed the Vistula at Gniew and
was advancing via Budzin on Straszewo.

Red's orders for 8 September called for continuing the
advance with the 1st and 2nd Divisions against Gross
Bellschwitz and Riesenburg.   The 1st Division, once it had
overcome resistance at Gross Bellschwitz, was to maneuver via
Rosenberg against the rear of the Blue force at Riesenburg.
The 2nd Division, meanwhile, was to pin the Blue 5th Division
at Riesenburg.   The newly arrived Red 3rd Division was
assigned the task of protecting the flank of I Corps against
the two Blue divisions advancing from the north.

Blue's orders for 8 September also called for an
offensive, with the 6th and 7th Divisions being ordered to
attack the north flank of the enemy in the morning.   The
missions assigned to the 5th Division and the Border
Protection Unit were the same as on the previous day.   5th
Division was to hold its position, while the Border Protection
Unit was to continue to secure the left flank of the division
against envelopment from the south.

In tactical terms, the centerpiece of the maneuver on 8
September was the assault of the Red 1st Division against the
Border Protection Unit.   Blue's five battalions took up a
formal defensive position between Gross Bellschwitz and
Langenau.   Numerical superiority was with the Red force, which
contained nine battalions.   The division attacked with two of
its three infantry regiments on the front line and one in
reserve.   Blue's troops were assumed to be entrenched, a
condition indicated by the men sticking their spades into the
ground, handles down. In addition, the Border Protection Unit
made skillful use of the terrain and camouflage to conceal its
actual position from Red's advance guards.

In keeping with the offensive spirit drilled in to the
Reichswehr by Seeckt, the Blue commander at Gross Bellschwitz
planned to deliver a riposte to the attacking Red force.   To
this end, he held out two infantry battalions in reserve.
When the Red attack reached the Gross Bellschwitz-Langenau
road, these reserves counterattacked against the enemy's right
wing.   The effectiveness of this counterthrust, however, was
lessened once Red's reserve regiment was brought up.   After
one hour of confused combat, Blue's advance was halted and its
two battalions were enveloped on both wings.   The Blue commander's strategy had been risky, and in this case he lost the
gamble.   Interestingly enough, General Seeckt himself was very
critical of the Blue counterattack on both tactical and strategic grounds.   The Blue forces, consisting of only five battalions, could not hope to reap any permanent success against
a force of nine battalions by means of a counterattack, but if
the Blue commander had employed the same forces in carrying
out a purely defensive policy, he would have been able to
maintain his main position for a much longer time and thereby
have carried out his mission more successfully.[74]   Clearly,
Seeckt was correct in his assessment.   Blue's orders to stand
on the defensive at Gross Bellschwitz did not mean that it was
surrendering the initiative to Red.   Blue still intended to
win by attacking, but the attack was to be a decisive blow
delivered by the two divisions marching from Nikolaiken.   The

most effective way for Blue's engaged forces to aid in this attack was to stand firm in the south and ensure that Red's attention was fixed on Rosenberg. As it actually happened, Blue's premature and outnumbered counterattack led to a decisive victory by Red at Gross Bellschwitz and freed Red's main body to deal with the Blue flanking force.

When the exercise ended at 2:00 p.m., 8 September, the commander of the 1st Division, Lieutenant General Wilhelm Heye, could be fairly proud of his troops. A wide variety of tactical, operational, and strategic problems had been analyzed during the six days of maneuvers, and the units involved had demonstrated that Germany once more had an excellent army. Colonel Conger was certainly impressed. "The maneuver was more like real war than any I have ever seen," he wrote at the beginning of a lengthy report to Washington.[75] Rather than concentrate on the strategy involved in the exercises, however, he was more interested in the tactical capabilities of the individual arms within the Reichswehr. He first discussed the cavalry:

> The 1st Cavalry Regiment is still armed with lances, and carried them in the maneuvers. . . . The cavalry also carried carbines, some of them slung over the back and some with the butt resting in a boot placed on the left hand side at the back of the saddle. I also heard that it is proposed to arm the cavalry with the bayonet as well as the carbine, but could not find out if this had been adopted. The cavalry privates all carried intrenching tools.
>
> The cavalry were very skillful in passing themselves off as infantry. Their horses were never in evidence from the side of the enemy and they produced quite as much racket of machine guns in proportion to their numbers as did the infantry. They were also accompanied by artillery--sometimes a single gun accompanying a patrol of 15 to 25 men. This flexibility of the cavalry made it impossible to tell, when one heard the rattle of the machine guns and the sound of artillery in a certain location, whether it was a reinforced cavalry patrol, or an infantry battalion or brigade that was holding the line.

The infantry, which bore the brunt of the fighting throughout the maneuvers, impressed Conger even more than did the cavalry:

> The backbone of the German army is its infantry. In appearance the men are hardy, very young on the average, and well disciplined. . . . The infantry moved along the roads in columns of squads but on arriving in the vicinity of the enemy went into columns of files, sometimes while still under the cover of the trees along the road. In moving forward, preparatory to deployment, and in following the attacking line as supports and reserves, I noticed that no movements were made of troops in larger units than a squad visible from the position of the enemy, or from the air, except at very long distances--3 to 4 kilometers from the enemy--where

the limit in the size of the body of troops moving
together was a platoon.

In moving forward to deployment there was no
attempt to observe regular sector lines between
units. Where woods in the general direction of the
attack afforded cover, the supporting troops would
take advantage of this cover, and then later on
would trickle back, a squad at a time, into their
sector. . . . The squads were checked irregularly,
and the men in each squad marched irregularly. The
idea seemed to be not to form a rigid firing line,
but to take the best advantage of cover and avoid
offering a target either for artillery or machine
gun fire.

In the advance there was little attempt at
rifle fire by the advancing infantry at any but very
close range; on the other hand machine guns were
firing all the time. When a higher ridge was
reached by attacking troops, machine guns would halt
and continue firing from the ridge, while the infantry would continue its advance. In covering forward
slopes or especially exposed places the squads would
open out still more, and when the enemy was firing
heavily would trickle down one at a time to the
nearest place offering cover. In such dashes sometimes a man would make a series of very short
dashes, as short as ten and even five yards,
evidently under the assumption that any movement
would attract machine gun fire, and the moment the
machine gun opened, he would have to drop. When
within assaulting distance, bayonets were fixed and
the charge made with a yell. In all phases of the
maneuver the infantryman took the keenest interest
and were very quick and alert in all their movements
of rising, running forward, and dropping to the
ground.

What is perhaps most interesting in Conger's description is
the use of infiltration tactics by attacking infantry.
Seeckt's return to a strategy of assault rested on firm foundations within the German army. The tactics to crack a fortified line were first devised by the German General Oskar von
Hutier during the First World War and used to great effect
against the befuddled Italians at Caporetto, the Russians at
Riga, and the Western Allies in Ludendorff's great spring
offensives in 1918.[76] The Americans had never really been the
object of a German infiltration assault during the war, which
would explain Conger's seeming amazement upon witnessing these
tactics for the first time. Although infiltration tactics did
not win the war for the Germans, they were still the best
method of infantry assault available, and they provided Seeckt
with a method of executing his strategic concepts on the
tactical plane.

Conger also made frequent mention of machine guns, whose
firepower was the cutting edge of infiltrating infantry. It
is clear from his report that whether on the offensive or the
defensive, the Germans relied almost exclusively on the
machine gun for fire support. "The general impression given
by the German troops," he wrote, "is that of machine guns
everywhere firing, and almost never visible from the side of

the enemy. The machine gunners seemed so well-trained that they were rarely given orders as to their position or target." Finally, Conger described the tanks which he had observed. It is clear from his observations that the German army was still a long way from Blitzkrieg in 1925, although he was impressed with at least the appearance of reality:

> The tanks used in the maneuvers were mounted on a pair of bicycle wheels, made of canvas properly camouflaged, and resembled the Renault tank with a turret and a heavy (dummy) gun at the top, and slits for machine guns lower down in front. A man in front of the tank walking along can, and some of them did, actually fire a machine gun from the front which aided in giving the tanks a semblance of reality.
>   The tank is actually operated by two men inside at the back of the tank, who push it forward. The back of the tank is left open for the convenience of these men. These tanks trundling along over rough ground on their two bicycle wheels, which are, of course, inside and out of sight, progress with all the mannerisms of movement of real tanks.

In his evaluation, Conger gave the Reichswehr high marks, in a curiously American way: "The officers and men of the 1st Division seemed to be of excellent morale, and to be well-trained. The majority of the German soldiers seemed very young but did not look essentially different from our own men in the 2nd Division in San Antonio." For one brief moment, the usually technical-minded Conger stepped out of his normal role to describe the nature of relations between the military and the civilian population in East Prussia. The description he gives is quite different than that of historians who write of the hostility between the Reichswehr and the nation:

> The population of East Prussia was as much interested in the maneuvers as were the troops. . . . Many children were present also and, from the ages of 8 to 18, seemed to take the same zest in observing the conduct of the operations and learning how the various movements were made as did the ex-officers and soldiers.[77]

It is obvious that, in this part of Germany at least, the Reichswehr was very much a popular institution. The events of the Seeckt years demonstrated conclusively that the Reichswehr was growing more and more confident in its ability to defend German soil.[78] Thus, Seeckt's tenure as Reichswehr commander was a total success. He, almost single-handedly, had preserved the tradition of German military excellence. Although he operated under severe disadvantages, Seeckt succeeded in creating an army capable of defending Germany's borders. In one sense, he was aided in his work by Poland's own defensive strategy. As we have seen, both Germany and Poland deployed their forces in a dispersed, strictly defensive manner. This permitted Seeckt the luxury of working slowly to perfect his forces without having to worry about a sudden

Polish attack.   Seeckt took roughly five years to form a truly
capable army.   The maneuvers of the 1st Division in   East
Prussia in 1925 were well executed; they indicated that   the
Reichswehr was once more an army capable of defending Germany.
      Seeckt's choice of strategies was instrumental in the
rebirth of the Reichswehr.   The first option open to Seeckt
was to educate his troops in the art of static defense.
Germany did possess some fortifications in the east, and these
could conceivably have formed the basis for a sort of
"Fortress Germany." As we have seen, however, these fortresses were neither adequately armed nor manned to play such
a key role in German defensive strategy.   Most of the forts
were old, constructed before the advent of heavy artillery,
and vulnerable to modern methods of assault.   Despite Polish
claims to the contrary, the forts were of limited tactical
value only.
      Whatever the state of the fortifications, Seeckt could
not have chosen a passive defensive strategy.   By temperament
and training, he was an advocate of maneuver warfare.
Although he realized that Germany's overall strategic posture
had to be defensive, he tempered this posture by schooling his
forces in the art of aggressive warfare.   This amalgam was an
"offensive-defensive" strategy, in which German forces would
seek to defend German soil by enveloping, encircling, and
destroying an invading army.   The training of the army in
aggressive defense was evident throughout the military exercises of the early 1920s, particularly the maneuvers of 1925.
In 1925, the 1st Division succeeded in repelling three
separate assaults by invading "Red" forces.   In each of these,
the defender launched a flank attack against the invading
forces and succeeded in halting their advance.
      While the maneuvers of 1925 were based on a more favor-
able balance of military force than Germany could reasonably
expect, they did demonstrate that by the middle of the 1920s,
the Germans had assembled an elite fighting force--well
trained, hardened, and highly mobile.   Furthermore, it was
geared to offensive action, at least in the context of an
overall defensive national strategy.   We have no evidence that
Germany was planning an aggressive war against Poland at this
time in order to win back the lands which it had lost in the
east as a result of the war.   Indeed, events such as Seeckt's
refusal to let the Reichswehr enter Upper Silesia in 1921
would seem to indicate that, for the present, the German
leadership understood the realities of the international situation and Germany's own powerlessness.   Seeckt was unwilling
to become engaged in any adventurous military gamble which
would probably result the loss of Germany's important western
industrial region to the French.   This is not to suggest that
the German military, including Seeckt, had surrendered all
thoughts of one day using force to regain Poznan and the
Corridor.[79]   Germans from every walk of life considered the
cession of these territories unjust, and military men were
particularly vehement in insisting that Germany must someday
regain the Corridor.   As long as Poland remained an ally of
France, however, Germany could not make war on its eastern
neighbor. Instead, the German army had to concentrate on what
appeared to be a much more likely prospect, a Polish invasion.
      But what of the Poles? During the 1920s, it was believed
within Germany that the Poles were planning a war of further
conquest against Germany, which would most likely occur in

cooperation with the French. The civilian population of Germany's eastern territories, as well as the irregular formations stationed on the border, was subject to periodic jitters over the prospect of a Polish invasion. The German government was also subject to the same nervous worries from time to time. Yet German military intelligence regarding Poland should have allayed some of these fears, since it showed clearly that the attention of the Polish army was directed mainly toward national defense, not aggressive war against Germany. While the Germans fretted over the possibility of a Franco-Polish invasion, the Poles worried just as much about a German-Russian one, and fashioned their military plans accordingly.

NOTES

1. Robert M. Kennedy, "The German Campaign in Poland," _Department of the Army Pamphlet_, no. 20-255 (Washington, 1956), pp. 48-49.
2. _Encyclopaedia Britannica_, vol. 18, "Poland" (Chicago: William Benton Publisher, 1958), pp. 129-154.
3. Kennedy, "German Campaign," p. 50; the _Slavonic Encyclopaedia_ (Philosophical Library, New York, 1949) entry for Poland states, "Whether it were Krakow in the Middle Ages, or Warsaw in modern and contemporary times, the capital [of Poland] was always connected with the axis of the Vistula and on it based the development of its political thought" (p. 390).
4. Report no. 8652, Conger to War Department, Berlin, 3 March 1927, Subject--Cities, in _United States Military Intelligence Reports: Germany, 1919-1941_ (Frederick, Md.: University Publications of America, 1983), microfilm reel 6, frames 759-761. Hereafter, documents from this collection will be cited as USMI (for United States Military Intelligence), followed by microfilm reel number and frame numbers. Using this notation, the above document would be USMI, 6, 759-761.
5. Report no. 8662, Conger to War Department, Berlin, 8 March 1927, Subject--Climate, USMI, 6, 709-712.
6. Report no. 8642, Conger to War Department, Berlin, 1 March 1927, Subject--Rivers, USMI, 6, 690-697.
7. Report no. 8652, Conger to War Department, Berlin, 3 March 1927, Subject--Cities, USMI, 6, 759.
8. "Seidlitz' Handbuch der Geographie, Deutschland," quoted in Report no. 8524, Conger to War Department, Berlin, 3 January 1926, USMI, 6, 670-671.
9. Ibid., USMI, 6, 669.
10. Report no. 7947, Conger to War Department, Berlin, 29 March 1926, Subject--German Frontiers, USMI, 6, 729.
11. Ibid., USMI, 6, 730-731.
12. Karl Werner, _Fragen der deutschen Ostgrenze_ (Breslau: Verlag von Wilh. Gottl. Korn, 1933), p. 11. Werner was a Silesian _Landrat_. His book is a collection of biased maps and nationalistic exhortations to the Germans regarding their lost eastern territories. It is a fascinating example of the romantic tendencies which used to dominate European geographic studies.
13. Report no. 8524, Conger to War Department, Berlin, 3 January 1926, Subject--Geographic, General, USMI, 6, 669.

14.   Report no. 7947, Conger to War Department, Berlin,
29 March 1926, Subject--German Frontiers, USMI, 6, 731. Ian
Hogg, Artillery in Color, 1920-1963 (New York: Arco Publishing, 1980), p. 16, maintains that the Germans did not actually
give up their antiaircraft guns, but kept them for training
purposes.
15.   Quoted in Edgar Graf von Matuschka, "Organisation
des Reichsheeres," in Handbuch der deutschen Militärgeschichte, vol. 6 (Frankfurt am Main: Bernard & Graefe
Verlag für Wehrwesen, 1970), p. 311.
16.   Hans Meier-Welcker, Seeckt (Frankfurt am Main:
Bernard & Graefe Verlag für Wehrwesen, 1967), p. 291.
17.   Georg Tessin, Deutsche Verbände und Truppen, 1918-
1939 (Osnabrück: Biblio Verlag, 1974), pp. 187-207. See also
Conger to War Department, Berlin, 23 December 1920, Monograph
Report no. 1109, Subject--Location of the Reichsheer, USMI,
13, 160-169.
18.   Service Report no. 1294, Conger to War Department,
Berlin, 2 February 1921, Subject--The German Army, USMI, 13,
248. See also Matuschka, "Organisation des Reichsheeres," pp.
325-327.
19.   "Monatsübersicht über die polnische Armee," February
1923, Akten des auswärtigen Amtes (Records of the German
Foreign Office), hereafter AA, reel 3758, serial K190, frames
K035 335-342 and 401-407.   In shorthand notation, these documents would be cited as AA/3758/K190/K035 335-342 and 401-407.
The German diplomatic representation in Lithuania received
these reports from the Lithuanian Intelligence Service in
Kovno.
20.   Service Report no. 1407, Conger to War Department,
Berlin, 23 February 1921, Subject--The Fortifications Question
in Germany, USMI, 24, 642-644.
21.   Ibid., USMI, 24, 642. For the German view of the
fortifications question, see AA/1606-1611/3170/D680 202-206,
264-266, 591-593, 766-769, and D681 189-193.
22.   Report no. 178A, initialed "E.Y.," to War Department, Berlin, 17 May 1920, Subject--German Frontier Fortress
Defenses, USMI, 24, 616-620.
23.   Quoted in Report no. 1407, Conger to War Department,
Berlin, 23 February 1921, USMI, 24, 642-644; also
AA/1606/3170/D679 815.
24.   Report no. 1407, USMI, 24, 642.
25.   Ibid., USMI, 24, 643.
26.   Actually, this number is not excessive for five
fortresses. As the German government reminded the Allies in a
note of January 1921, German forces had captured 857 guns at
Kovno, 1,100 at Warsaw, and 412 at Maubeuge during the war.
Report no. 1212, Conger to War Department, Berlin, 14 January
1921, Subject--German Fortifications, USMI, 24, 639-641.
27.   AA/1606/3170/D679 489 and 815.
28.   Matuschka, "Organisation des Reichsheeres," p. 327,
lists the 16 antiaircraft guns in Königsberg as including 12
88mm and 4 105mm guns. The 10 guns in Pillau included 4
105mm, 4 88mm, and 2 76.2mm guns.
29.   AA/1606/3170/D679 817.
30.   Report no. 330, Attache to War Department, Warsaw,
20 December 1926, Subject--Violations of Treaty of Versailles,
USMI, 24, 697-698.

31.   Report no. 8867, Conger to War Department, Berlin,
25 July 1927, Subject--The Fortress of Königsberg, USMI, 24,
708-711.
32.   Report no. 350, Attache to War Department, Warsaw,
26 February 1927, Subject--Character of German Fortifications
on Eastern Frontier, USMI, 24, 706-707.
33.   Report no. 11,878-W, Attache to War Department,
Paris, 24 January 1927, Subject--Fortifications on the Polish
Frontier, USMI, 24, 699-701.
34.   AA/4041/L129/L026 343.
35.   The text of this fascinating and lengthy article is
to be found in AA/4041/L129/L026 491-500.
36.   Comment no. D-8617, attached by Conger to Report no.
11,878-W, Attache to War Department, Paris, 24 January 1927,
USMI, 24, 702-703.
37.   Comment by Conger, Berlin, on Report no. 330,
Attache to War Depart-ment, Warsaw, 20 December 1926, USMI,
24, 704-705.
38.   Ibid., USMI, 24, 704.
39.   Gordon A. Craig, The Politics of the Prussian Army,
1640-1945 (London: Oxford University Press, 1975), pp. 382-
383.   See also USMI, 13, 364-365, for a summary of Seeckt's
career.
40.   "Modernes Heer" was reprinted in Hans von Seeckt,
Gedanken eines Soldaten (Leipzig: von Hase und Koehler
Verlag, 1935), pp. 51-61. For the quote on "cannon fodder,"
see p. 56; the quote on the poor maneuverability of mass
armies is on p. 54.
41.   Hans von Seeckt, "Schlagworte," reprinted in
Gedanken, pp. 9-18, illustrates Seeckt's contempt toward the
military dilettantes who coined such slogans.
42.   Hans von Seeckt, "Neuzeitliche Kavallerie,"
reprinted in Gedanken, pp. 99-116, especially pp. 101, 110.
43.   Hans von Seeckt, "Modernes Heer," in Gedanken, p.
56.
44.   Hans von Seeckt, "Grundsätze moderner Landesverteidigung," reprinted in Gedanken, pp. 62-85. The quote is
taken from p. 77.
45.   Craig, Politics of the Prussian Army, p. 396.
46.   Friedrich von Rabenau, Seeckt: Aus seinem Leben,
1918-1936 (Leipzig: von Hase und Koehler Verlag, 1940), p.
297.
47.   Seeckt, "Neuzeitliche Kavallerie," in Gedanken, p.
102.
48.   Rabenau, Seeckt: Aus seinem Leben, pp. 284-285,
contains Seeckt's speech to the officers of the Defense
Ministry upon his return from Spa.
49.   Ibid., p. 316.
50.   Ibid., p. 184.
51.   Quoted in Harald von Riekhoff, German-Polish
Relations, 1918-1933 (Baltimore: Johns Hopkins Press, 1971),
p. 31, and Rabenau, Seeckt: Aus seinem Leben, p. 316-318.
Rabenau's biography contains almost the entire text of the
promemoria.
52.   Rabenau, Seeckt: Aus seinem Leben, p. 317.
53.   Monthly Intelligence Bulletin no. 148 8 1/2, April
1922, Headquarters, American Forces in Germany, Coblenz, USMI,
15, 473-488.
54.   See Riekhoff, German-Polish Relations, pp. 41-47,
who argues for the interpretation of a spontaneous Polish

national uprising. Jacques Benoist-Mechin, Histoire de l'Armee Allemande, vol. 2 (Paris: Editions Albin Michel, 1938), pp. 160-204, argues that it was Korfanty and the French who were mainly responsible for starting the uprising.

55. Benoist-Mechin, Histoire de l'Armee Allemande, vol. 2, p. 180.

56. Rabenau, Seeckt: Aus seinem Leben, p. 301.

57. Ibid.

58. Benoist-Mechin, Histoire de l'Armee Allemande, vol.2, p. 184.

59. Rabenau, Seeckt: Aus seinem Leben, p. 302. Throughout this period, Seeckt was worried about the effects of naive pacifism, as embodied in the Social Democratic party, on the German nation. He had, on first seeing the peace terms, remarked that the treaty provisions for German disarmament reminded him of the Social Democratic Erfurt Program (Rabenau, Seeckt: Aus seinem Leben, pp. 169-170). Seeckt considered "pacifism" to be a mere slogan, devoid of objective reality, and not a suitable goal for a political program (Gedanken, pp. 10-11).

60. Quoted in Riekhoff, German-Polish Relations, p. 46.

61. Quoted in Rabenau, Seeckt: Aus seinem Leben, p. 299, note.

62. Report no. 7947, Conger to War Department, Berlin, 29 March 1926, Subject--German Frontiers, USMI, 6, 732, goes much too far in asserting that

> should war break out in the next five years, the German plan of campaign is to take the offensive against Poland--and if necessary against Czechoslovakia--and the defensive against France. They count upon being able to reduce Poland in a campaign of a few months and in the meantime raise and start the equipment of an army to recover such German territory as France had gained possession of in the meantime.

In reality, we have no evidence that Germany planned, on the outbreak of a new war, to invade Poland. The foolhardiness of such a strategy, given Germany's military weakness, can scarcely be overestimated.

63. USMI, especially reels 14-17.

64. Rabenau, Seeckt: Aus seinem Leben, p. 277 and photographs facing p. 273.

65. Information Digest Report no. 4852, Conger to War Department, Berlin, 15 October 1923, Subject--Field Exercises 1923, German Army, USMI, 15, 713-718.

66. Ibid., USMI, 15, 717.

67. Report no. 7550, Conger to War Department, Berlin, 16 September 1925, Subject--Maneuvers, First Division, USMI, 14, 184-233. This lengthy report contains maneuver problems and orders for both sides taking part in the maneuvers, comments on the maneuvers for all five days, and general comments, as well as Conger's answers to a Department of the Army questionnaire.

68. Comments on the Manuever of the 1st Division, 3 September 1925, USMI, 14, 187.

69. Maneuver Exercise on 4 September, USMI, 14, 189.

70. The presence of air forces was indicated by the raising and lowering of red, white, blue, and green toy

balloons, fourteen meters in diameter, which indicated the presence of combat planes, observation planes, pursuit planes, and bombing planes, respectively. Whether the aircraft was hostile or friendly was indicated by a red or blue pennant attached to the cord near the end of the balloon (USMI, 14, 222-223).

71.   Blue: Situation for 5 September, USMI, 14, 200.

72.   Maneuver of the 3rd Day (5 September), USMI, 14, 204.

73.   Ibid., USMI, 14, 205-206.

74.   Maneuver of the 5th Day (8 September), USMI, 14, 221.

75.   Comments on the Maneuvers of the 1st Division, USMI, 14, 223.

76.   For an analysis of "Hutier tactics," see Colonel T. N. Dupuy, USA, Ret., A Genius for War: The German Army and General Staff, 1807-1945 (Englewood Cliffs, N.J.: Prentice-Hall, Inc., 1977), pp. 170-172.

77.   Conger's fascinating report is found in USMI, 14, 222-229.

78.   Gaines Post, Jr., The Civil Military Fabric of Weimar Foreign Policy (Princeton, N.J.: Princeton University Press, 1973), p. 107. See also Harold J. Gordon, The Reichswehr and the German Republic, 1919-1926 (Princeton, N.J.: Princeton University Press, 1957), p. 215.

79.   Post, Civil-Military Fabric, pp. 98-100, maintains that the Corridor remained, in German eyes, a legitimate cause for war throughout this period.

3
The Polish Army in the Eyes of German Military Intelligence, 1921-1933

Throughout the interwar years, it has been assumed, German military leaders felt a serious threat from the Polish army. In numerical terms, of course, the Polish army was far superior to the German; indeed, the Poles could count on achieving a potentially decisive quantitative superiority on any sector of the German border which they chose to attack. In terms of quality, however, it was clear to both the German and Polish military leadership that the Polish army, by itself, was incapable of fighting and winning a war against Germany. German military intelligence regarding the Polish army indicated clearly that Warsaw lacked confidence in the offensive capability of its forces. In Polish wargames and maneuvers of the period, the results of which were made known to the German government by its agents abroad, Poland's forces showed consistently that they were unsuitable for offensive warfare. Likewise, interviews and interrogations of Polish deserters indicated that the Polish army was lacking in the modern equipment and realistic training which would enable it to pull even with the Reichswehr in terms of quality. While the Germans respected the Polish cavalry and infantry, they had much less respect for the other arms of the Polish army. In particular, the Polish artillery was seen as ineffective because of obsolete equipment and outmoded tactics. While the Polish infantry received high marks in terms of march discipline and physical toughness, it also suffered from poor training and an underdeveloped tactical system which failed to stress combined-arms tactics.

The principal reason for the low quality of the Polish army was the poor state of Poland's economy. Neither the German nor the Polish economy could be characterized as robust during the interwar period. Given the respective size and industrial development of the two states, however, it was obvious that the economic burden of supporting a 100,000-man force was much lighter on Germany than the burden on Poland of supporting an army three times as large. Toward the end of the 1920s, as the world's financial and economic problems turned catastrophic, Poland's capacity to field a large, powerful army became ever more limited. In addition, Poland lacked the industrial base to produce its own weapons. Poland was dependent on foreign sources, particularly France, for armaments.

As early as 1921, the Germans were aware of the problems which plagued the Polish army. Through the interrogation of Polish deserters, German military intelligence learned much about the weakness of the Polish forces. The earliest documented interrogation involved one Stanislaus Szlachta, a nineteen-year-old German-speaking chauffeur from Torun. Szlachta had been drafted into the army in August 1920, that is, at the height of the Russo-Polish War. He belonged to the 63rd Infantry Regiment, stationed in Torun, and served there until April 1921. As a result of the Polish demobilization after the Treaty of Riga, he received his discharge from the service. He was, however, kept on the reserve rolls and was thus eligible to be recalled in case of mobilization or national emergency along with the classes of 1890-96 and 1901-3. Along with the 63rd Infantry Regiment, there were in Torun the 64th, 65th, and 69th Infantry Regiments, the 64th Marine Brigade (consisting of eight thousand men), the 8th Uhlan Regiment, and a headquarters unit. The commanding officer of the headquarters, Szlachta stated, was a French general, whose name the deserter could not remember. There was also a sizable force in Grudziadz, which together with the regiments in Torun formed a potential threat to German Pomerania. The Grudziadz force included four infantry regiments, the 59th, 61st, 62nd, and 67th; a motorized troop of twenty men, four tanks, and ten trucks; and the 7th Uhlan Regiment with eight hundred to one thousand horses and fifteen to twenty machine guns. Szlachta's most detailed information concerned his own regiment, the 63rd, and the other units in Torun. His regiment had eight infantry companies and one machine gun company, fifteen hundred men in all. In case of mobilization, however, its complement would be expanded by three or four assault companies, each of which possessed three flamethrowers. As to the equipment of these formations, Szlachta's report was comforting to the Germans:

> The 63rd Infantry Regiment is equipped with Russian, French, Czech, and German rifles. Ammunition is very scarce and is not even handed out to those on guard duty. The clothing consists for the most part of English uniforms. The horses are good, but there are not enough of them. The 8th Uhlan Regiment has only around 50 horses for a complement of 600 men. The overwhelming majority of its wagons are unharnessed, and those which are harnessed possess only a single horse rather than a team. In Torun, there are two 210mm artillery pieces hooked up to a team of eight horses. The light pieces, 75mm and down, are dragged through the streets by the men themselves.
>
> The uniforms are miserable; there is a serious lack of shoe leather. Often, troops carry out their service in the barracks square in their bare feet. The food is insufficient. The men receive two pounds of bread per day, sometimes with a bit of jam. Each man is paid 50 Polish marks, plus an extra 30 per day of leave. Leave is given very seldom.

Szlachta's interview is a useful corrective to the commonly held assumption of Polish military superiority against

Germany.   Clearly, an army unable to provide transport teams
for its artillery pieces had little reason to call itself a
modern force.   Likewise, a uhlan regiment with only fifty
horses was not a cavalry formation at all, nor were soldiers
without shoes modern infantry.
     Of even more interest to the German interrogators was
Szlachta's interesting description of the low morale of the
Polish troops. A poorly equipped army is typically an unhappy
one, but in the Polish army national and regional conflicts
combined with the poor logistical circumstances to create an
explosive situation:

> The attitude of the troops is very poor, since the
> Pomeranian troops and those from Congress Poland
> cannot agree on anything.   About three weeks ago,
> officers from Congress Poland were driven from the
> city by Pomeranian troops, under the leadership of
> officers from the region of Poznan, since the
> officers from Congress Poland wanted to introduce
> corporal punishment.   Speaking German to one's fel-
> lows is strictly forbidden.   I myself received four
> days close arrest, since I answered in German to an
> officer's question which had been delivered in
> Polish.   The attitude of the troops toward Germany
> is favorable; however, that of the officers is
> extremely hateful. [1]

     Much of Szlachta's testimony was corroborated by a second
deserter, who was interrogated by German intelligence in
September 1921.   This soldier had been a member of the cavalry, specifically the 2nd Squadron, 15th Uhlan Regiment,
stationed in Poznan. The regiment possessed six squadrons and
was under the command of the 17th Infantry Division.   Its
first four squadrons were pure cavalry formations, with a
strength of eighty men each.   Each trooper in these squadrons
was equipped with a carbine, lance, and short dagger. The 5th
Squadron was a machine-gun formation with a strength of over
one hundred men and about thirty machine guns.   The 6th
Squadron was the regiment's Technical Squadron, and its men
were equipped with carbines and daggers.   The Uhlan Regiment
possessed no other supporting formations such as horse artillery batteries or pioneer units.   Thus, in an important
qualitative sense, the German cavalry, which always was
equipped with supporting artillery and pontoon bridge formations, was superior to its Polish counterpart.
     The deserter's report went beyond matters of organization,
however, to the equipment and morale of the Polish forces.
Like Szlachta, this second deserter painted a very unflattering portrait of the Polish army:

> Clothing is very frugal. Each man has only a single
> pair of fatigues and a single pair of boots. . . .
> The attitude of the troops in Poznan is very
> divided, since there are many troops from Congress
> Poland.   The Poznan troops all wish for union with
> Germany.   In a war with Germany, the Poznanian
> troops could not be used, since the larger part
> would desert.   Desertions are listed in the orders
> of the day; in addition, the number of German sol-
> diers who commit suicide is very high.

Like the soldier Szlachta, this deserter pointed out the gravest weaknesses of the Polish armed forces: poor equipment, lack of supplies, and tensions arising out of the multinational character of the Polish state.

Each army is a reflection of the society which it serves. As reconstructed in 1918, Poland was a land of large numbers of ethnic minorities. The two largest non-Polish groups in Poland were the Germans and the Ukrainians. Large numbers of the latter group, of course, were added to the state as a result of Pilsudski's successful war against the Bolsheviks in 1920. The German presence in Poland was the result of the Versailles settlement. Both nationalities remained disaffected segments of the population of Poland throughout the interwar period. Thus, the Polish army contained large numbers of troops whose loyalty would have to be considered doubtful in the case of a war. In addition, the presence of a large German community in Poland's western districts raised the possibility that Polish army operations in these areas might be hindered by an unfriendly citizenry. From the reports of the two deserters, it is evident that Poland had not yet succeeded in assimilating its German population in general or its German soldiers in particular. While it could be argued that the Poles had not had sufficient time to mold their subject nationalities into a state, forging a strong army out of Poland's disparate national groups would remain a major challenge to the leadership. In addition, a caveat should be appended to the interrogations of these deserters. Both were ethnic Germans, and it is quite possible that they were to a certain degree merely telling their questioner what they felt he wanted to hear. Also, subjects of a military interrogation are likely to say anything to preserve their good health. Yet the very plausibility of the deserters' responses makes it likely that Szlachta and his compatriot were telling the truth. The third Polish uprising in Upper Silesia had occurred but a short time before, and national tensions between Germans and Poles ran high wherever the two groups were in contact. This tension formed the backdrop for the outbreaks of violence between German and Polish soldiers which Szlachta described.

The ubiquitous presence of French officers in the Polish army only served to fan the hatred between Germans and Poles. The report of the second deserter contained the following description of the French presence:

> French officers are found in every company. The Polish company commander may not initiate disciplinary measures by himself, but must first request permission of the French officer, who usually doubles the punishment. These French officers harangue the Poles constantly about Germany. They declare again and again to the troops that it is high time to march against Germany. Germany, they say, is growing stronger by the day, and Upper Silesia is the only justification such a war would need. Without Upper Silesia, explain the French officers, Poland cannot exist. Therefore, Poland must have the entire province.

Of course, the French officers were merely acting out on a somewhat lower plane the grand strategy of their nation, which was to ensure that in the event of a future war, a hostile Poland would face Germany's eastern frontier.

The deserter then went on to describe what he believed to be the Polish preparations for a drive on Upper Silesia:

> It is known to me that about fourteen days ago the 23rd Infantry Division was sent to Upper Silesia. Among other units, the 57th and 58th Infantry Regiments are part of this division. The 17th Infantry Division, from Warthelager, is supposed to be sent to Upper Silesia within a week. According to the placards which are hanging everywhere, all 18-year-olds in Poland are to report to their mobilization areas. The official justification for this is the possibility of war with Germany and the renewed border violations near Brest and Lwow committed by the Bolsheviks.

Perhaps without realizing it, the deserter had identified Poland's overriding strategic problem. Just as Germany faced encirclement from Poland and France, Poland faced encirclement by the Soviet Union and Germany. Although this interrogation took place before the signing of the Treaty of Rapallo, the thrust of the information which the deserter provided was that the Polish army was as concerned with the security of Poland's eastern border as with that of the western border. Hence, this mostly fictional account of a massive Polish deployment against Upper Silesia, which appears to be nothing more than a compilation of the various rumors circulating amongst the Polish troops, ends on a note of reality regarding Poland's true strategic weakness:

> At the same time, telegrams are arriving in Poznan from Grodno and Lida, asking for reinforcements, since the local troops are facing a very powerful Bolshevik force. According to some telegrams, Minsk has already fallen to the Bolsheviks. Newly formed units, to which each company had to give several men, have already departed for the East.[2]

The information provided by the deserters indicated that the Polish army, in its underequipped and undertrained state, was no match for the Reichswehr in terms of quality. Its greatest asset, its size, was more than counterbalanced by its low quality and by Poland's difficult geographic position.

Both the Polish and German military officials were aware of the sad state of Poland's army. As early as 1921, German military intelligence officials obtained documents concerning Polish military planning. These documents detailed Polish mobilization plans, operational tendencies, and tactical doctrine, and the development of Poland's extramilitary intelligence service, the Dywersja. German officials in Warsaw sent the material to the Truppenamt in Berlin, where it was evaluated and relayed to the Foreign Office, the Ministry of the Interior, and the Regional Border Police (Landesgrenz-polizei). These documents indicate quite clearly some of the difficulties which the Poles faced in fielding a modern army.

Perhaps the most instructive of the documents from the immediate postwar period was that which explained the role and function of the Dywersja, or Diversionary Section of the

Polish General Staff.   The Diversionary Section was in some
ways similar to the intelligence-gathering bodies in all the
European states.   In the Polish system, however, the
Diversionary Section had responsibilities which went beyond
simple intelligence-gathering operations.   The mission of the
section was fourfold: "To form the conditions under which the
deployment of the enemy's forces is impossible; to disturb
enemy troop concentrations and movements; to impede enemy
transport; to demoralize the enemy." The Poles recognized
that the success of these activities in wartime was impossible
without a great deal of preparatory work in peacetime.   These
preparatory activities might even extend to actual
diversionary operations on foreign soil.   Any covert operations carried the risk of discovery, however, and could proceed only upon the order of the General Staff.   Among the
preparatory tasks of the Diversionary Section, reconnaissance
and spying activities received the highest priority.   These
activities included reconnaissance of important strategic
points, such as fortresses, fortifications, munitions
factories and other war industries, railroad lines and
stations, bridges, dikes, and dams; photographing these
strategic points; and enlisting sympathetic agents.

These peacetime activities, of course, were no different
than those carried out by the intelligence services of any
country.   It was in wartime, however, that the true nature of
the Diversionary Section would have become apparent.   In fact,
the section was a sabotage organization, an extramilitary
fifth column whose mission was to discomfit the enemy in any
way possible.   At the outbreak of the war, the Diversionary
Section's first target was the enemy's mobilization, especially the transport of troops to the front.   Suggested
"effective actions" for the section included the following:

1. Demolition and arson in enemy munitions factories
or factories which support the war effort
2. Destruction of enemy's stores of food and forage
3. Destruction of enemy's merchant steamers; false
rail signals which result in train wrecks
4. Demolition of docks and rail depots
5. Demolition of rail bridges; destruction of rails;
demolition of munitions trains
6. Destruction of telephone and telegraph nets
7. Acts of terror against the enemy's population
8. Organization and subsidy of guerrilla warfare
units
9. Organization of strikes and acts of sabotage;
spreading false rumors and sowing panic

Obviously, the Diversionary Section would have to rely
upon stealth, quickness, and surprise to achieve its goals
during wartime.   In addition, the section's work with explosives and arson required a large number of trained specialists.   These specialists were divided into six departments.
The Railroad Department was concerned with any actions
involving enemy railroads, especially the destruction of
locomotives, rails, switches, and depots.   The Explosives
Department concerned itself with demolition work, especially
the destruction of enemy bridges and munitions dumps.   The
Arson Department was to destroy enemy coal dumps, oil depots,
and gasoline dumps.   Its mission also included the destruction

of the enemy's wood bridges and stores of hay.   The Intelligence Department was to identify flammable enemy targets.   The
Political Department was to organize strikes and sabotage and
spread false rumors and panic.   Finally, the Guerrilla Department was to organize guerrilla and terrorist units.   Entry
into these departments was open only to "patriotic volunteers," and special care was taken to ensure that the talents
of the recruit would suit the department in which he would
serve.[3]
      It is an axiom of military affairs that small, weak
states must rely upon their intelligence services to protect
them.   Seen in this context, the Diversionary Section was part
of the traditional search for security by a weak nation which
felt itself unable to rely upon its regular forces for protection.   In specific terms, the mission of the Diversionary
Section was an attempt by the Polish army to make up for some
of   its   own   deficiencies--insufficient   supplies,   an
underdeveloped communications net, and a disorganized mobilization procedure--by recasting any potential enemy army in its
own image.   If these diversionary activities succeeded in
disrupting enemy mobilization, rail movement, and logistical
transport, the Poles would not be at such a disadvantage in
these crucial areas.   Other activities of the Diversionary
Section were not as directly related to Poland's own weaknesses, but still held interesting possibilities should Poland
and Germany go to war.   The plan to organize a guerrilla
force, presumably of Poles living in German territory, was a
potentially effective method of disrupting public order on the
German side of the border.   However, guerrilla warfare conducted by disaffected minority nationalities was the
proverbial two-edged sword for the Polish state.   The Germans
could have easily retaliated against the Poles by organizing
guerrilla formations from among the numerous Germans living in
Poland's western districts.   Finally, the generically designated "acts of terror" which the Diversionary Section was to
carry out were likely to be of no real military or political
utility, if the numerous examples of terrorist acts in this
century may act as a guide.   Still, whatever the potential
effectiveness of the Diversionary Section, the stress placed
upon extra-military activities indicated that the Polish
General Staff was well aware of the deficiencies of its
regular forces.
      While the possibilities of sabotage and terrorism during
a war worried the Germans, military officials in Berlin took a
rather calm view of the military situation in the east.
Correctly reading the heavy Polish reliance on institutions
such as the Diversionary Section as a sign of Polish weakness,
the German Defense Ministry was always highly skeptical of the
reports of Polish troop concentrations which it received from
Warsaw and the German border districts.   In September 1921,
for instance, the defense minister received a cable from the
German ambassador in Warsaw in which the latter reported on a
conversation with a Polish general.   The general stated that
in the region Czestochowa-Sosnowiec-Krakow, as well as in the
vicinity of Wongrowiec in Poznan, large Polish troop concentrations had recently taken place, chiefly consisting of
infantry.   The number of infantry gathered was listed as
120,000 men, plus six or seven regiments of cavalry, each
consisting of about 900 troopers.   In addition, a large number
of field guns and aircraft were present.   The purpose of

concentrating these troops was so that they could be used if a war between Germany and Poland broke out as a result of the Upper Silesian question. If the decision of the Allies regarding Upper Silesia was totally unfavorable to the Poles, as appeared more and more likely to the Polish government, then a war could start at any time. According to the general, if war broke out between Germany and Poland, then the Poles would order a general evacuation of all western territory up to the Netze district:

> The reason for this evacuation is that the Polish government fears the predominantly German population of this area, and is worried about resistance and assaults against Polish forces by the population, especially if German forces enter the region. As a justification for this strategy, Polish leaders point to the statement by the Commissioner of the Free City of Danzig, General Haking, that the entry of German troops into the western regions would be greeted by the local population with jubilation.[4]

At the moment, reported the general, the evacuation of the northern garrisons in Dirschau, Starogard, Grudziadz, Torun, and Bydgoszcz had freed the troops who had been transferred south to Czestochowa, where they protected Polish interests in Upper Silesia. If the final Allied decision regarding the disputed territory was not in Polish interests, he concluded, then the entry of regular Polish troops into the province was likely.

The defense minister in Berlin denied the likelihood of the events discussed in the report and stated that "the entire thing is unbelievable." Specifically, the minister took issue with the report of Polish troop concentrations in the Krakow-Czestochowa region as well as the discussion of Polish strategy in the event of a new war:

> The deployment of Polish forces on the Upper Silesian border in the Krakow-Sosnowiec-Czestochowa region has remained the same for a long time. . . . The total strength of the regular forces and insurgents is around 75,000 men. In the vicinity of Wongrowiec there are no forces at all.
>
> If the Upper Silesian question is resolved unfavorably for Poland, a new uprising would perhaps result, but only if France approves. Due to the present quiet situation within Upper Silesia, a new uprising in the province would have to be carried out by the insurgent forces already placed on the Upper Silesian border. Whether the Polish government would use regular troops to support a new uprising, in the process declaring war upon Germany, appears very questionable. Should it come to a war against Germany, it is improbable that Poland would evacuate West Prussia, thereby uncovering the rear of its assault forces advancing from Poznan into middle Silesia. The reason mentioned in the report for such a strategy, fear of the German population, does not hold water.[5]

From this exchange of correspondence, we see a pattern emerging. Time after time, German officials, either in Warsaw or in the border regions, predicted a Polish military aggression against Germany. Rather than causing a panic, their reports were dismissed by the better-informed Truppenamt or Defense Ministry. Germany's military officials simply did not judge the Polish army worthy of consideration as a serious adversary.

Even Poland's principal ally, France, seemed to have doubts about Polish military power. According to a report from the police director in Königsberg in 1923, for instance, Field Marshal Foch's trip to Poland in June of that year had resulted in a "great fiasco." Foch had made the trip to determine if the huge sums of money which France had provided to the Polish army were being used wisely. His stay in Warsaw, which included a grand review of the Polish troops, left him with an unfavorable impression. The general did not hesitate to speak his mind on the issue of French monetary assistance to Poland. While still in Warsaw, he claimed that "it was apparent that a large part of the money had been used for non-military purposes and that much of it had found its way into the pockets of Polish officials."[6]

The interallied tensions aroused by Foch's comments were evident in a series of conversations between the head of the French military mission to Poland, Colonel Baron de Gayl, and the German consul in Poznan, Stobbe. Stobbe's reports on these talks received wide circulation among the German officials responsible for eastern affairs. The Germans thought it likely that the French government had approved Gayl's remarks in advance, which cast serious doubt on France's resolve to support Poland in a crisis.

The conversations began with a general review of Franco-German relations. The central point which Gayl wished to make was that France was trying seriously to come to a reconciliation with Germany. Anti-German rhetoric of the sort indulged in by the French president, Raymond Poincare, was nothing more than an electoral maneuver, a device by which the president rallied public support behind his policies. Gayl then turned the conversation to the Polish army, with which he was not at all impressed. Above all, he stressed the poor quality of its artillery. During the Russo-Polish campaign, in which Gayl had participated personally, the Russians had often employed envelopment tactics against the Polish forces. In this situation, the Polish artillery had been totally helpless. The artillery never attempted flanking fire against the enveloping troops, but instead tried to retreat, almost always without success. Today, noted Gayl, the forces which one saw in the parades in Poland were naturally drawn from the best elements in the army. In fact, he stated, everything impressive in the Polish army, especially in matters of tactics and discipline, was attributable to former members of the old imperial German army. In the Polish army, Gayl noted sadly, former German officers were not numerous. Most officers had seen duty previously in the Austrian or Russian armies. Interestingly, Gayl mentioned that since he spoke no Polish, and since most Polish officers spoke no French, all of his conversations with Polish officers had taken place in German. The Poles, however, would speak German with him only "in private."

Gayl also spoke at length about Pilsudski. At the time, it was rumored that Pilsudski would run for the presidency

after the establishment of the Polish constitution.   Although
the marshal declined the opportunity to run, Gayl's characterization of   the Polish leader was significant for Franco-
Polish relations after the coup of 1926.   Quoting from
Stobbe's report:

> Pilsudski is remarkably ambitious; he hangs on fer-
> vently to his power, and is unscrupulous in his
> means. In close contact, he gives the impression of
> a very clever, but practically insane personality,
> who loves play-acting and intrigue.   Often he sits
> for half the day lost in thought without doing a
> thing;   toward evening he becomes a bit more lively,
> and then suddenly a restless energy overtakes him.
> The last time Pilsudski participated in an official
> reception in Poznan, he practically ignored Baron
> Gayl.   Gayl was furious and let Pilsudski know it,
> whereupon Pilsudski asked him to sit down at a small
> table.   The two men then discussed the current
> political situation for almost two hours.   Baron
> Gayl oberved that Pilsudski at first appeared apa-
> thetic and only gradually, with the aid of strong
> tea and cigarettes, became more lively and acces-
> sible.   As they spoke, Pilsudski consumed thirteen
> cups of tea and smoked twenty-six cigarettes.   "Il
> se dope," remarked Gayl, just as others need mor-
> phine or cocaine.

Gayl concluded by noting that Pilsudski spoke German well, was
not hostile to Germany, and had practically forgotten his
imprisonment in Magdeburg. He recognized that Poland's health
was not to be found in a narrow alliance with France, since
such an alliance threatened Poland's relations with Germany
and Soviet Russia.[7]
    The visit to Paris of Polish war minister Wladyslaw
Sikorski in late 1924 aroused great interest in Germany,
especially since German military intelligence had reported to
Berlin that the purpose of the visit was to negotiate the
terms of a new French loan for the improvement of the Polish
army.   The actual course of the trip and its aftermath,
however, did not indicate any strengthening of the Franco-
Polish tie.   Instead, the French made clear that any increased
aid for Poland would have a price--complete French direction
of Polish military policy.   In particular, France would allow
no weakening of Poland's defenses on the German frontier.   A
report on Sikorski's trip from the German Foreign Office
Archives quotes Sikorski:

> I acknowledge frankly our complete military super-
> iority over Germany in the West, and I believe that
> we are therefore able to transfer troops to the
> East, where the situation is much more critical. I
> cannot recommend this action, however, due to polit-
> ical reasons.   I have just returned from Paris,
> where I discussed new French credits for our
> military.   The French will grant new credits, but
> only if we agree to strengthen our garrisons in the
> West, and to behave as if we feel a constant threat
> from Germany.   The leading circles in Paris hold to
> the fiction that Germany is building up its armed

forces in the East,   while it disarms in the West.
We Poles must contribute to the maintenance of this
fiction in the interests of our French allies, by
guarding our western border in a demonstrative
fashion.[8]

Commenting upon this report, the German ambassador to
France agreed that the Poles had to keep their forces facing
Germany strong if they were to receive more French aid:

There is no doubt that France feels that aid to
Poland is only justified if Poland remains strong on
the German border.   It also corresponds to French
wishes that, by the preservation of a strong armed
force on the German border,   the feeling grows among
Poles that they are threatened by Germany.[9]

The German minister in Warsaw likewise commented that it
was improbable that Sikorski had negotiated new credits in
Paris. He stated, however, that

it is certainly not impossible that, in view of the
calm situation upon the German border, the Poles are
considering transferring troops to the East.   As
Sikorski pointed out, however, the terms of the
alliance treaty between Poland and France specify
that Poland is to maintain a certain number of
divisions upon the German border.[10]

The minister considered it likely that the Poles would rely
upon border defense units for protection in the east. At this
time, he reported, the Poles had an irregular border force of
ten battalions of infantry and ten squadrons of cavalry already deployed in the east, of a total planned force of thirty
battalions and thirty squadrons.

The implications of the Sikorski affair were plain.
France would demand, as the price for any increased aid to
Poland, the continued presence of large numbers of Polish
troops on the German border, even while the Poles felt their
main threat from the Soviet Union.   Just as France had
attempted to institutionalize German-Polish enmity through the
Treaty of Versailles, so it now desired to play the role of
the financier of tension between Germany and Poland.   The
Poles learned during this period that their own security
interests were not always identical with those of the Great
Power benefactor.   The period commencing with Pilsudski's
seizure of power in 1926 and ending with the German invasion
of Poland in 1939 was one in which Polish statesmen, tenta-
tively at first and then more and more boldly, attempted to
assert their independence from France and to conduct a military and foreign policy more in line with Polish national
interests.

The conditions which produced Poland's independent strategy were present even in the 1920s.   To be sure, Poland in
some ways benefited from the French alliance.   France needed
Poland's friendship to maintain the international system built
at Versailles and was willing to pay for that friendship with
loans, credits, and industrial help.   The massing of the
French army on Germany's western flank, for instance,
prevented Germany from presenting a serious threat to Polish

security.   But Poland had no such counterweight against its
troublesome eastern neighbor.   Therefore, Polish leaders felt
it necessary to improve their defenses against the Soviet
Union.   It soon became apparent to Warsaw, however, that any
attempts to strengthen the East at the expense of Polish
garrisons in the west would lead to hostility from France.   At
the same time, French actions were not altogether pleasing to
the Poles.   Attempts by France to reach a reconciliation with
Germany, most notably the Treaty of Locarno in 1925, caused
consternation in Poland.   The so-called "spirit of Locarno," a
slogan supposed to represent a new era of good will between
nations, never found any echo in Poland.   The Locarno pact,
since it guaranteed Germany's western border, was a violation
of the spirit, if not the letter, of the Franco-Polish
alliance.   Before 1925, the most likely scenario for a new war
in central Europe, as seen from Warsaw, was a German-Polish
conflict over the territories which Germany lost in the peace
treaty.   After the Treaty of Locarno, a French entry into such
a war would be illegal, as the Franco-German border was now
guaranteed by Britain and Italy.   The cavalier treatment of
the Polish delegation at Locarno by the French, as well as the
explicit refusal of the German government to consider any sort
of "eastern Locarno" to guarantee the Polish-German border,
caused the Poles to question seriously the value of the tie
with France.[11]
In the military sphere, where the alliance with France
was of the highest potential value to Poland, French aid
consisted basically of loans, supplemented by the shipments of
modest amounts of materiel.   In April 1922,for instance,
"reliable sources close to the Entente" reported that a French
steamer left Marseilles on 28 March conveying a load of
weapons munitions for Poland.   The materiel consisted of
80,000 rifles, 2,200,000 nickel cartridges, and 1,115,000 dum-
dum cartridges.   In addition, the steamer carried a series of
modern searchlights.   The materiel was accompanied by four
officers from the War Ministry in Paris.[12]
This rather modest contribution to the Polish military
establishment was partially supplemented by Poland's own
nascent military industries.   The Poles were clearly not
satisfied with the quantity or quality of the arms which they
received from France.   Compounding this dissatisfaction was
their recognition of the stakes of any future war.   During an
interview with the Petit Parisien in 1925, Sikorski declared
that the Polish army must remain strong because any future war
must have a successful conclusion for Poland; a defeat would
mean the loss of independence.   In case of a war, he declared,
Poland was capable of tying up twice as many German troops as
had the Russians in 1914.   But Poland had to be careful not to
be surpassed in the arms race by any of its neighbors.[13]
Sikorski was especially concerned that Poland increase its
stocks of artillery and construct an air fleet.   To achieve
this, however, France had to increase its aid to Poland.
In the meantime, Poland depended for its security upon
two things: its own industrial capacity and, as in Germany,
the recruitment of irregular border guard forces.   These two
trends in Polish military planning were evident in a report
drawn up by the Prussian minister of the interior in 1925:

The weapons factory at Warsaw is producing a copy of
the French infantry rifle Model 24.   This infantry

weapon will be introduced into the Polish army during the next year. For the time being, a battalion in Warsaw is using the weapon on an experimental basis. The weapons formerly in use in the Polish army, mainly old German Model 88 and 89 rifles, are to be given to the veterans organizations. Recently, in the Polish areas bordering Germany, groups of veterans of the War and the Upper Silesian uprisings have been formed. These groups are to act as border defense forces in the event of a war, and each member is to be armed with a rifle.[14]

Unlike the German army, it appears that the Poles planned a more active role for their border defense units. Information obtained from a Polish official indicated to the Germans that irregular Polish units would not hesitate to take part in operations on German soil:

In Polish mobilization plans, a "preliminary defense" of the western border is mentioned. Its task is to secure the border in case of mobilization before regular troops have arrived. Once regular troops arrive, the task of the border defense will be to support them. The organization is arranged along purely military lines and relies chiefly upon the patriotic leagues. The military leadership is in the hands of the General Staff of the VII Army Corps in Poznan. The border defense forces are divided into divisions and subdivisions. Division leaders are former officers of the Polish army, who either hold leadership posts in the customs police or live in the border district. There are known cases where a division leader has been provided with a farm and the state has paid the former owner for the land. The leaders of the subdivisions are usually former non-commissioned officers who now hold positions in the customs police.

The formation of the border defense has been undertaken energetically since March of this year, when several Polish officers toured the border areas and gave special instructions to the division leaders. The members of the organization, in so far as they are not officials, are all reliable persons of Polish nationality, who take a pledge to the organization by means of a handshake. The subdivision leaders give all orders orally; their special task is the care of all weapons. The tasks of the border defense extend from occupying important Polish mobilization centers to preventing the concentration of the German paramilitary organization in the German border regions. It is the special duty of the border defense to seize the weapons stored in the German border areas.[15]

The Poles were, of course, in greater need than the Germans of irregular supplements to their armed forces, since the quality of the Polish army was so much lower than that of the Reichswehr.

The most serious deficiency of the Polish army was the lack of a cohesive, homogeneous officer corps. While Polish officers often had war experience, gained during the First World War or the Russo-Polish War, and were personally brave, they lacked instruction in the techniques and tactics of modern war. It should also be mentioned that after Pilsudski's withdrawal from public life in 1922, the Polish army had no soldier with either the prestige or the strategic insight to compare with Germany's General Seeckt. Pilsudski would be heard from again, in 1926, and it is no coincidence that the post-1926 period was a much more vibrant era for the Polish army in terms of planning, training, and procurement of modern equipment.

In a wide-ranging discussion of Poland's military weakness which took place in 1924, a Polish officer recognized the problems of the Polish officer corps:

> The present officer corps is at a low level of education and is not cohesive. Because of a lack of suitable officers candidates, the army command has raised many school-age German nationals to the rank of officer. These have often received only a rudimentary training. Even the training of the General Staff officers leaves much to be desired. They possess no individual initiative and are merely the servants of their French instructors. The deficiencies of the Polish officers are very noticeable in comparison with the former German officers in the Polish army.

The anonymous Polish officer was just as negative with regard to the soldiers and equipment of the Polish army:

> There is a terribly large number of illiterates among the soldiers, especially those from the eastern areas. The formations currently stationed in Poznan contain members of practically every nationality in Poland: Ukrainians, White Russians, Ruthenians, Germans, and others. The Polish formations, though, tend to be transferred to the East. In general, the personnel is very unreliable. In case of a war, many men will probably desert. In addition, the political reliability of the troops is very doubtful. Communist agitators have repeatedly been apprehended while among the troops. . . . The equipment of the Polish army is also very deficient. There is a serious lack of heavy artillery. The heavy artillery regiments in Poznan and Grudziadz possess for the most part obsolete guns. The most serious deficiency in the machine gun sections is the presence of different systems of armament. The French equipment has greatly disappointed military circles here, since France usually sends obsolete and unusable materiel. The Poles prefer German materiel, which surprisingly is still found in large amounts and in some cases is still being shipped (cartridges). Many shipments from France contain old German materiel.[16]

The opinions expressed by this Polish officer are important on two levels. First, the Polish army possessed grave
deficiencies with regard to training, organization, leadership, and equipment; members of the army were quite aware of
these deficiencies. Second, the Germans were aware of
Poland's military weakness, as well as the resulting unlikeli-
hood of a Polish attack on Germany's eastern regions. In
addition, the absence of any operational plans or maneuver
reports from the files of German military intelligence was a
further indication to the Germans that they had little to fear
from the Poles.

On the local level of German government, however, the
military situation appeared much more threatening. The German
population of the eastern regions felt that the threat from
Poland was indeed acute. Report of Polish military preparations also originated with German travellers to Poland. In
April 1925, for instance, a local German industrialist
reported to Herbert von Dirksen that "during a trip to Poland
in the night of 10-11 April, he saw five large freight trains
on the Lodz-Kalisz railway carrying heavy artillery, American
guns apparently, with surprisingly high mounts, teams of
horses, but no personnel among them."[17] In fact, the German
records are filled with information regarding Polish troop
movements. This information was false more often than not,
and on the rare occasions when it was true it was almost
always misinterpreted by its source to signify an imminent
Polish attack upon Germany. A report on the military situation in Polish Pomerania from early 1925, for example,
described a kind of "war fever" in Poland:

>   The formations stationed in Starogard have entered a
>   definite state of readiness. In one of the rooms at
>   the fortress of Gurbierc, there is a relief map of
>   northern Poland, East Prussia, and Pomerania. Upon
>   the map, there are operational plans for a march in
>   the direction of Stolp and Königsberg. Officers and
>   enlisted personnel are instructed inside this room
>   daily. The troops have recently participated in
>   many firings and field exercises, and have been
>   trained in the methods of gas attack. The military
>   activity of the organizations in Grudziadz has been
>   heavy. There even exists a "National Air Defense
>   League" which is so well equipped that it operates
>   with aircraft.[18]

Likewise, numerous reports of Polish mobilization measures, including one bizarre report which spoke of the enlistment of all Polish men fifty years of age or younger,
indicated that officials of the German border regions remained
very worried about the Poles. These reports failed to have
similar influence in Berlin, where officials knew that the
Poles were having a difficult enough time paying the soldiers
they had already inducted. Throughout this period, to be
sure, the Poles tried to compensate for the low quality of
their army by increasing the size of their forces. This was
usually done by calling up a class of recruits before its
scheduled induction date. As a result of budget difficulties,
however, the army often had to let these men go before their
two-year term of service was completed.[19]

In general, civilian officials in Weimar Germany tended to worry much more than military officials about "the danger from Poland" (Polengefahr). While German military circles refused to consider the Polish army as a power factor in Europe, many civilian members of the German government did. The German minister in Warsaw, Ulrich Rauscher, was at first susceptible to the illusions of Polish power. In 1925, the Poles held their first large army maneuver, which took place near Warsaw. Rauscher was impressed, albeit not unreservedly, with what he saw:

> The intention of the Polish government to prove, in front of a large host of drunken guests, that the young Polish army has been transformed in the last several years from something out of an operetta to a factor in European strategy has doubtless succeeded. The credit for this transformation goes to the iron hand of the French military mission.
> Poland has created a more or less unified army. In its fighting ability, this new force noticeably surpasses the force which fought in the Polish-Bolshevik War. The French military mission, up to now the driving force behind the organization of the Polish army, is well aware that the inner structure of the army, apart from its purely technical training, still leaves much to be desired. These deficiencies include the standardization of the officer corps, its economic position within the army, and not least the level of morale among the troops. In cooperation with the Polish High Command, the French work tirelessly to solve these problems. The ably chosen maneuver problem stated that the engaged Polish forces were to protect the mobilization of their army against one enemy advancing from the Ukraine and another advancing from East Prussia. The problem was designated as "solved" by the leadership. The judgment of the foreign guests was that . . . the conduct of the maneuver by all arms, the spirit of the soldiers, and their equipment were all very good.

Rauscher turned to a discussion of the individual arms within the Polish army. He was impressed with the cavalry and the infantry, less so with the artillery:

> The infantry is trained according to modern concepts and makes in general a well-disciplined impression. Certainly, one should not overlook the fact that, in general, only the Warsaw corps and troops from the former German areas participated. The corps from Poznan and Thorn are regarded both in public opinion and military circles as elite troops. The rest of the Polish forces, above all those from Galicia and the eastern regions, remain far behind them in military prowess.
> The most popular and best-trained Polish troops are the cavalry. These units proved themselves especially fit during the maneuver. The cooperation among units in the cavalry divisions and their training in dismounted combat were both excellent.

Several attacks, carried out with great elan, show
that not only do the Poles remember the battle of
Sommo-Sierra, but that they still consider mounted
combat possible, at least in the eastern theater of
war.
     It is difficult to give a judgment on the
ability of the artillery.   One feels instinctively,
however, that the very brilliant parade training
given to the artillery has left little time for pure
schooling in gunnery.   Also, if a real war breaks
out, problems in ammunition procurement, which have
recently grown into an official scandal, will cause
difficulties.

Rauscher also called special attention to the technical training of the Polish army, an issue which would in the future
cause the most concern in Germany:

     The French military mission has made special efforts
     to train the technical troops of the Polish army in
     the modern sense.   These efforts have borne fruit,
     as witnessed by the achievements of the pioneer
     troops in bridge-building and by the construction of
     temporary positions.   The cavalry division present
     was provided with fourteen tanks.   The air force
     suffered one casualty, when an officer was killed
     during a failed landing.   Lastly, near Thorn, a
     retreating force attempted to cover its retirement
     through the use of smoke.[20]

     Other observers, even Polish military men, were less
impressed than Rauscher by the Polish army.   One document in
German intelligence files tells of a conversation by a Polish
general soon after the maneuver:

     The subject of the conversation was the recent
     maneuver in Upper Silesia.   The men had made a good
     impression, he said, especially the Upper Silesian
     forces, but the higher leadership, indeed the
     leadership at all levels, was very poor. There was
     a shortage of technical troops and the large cavalry
     movements had ended in total disorder.[21]

     By 1924, it had become ever clearer that Poland's mili-
tary strength was more illusory than real.   Reports filtered
into Berlin that Poland's financial troubles would soon cause
a reduction in the size of the Polish army. On Christmas Eve,
1924, Rauscher wired the Foreign Office in Berlin:

     I have been told by a well-informed source that the
     French government is exerting influence on the
     Polish government to cut down the size of its army
     to the level agreed upon by both sides in 1919,
     around 144,000 men.   I request a report as to the
     probability of this information being true.[22]

     Neither Rauscher nor the German ambassador in Paris be-
lieved this report of French pressure upon Poland.[23]   Still,
Rauscher believed that although France did not want a
reduction in the size of the Polish army,

recently, France appears to have accepted the fact
that the reduction of its ally's army is an unavoidable necessity for financial reasons. In order to
save what is possible, the French military mission,
as another well-informed source told me, has offered
to give assistance during the army reduction.[24]

Whatever the French attitude, the signals coming from
Washington and London were much less equivocal. A telegram to
the Foreign Office from the German ambassador to the United
States contained a wire service report concerning the reduction of the Polish army:

Practical disarmament is one of the urgent requirements laid down preliminary to rehabilitation of
Polish government finances by American banking
interests in negotiations involving new credits to
Poland. Poland's difficulties are complicated by
the fact that France has already done so much to
build up the Polish army that the Poles fear to take
actual steps toward disarmament which might antag-
onize their ally. As the situation is understood
here, Poland urgently needs additional foreign
credits. American bankers are unwilling to grant
these until there have been drastic cuts in
expenditures.[25]

Likewise, the Manchester Guardian reported on 16 March 1926
that the English War Ministry, working through the English
ambassador to Warsaw, had demanded a reduction in the size of
the Polish army.[26]
     This was a critical period for the young Polish army and
for the Polish state in general. The army had already been
reduced in size to about 300,000 men following the Russo-
Polish War.[27] A further reduction to the suggested level of
144,000 men, or about twelve divisions, would have left the
state practically powerless against its neighbors, particularly the Soviet Union. It is against this backdrop that the
events of May 1926 must be viewed. Jozef Pilsudski, still
Poland's first soldier despite his retirement from political
life, decided that only he could save the state and especially
the army. After assembling a small force of about
two thousand men, including portions of the 22nd Infantry and
7th Uhlan Regiments, he marched on Warsaw.[28] At Praga, his
forces clashed with a company of cadets from the Infantry
Officers School as well as regular cavalry loyal to the Warsaw
government. Lives were lost on both sides, but by the evening
of 13 May, Pilsudski's troops were masters of Warsaw. What
had appeared to many observers as the inevitable had happened.
The Germans were certainly not surprised. As early as 1922,
German military intelligence had the impression that
Pilsudski's disappearance from power was not necessarily
permanent.[29] Now, Pilsudski had resorted to the sword to
reassert what he felt was his legitimate claim to be leader of
Poland.
     Opinion within the German army was divided about the
effect upon the Polish army of Pilsudski's coup. Some felt
that Pilsudski's hostility against his political enemies would
carry over into military affairs and thereby tear apart the
army. Others feared, however, that Pilsudski would strengthen

and enlarge the Polish army and put it on a war footing.   The
earliest indication we have of the German reaction to the coup
was   a   report from Rauscher on 21 May concerning   the   actual
military   conduct of the combatants.   Rauscher was   impressed
with the troops he saw in action:

> As   far as a 2 1/2-day struggle allows us to make   a
> judgment   about the behavior of an army during   war-
> time,   the   events   of the last few days allow us   a
> glimpse into the soul of the Polish army,   since the
> battles   were   fought right before   our   eyes.   One
> couldn't   help   but notice that the troops   on   both
> sides fought bravely and cleverly.   The infantry and
> the reserves manned their machine guns under hostile
> fire,   participated   in battles with hand   grenades,
> and used camouflage well.   The cadets and the Poznan
> regiment   fought especially   well.   The   artillery,
> apart   from   a few direct hits,   did not exert   much
> influence upon the battle.   Aircraft did not distin-
> guish themselves;   the bombs dropped fell on private
> houses,   much   to   the   anger   of   the   civilian
> population.

According   to   Rauscher,   the leaders of both   sides   deserved
severe criticism. The government's General Staff deployed in a
vital   strategic point a battalion whose friendly attitude   to
Pilsudski was well known.   This unit deserted at the outset of
the coup.   Pilsudski had also erred:

> Pilsudski,   for   his   part,   did not reckon with   the
> resistance   put   up by the cadets.   He possessed   a
> decisive superiority on the first night,   so that   a
> speedy advance could have led to the crushing of all
> opposition.   Through   his   hesitation,   the   cadets
> received   reinforcements   and   both   sides   suffered
> heavy losses.   The fact that this did not lead to an
> actual civil war was just luck.

Rauscher   saw   the coup as having a generally negative   impact
upon   the Polish army,   despite the prestige   which   Pilsudski
possessed amongst the troops.   In addition,   Rauscher   stated,
the   success   of the coup pointed up a basic weakness   of   the
Polish state:

> The   coup has opened up a wide chasm which will only
> be healed through time and work.   Pilsudski's   name
> still holds its magic with the troops.   We need not
> go   into the many reasons which led him into   rebel-
> lion   against the legal   authorities.   However,   it
> should   be   mentioned that   the   decision "for   or
> against Pilsudski" was very much an officer's   pre-
> rogative;   the   men   simply obeyed their   immediate
> superiors.

That   the power of the state was dependent upon the   decisions
of lower ranking officers,   noted Rauscher,   should be a matter
of great concern to the new government.[30]
The difference of opinion in German circles regarding the
effect   of   the coup upon the army was a reflection of a   disagreement over Pilsudski's abilities.   On the one   hand,   the

Germans recognized him as a strong, fearless, and charismatic--if not necessarily wise--military leader, who would undoubtedly do all in his power to strengthen the Polish army. On the other hand, German officials thought that his personal idiosyncracies, especially his tendency to carry a grudge, were fatal weaknesses in a national leader. The method by which he came to power, a coup which almost destroyed the army he desired to save, only confirmed German suspicions about his basic unfitness for high office.

Pilsudski's actions immediately after seizing power reinforced the negative opinion in German military circles. In one sense, the work of rebuilding and healing the Polish state could only have been performed by Pilsudski, since only he held the necesary charisma with the common foot soldier. The architect of "the miracle on the Vistula" now had the task of reconstructing the army he had created almost singlehandedly in 1920. The first major task was liquidating the coup. He had two options with regard to those who had opposed him in May: reconciliation or exclusion from the army. Characteristically, Pilsudski chose the latter, and attempted "to unite the army through a series of appointments, reckless firings, and transfers," in Rauscher's words:

> In almost all of Poland, the higher leaders who did not stand behind him, whether out of loyalty or out of personal enmity, have been demoted to commanding regiments or have been transferred to formations loyal to Pilsudski, and thereby completely paralyzed. In the last weeks, twenty regimental commanders have been replaced. Only in the province of Poznan has this process of "Pilsudskification" of the army not proceeded in the same fashion.[31]

Another method by which Pilsudski strengthened his position in the army was the creation of twelve army inspectorates. Rauscher estimated that at least eleven of these appointments went to Pilsudski's most loyal supporters. Eight of them sat in Warsaw, with one each in Wilno, Poznan, Krakow, and Lwow. The inspectors were responsible for forces within their territories and would command those same forces in wartime. Thus, corps commanders found their powers limited seriously, since they were now responsible to the inspectors.

Another of Pilsudski's stratagems, his plan to raise the salaries of his officers, caused much less opposition. He requested a total of twenty million zloty for this purpose during his first six months in office and ignored the protests of his finance minister that the budget could not bear the increase. In addition, Pilsudski attempted to secure better housing for his officers and instituted a system of benefits for all ranks, including free passage for vacations and free tickets to the theater.[32]

It is clear that Pilsudski was successful in making the army his personal instrument and in securing his own position of power. He achieved this by appointing individuals loyal to him as well as by the sheer force of his personality. Needless to say, the effects on the army were not totally positive. Again, a report from Rauscher several years after the coup is instructive:

The military circle around Pilsudski is assembled
from completely heterogeneous elements. They are
held together only by his personality, which can
only be described as "mystical." It is an extreme
hazard for the Polish army that selection into high
posts is made on the basis of personality rather
than military ability. Thus, one finds, besides
militarily capable men with initiative and spirit,
many who obey Pilsudski blindly. The latter serve
Pilsudski more like medieval courtiers than officers
in a modern army.[33]

One result of Pilsudski's appointment policy was that the
former officers of Pilsudski's legion now began to play a more
important part in Polish military affairs. The new prominence
of Pilsudski's old comrades took place at the expense of
former officers in the Russian and Austrian armies. Before
1926, this latter group had dominated the army administration.
After the May coup, with Pilsudski's approval if not his
direct participation, a purge of these "Austrian" and
"Russian" elements proceeded with great vigor. Indeed, this
process was still under way when Adolf Hitler took power in
Germany in 1933. While the purge ensured that Pilsudski would
maintain total control over the army, it also excluded many
able and experienced officers from continuing on active duty.
Rauscher wrote:

Those who remain know that their military ability is
not as important as is proof of their 100%
"Pilsudski-ism," which they therefore try to demonstrate constantly. They try so hard that one gets
the impression that, instead of seeking to improve
its war-fighting ability, the army is trying to
increase its efficiency in domestic politics.[34]

Despite the problems of sycophancy and the lack of
initiative which the Germans identified, many in Berlin felt
that Pilsudski was capable of bringing about real improvement
in the Polish army. The central problems facing the Polish
army, as viewed by Pilsudski, were its poor equipment, organization, and training. Pilsudski ordered industrial activity
within Poland stepped up to produce more and better equipment,
and he also searched for alternative sources of equipment
since French aid in this area was unsatisfactory. Under
Pilsudski, the Polish army took its first, hesitant steps
toward mechanization, although the great expense of mechanized
weapons prevented more of them from being introduced into
frontline units. In fact, the economic weakness of the Polish
state, particularly after the onset of the Great Depression,
made any material improvements in the army extremely difficult. In the matter of organization, Pilsudksi's appointment
of inspectors has already been discussed. The next several
years would see several reorganizations of the General Staff
and the cavalry forces in an attempt to streamline and
modernize them. Finally, and perhaps most importantly,
Pilsudski improved the training of his officers and men by
establishing regular wargames and maneuvers after 1928. Just
as the Germans relied upon maneuvers in order to plan strategy
and tactics for a war against Poland, the Poles used them to
plan for a possible war against Germany. All of these

attempts to improve the capabilities of the Polish army, of course, bely one fact: Pilsudski believed that, as matters stood, Poland had no hope of waging a successful war against Germany.

The most pressing deficiency of the Polish forces was the lack of modern equipment. To remedy this shortage, Pilsudski moved with dispatch to set up a national arms industry within Poland. By November 1927, a number of arms factories had been constructed or expanded. Other nationally owned factories were put under independent direction to increase their efficiency. These included the state nitrate works at Chorzow, the munitions plant at Zagozdom, the small arms factory at Radom, the rifle and carbine factory at Skarzysko, the munitions factory at Warsaw, and the nitrate factory at Tarnow.[35] In addition, Poland ordered 164 light (104mm) Model 19 field howitzers from Czechoslovakia's Skoda works. These pieces were reconditioned old Model 14 howitzers from the Austrian army. Skoda also contracted to recondition 300 more Model 14 pieces already owned by the Poles. By 1930, almost 250 of these howitzers had been distributed to the active regiments or to reserve stocks. Their ammunition was produced at Skarzysko.[36] At the same time, the Poles placed another order for howitzers with the French firm of Schneider-Creusot.[37] While these measures helped to overcome the howitzer shortage, the main gun employed by the Polish army continued to be the old 75mm French cannon. This gun partially made up for its light weight of metal by a quick rate of fire, but was inferior to the German 105mm gun.

Another item in short supply in the Polish arsenal was the machine gun. Rauscher reported in 1929 that "there are so few light machine guns that the troops use dummies during maneuvers and exercises."[38] During the 1929 fall maneuvers, he stated, light machine guns had not been present at all. Rauscher had heard rumors that the Poles had struck a deal with the Belgian Browning munitions firm along the following basis: the firm would transfer five thousand light machine guns to Poland immediately; at the same time, Browning pledged to open a factory in Poland which would produce a further twenty thousand. Along these lines, Rauscher informed Berlin that light machine gun tactics and the operation of the Browning had recently been added to the curriculum at all Polish military schools. While it appears that nothing ever came of the plan to build a Browning plant in Poland, the shipment of the five thousand weapons took place almost immediately.[39] At the same time, the Polish government ordered the production of a new heavy machine gun. This weapon was provided to several companies of the army as a test weapon, but did not arrive in frontline units until 1933. The Mauser heavy machine gun upon which the Poles had relied since 1918 had a rate of fire of only four hundred rounds per minute; the new piece could fire six hundred rounds per minute. Because of the thickness of its cone of fire, the Poles were also able to use it as an antiaircraft weapon.[40]

Pilsudski thus had achieved much in terms of increasing his army's firepower and expanding his country's industrial potential. Both of these improvements were of great concern to the Germans. Especially worrisome, in the long run, was Poland's development of an "arms industry triangle" to the south of Warsaw. Hans-Adolf von Moltke, minister to Warsaw, commented in 1931 that "Poland has in the last five years made

great strides forward in its war industries.   There exists no
doubt that it will hold fast to its goals of self-sufficiency
in wartime and freeing itself from dependency upon arms imports in peacetime." For the short term, however, the Germans
seemed to realize that spiralling costs and the economic
depression would smother this Polish industrial revolution.
Moltke believed that in peacetime, Poland was dependent on
arms from abroad in the following categories: guns of all
types, tractors, medium and heavy tanks, and bombers. During
wartime, Poland would also have to import medium and heavy
artillery ammunition, gas masks, poison gas, and airplane
motors. In case of a war, the country was capable of
producing rifles, machine guns, small arms ammunition, hand
grenades, aircraft (without motors), and possibly light artillery ammunition.[41]

One index of Poland's success in developing a domestic
arms industry was the degree to which Polish arms had entered
the export market by 1932. A report from the German legation
in October of that year declared that the Poles were exporting
arms to Greece, Bolivia, Brazil, and Romania. The Greeks were
interested in small arms and artillery munitions, especially
shells for their 105mm cannon. Bolivia had placed an order
for 5,000,000 small arms cartridges and about 30,000 rounds of
various light- and medium-caliber gun ammunition. Brazil had
ordered 25,000 rounds of 75mm ammunition for its French-made
guns; these shells were loaded at Gdynia and transported to
Brazil by the end of 1932. Romania was interested mainly in
aircraft bodies and various munitions.[42] While the quantities
purchased by all of these nations were not large, the very
fact that Poland had become an arms exporter indicated that in
one small way at least, Pilsudski had been successful in
erecting a Polish arms industry.

By 1932, the figures for Polish stocks of medium- and
heavy-caliber artillery were still quite modest. Of course,
in comparison to the German army, which was permitted no heavy
weapons at all, the Polish army was relatively well equipped.
But included in the Polish arsenal of medium and heavy guns
were a number of obsolete Russian mortars and only two modern
railroad guns (table 3.1).[43] Pilsudski did succeed in forming
a fairly large artillery force. There was even one antiaircraft regiment, with nine batteries, and three independent
antiaircraft batteries.[44] Altogether, then, the Poles had
over fifteen hundred pieces of artillery. Still, it should be
pointed out that the aged 75mm French gun made up almost half
of this total and that the semi-obsolete pieces of the
Austrian and Russian armies formed an additional third (table
3.2).

Besides increasing domestic production of armaments, the
Poles also attempted to broaden their base of foreign arms
suppliers. Business with the United States increased. In the
spring of 1932, the Poles placed an order for one hundred
antiaircraft guns with an American firm. These were Driggs
guns, modern two-inch pieces with a muzzle velocity of three
thousand feet per second. At first, the Poles had considered
placing their order at Schneider-Creusot, but the prototype
sent to Poland had experienced difficulties. Although it
performed well in its first trial firing at Rembertow, its
wheel carriage collapsed. After the Poles replaced the
wheels, they found that the calibration of the gun was not as
precise as it needed to be; indeed, the weapon would no longer

Table 3.1
Polish Medium and Heavy Artillery

Type	Number	Active	Reserve
155mm howitzer	218	168	50
120mm/79 cannon	40	--	40
180mm cannon (Italian origin)	60	60	--
210mm mortar	30	18	12
240mm mortar (Russian origin)	8	--	8
240mm railroad guns (purchased from France)	2	--	2

Table 3.2
Polish Artillery Formations

Formation	75mm	3-inch	104mm	105mm	150mm	155mm	210mm
45 Field Regts.	720	--	--	360	--	--	--
10 Heavy Regts.	--	--	60	--	--	120	--
1 Very Heavy Regt.	--	--	--	--	--	--	18
3 Mounted Regts.	36	--	--	36	--	--	--
13 Horse Batts.	--	156	--	--	60	--	--
10 Foot Comps.	--	--	--	--	60	--	--

shoot straight.   Although the French were highly indignant,
the Poles decided to purchase the guns from the United
States.[45]

In June of the same year, perhaps as a result of its
satisfaction with the American guns it had bought, the Polish
government decided to purchase heavy railroad guns from the
Americans.   Again, the party edged out was France, which had
in the past supplied Poland with the only two heavy railroad
artillery pieces in the Polish arsenal.   The new American guns
were of twelve-inch caliber (about 300mm) and were used by the
American army as coastal batteries.   The Poles felt that these
guns would be useful for the defense of their Baltic coast.[46]

Beyond Pilsudski's struggle to increase the quantity and
quality of his artillery, he was also concerned with the
effect of mechanized technology upon his army.   The Poles did
possess a small armored force at the time of Pilsudski's coup,
which consisted mainly of French Renault tanks of World War I
vintage.   Polish tanks and armored cars had participated in
many battles against the Red Army, and Pilsudski seemed more
aware of their potential than many contemporary French
generals.   As the Germans were permitted no tanks at all, they
watched the growth of Poland's armored strength with much
interest.   As with its artillery program, however, the Polish
army's acquisition of armor never reached the desired level
because of economic problems.

In keeping with the Polish cavalry tradition, the first
armored formations in the Polish army were attached to the
cavalry.   During the pre-1926 period, the armored formations
were not standardized, either by type of vehicle or by organization.   Pilsudski took the first steps toward standardizing
these units.   In February 1927, the armored car units were
reorganized into "armored squadrons" of ten to twelve armored
cars each.[47] It soon became apparent, however, that attempts
to build a large armored force were doomed from the start.
Money was the foremost obstacle; in the 1920s, just as today,
the tank was an expensive, high-technology item, and the
fragile Polish budget could not stand the purchase of more
than about twenty tanks a year.[48] In addition, the Polish
leaders, including Pilsudski himself, seemed unable to decide
which tank they wanted to deploy.   Finally, Pilsudski's desire
to construct an indigenous Polish arms industry worked against
an increase in armor capability, since the Poles demanded that
any foreign producer of tanks build facilities within Poland
for tank construction.   This demand led to lengthy negotiations with several foreign firms, which delayed the actual
production of tanks in Poland until well into 1932.

The Germans watched carefully Poland's efforts in the
sphere of armor.   In April 1931, Emil von Rintelen, the
counsellor to the German legation in Warsaw, noted that the
armored formations had "undergone significant change in the
past few years." He identified the commander of the armored
units as Colonel Tadeusz Kossakowski, who commanded the following forces: one tank regiment, which had recently been
transferred from Galicia to Poznan; two armored car sections,
located in Brzesc and Przemysl; two armored train sections,
consisting of one old Russian and one old Austrian train; and
the training school for armored forces in Warsaw.   The tank
regiment was the principal unit and consisted on paper of one
heavy and two light battalions of three companies each.   Each
company contained three platoons of four tanks each.   In

reality, not all of these tanks were present in the regiment. The equipment of the heavy battalion was very incomplete; it was really just a cadre with several old German tanks as well as a few heavy Vickers tanks.[49] According to Rintelen, a Polish official had recently stated that the Poles had the capability to produce their own tanks. However, not one foreign military attache had seen a single Polish-made tank. Rintelen speculated that the remark might have been meant only as a theoretical possibility. The two armored car sections consisted of six or seven squadrons of three platoons each. Each platoon contained two cars. The equipment of the Brest section, Rintelen had learned, consisted of small Vickers "one-man tanks." These sections, as mentioned above, were assigned to the cavalry.

Altogether, the Poles had assembled a force of 380 tanks by 1932. This force consisted of three tank regiments, located at Poznan, Zurawica, and Modlin. Included in the total were 35 Char 2Cs, 100 Renault Model 17s, 160 Renault Model 27s, 50 Renault M. C. 27s, all French, plus 20 Italian Medium 2 Mark Vs, and 15 German A VII Mark Vs. Of this relatively large number of tanks, however, as many as half were obsolete by 1932. The Renault Model 17 and the A VII Mark V tanks were of particularly little value.[50] As with their artillery, the Poles succeeded in achieving quantity, but not quality, in their armored forces. Despite Pilsudski's efforts, the Polish army remained an infantry-cavalry force in the 1930s.

While success in improving the material condition of the army eluded Pilsudski, he also endeavored to improve its organization. Both Pilsudski and the many foreign military observers in Poland were well aware that the Polish army was deficient in matters of organization. In particular, logistics, rail movement, and the composition of units were the subject of criticism from many quarters. There were two principal fields for his reorganizing efforts: the cavalry formations and the high command. The reorganization of the high command centered around the creation of the army inspectorates and has already been discussed.

The reorganization of the cavalry was one of the most confusing activities of Pilsudski's tenure in office. When the marshal seized power in 1926, the Polish cavalry was organized into brigades. He apparently felt that these brigades lacked the firepower and endurance to engage in combat on the modern battlefield. Hence, during the summer of 1926, almost immediately after the coup, Pilsudski ordered the merger of the cavalry brigades into divisions. This process resulted in the formation of four cavalry divisions (table 3.3). In addition, the 2nd, 3rd, 5th, 6th, and 9th Independent Cavalry Brigades remained in existence, stationed at Rowno, Wilno, Krakow, Stanislawow, and Baranowiczi, respectively.[51]

The advantages of this new arrangement--greater concentration of firepower and fewer cavalry units--soon turned out to be more apparent than real. The cavalry divisions showed themselves in maneuvers to be far too cumbersome. In the face of the awesome firepower of the modern battlefield, cavalry could operate only in dispersed formation, a fact which the Germans had made the basis of their new cavalry tactics. General Seeckt's design for quick mounted maneuver combined with dismounted combat by small groups of cavalry, supported

by machine guns and artillery, was the real future of the
mounted arm.   The leadership of the Polish army seemed to
accept these facts after the fall maneuvers of 1928.   During
the spring of 1929, the Polish General Staff devised another
reorganization plan for the cavalry, which basically cancelled
the 1926 reorganization.[52] Cavalry brigades once more made
their appearance, and only one cavalry division, the 2nd at
Warsaw, remained in existence.   Polish cavalry now consisted
of eleven independent brigades, and it would carry this organization into the Second World War.   Yet the struggle within
the Polish army over the role and function of cavalry would
continue.   One German observer wrote that, in his opinion,
"the struggle over the final fate of the cavalry is still not
complete." He continued:

> There is no shortage of voices who argue for a
> reduction in the size of the cavalry forces.   Among
> the influential proponents of this point of view is
> the head of the Polish air force, who argues for an
> increase in the air force at the expense of the
> cavalry.   The cavalry has its own influential
> defender in General Gustaw Orlicz-Dreszer of the
> Army Inspectorate.   He has prevented any reduction
> in the number of cavalry regiments and it is thanks
> to him that the Warsaw cavalry division still
> exists. General Dreszer, who possesses the trust of
> Marshal Pilsudski, also believes that in war,
> especially a war in the East with the Soviet Union,
> the use of large bodies of cavalry is necessary. It
> is therefore very possible that in case of war, the
> cavalry, after it has performed its preliminary
> tasks of securing the border and protecting the
> deployment of the Polish army, will again be formed
> into divisions.   Then it might again find a stra-
> tegic use. For the time being, however, Dreszer has
> had to give in to the enemies of cavalry and agree
> to the dissolution of the cavalry divisions.[53]

In fact, the entire process of cavalry reorganization
indicated the basic indecision on the part of the Polish
leadership as to the use of mounted troops. Of course, the
1920s was a period of great theoretical ferment and experimentation in all European armies, and the cavalry question was
among the foremost debates of the era.   While most countries
made the decision to replace horse cavalry with mechanized
forces, Poland did not follow suit; indeed, Poland entered the
Second World War with more cavalry than any other European
country except the Soviet Union.   On the simplest level, the
Poles kept their cavalry because it had been effective for
them in the past, most recently in the Russo-Polish War.
Tradition is always a powerful motivating factor in armies;
the tendency to keep doing things the old way is even stronger
when it appears that the old way works.   At any rate, the
Poles had little choice other than to maintain their cavalry,
because the state lacked the money to mechanize their forces
more extensively.   As subsequent events were to prove, however, mounted forces were by the 1930s an inadequate
substitute for tanks as a striking force.
    The mixed success of Pilsudski's attempts to reform the
Polish army was evident in the large summer maneuvers of 1928,

Table 3.3
Polish Cavalry Divisions, 1926-1929

1st Cavalry Division
Bialystok

4th Cavalry Brigade--Wolkowysk
    2nd Uhlan Regiment--Suwalki
    3rd Light Horse Regiment--Suwalki

8th Cavalry Brigade--Bialystok
    10th Uhlan Regiment--Bialystok
    3rd Mounted Rifles--Wolkowysk

11th Cavalry Brigade--Augostowo
    1st Uhlan Regiment--Augostowo
    9th Mounted Rifles--Grajewo

2nd Cavalry Division
Warsaw

1st Cavalry Brigade--Warsaw
    1st Light Horse Regiment--Warsaw
    1st Mounted Rifles--Warsaw

12th Cavalry Brigade--Ostroleka
    5th Uhlan Regiment--Ostroleka
    7th Uhlan Regiment--Minsk-Mazowiecki

13th Cavalry Brigade--Plock
    11th Uhlan Regiment--Czechanow
    4th Mounted Rifles--Plock

```
          3rd Cavalry Division
          Poznan

7th Cavalry Brigade--Poznan
     15th Uhlan Regiment--Poznan
     17th Uhlan Regiment--Lissa

14th Cavalry Brigade--Bydgoszcz
     16th Uhlan Regiment--Bydgoszcz
     7th Mounted Rifles--Poznan

15th Cavalry Brigade--Grudziadz
     18th Uhlan Regiment--Grudziadz
     8th Mounted Rifles--Culm


          4th Cavalry Division
          Lwow

10th Cavalry Brigade--Przemysl
     20th Uhlan Regiment--Rzeszow
     10th Mounted Rifles--Lancut

16th Cavalry Brigade--Lwow
     14th Uhlan Regiment--Lwow
     6th Mounted Rifles--Zolkiew

17th Cavalry Brigade--Hrubieszow
     24th Uhlan Regiment--Krasnik
     2nd Mounted Rifles--Hrubieszow
```

which took place near Rozan north of Warsaw.[54] Foreign military attaches received invitations, but they had to swear not
to reveal anything of what they had seen. The German minister
attributed the need for secrecy to the presence of the Soviet
attache. The leadership of the forces involved in the
maneuver was in the hands of Pilsudski protege General Edward
Rydz-Smigly, who "proved himself to be a very capable
general." The composition of the two forces and their
starting situations were as follows. Playing "Blue" was the
8th Infantry Division, with attached units: an independent
cavalry brigade, one training battalion, two independent
machine-gun battalions, one heavy artillery battalion of six
batteries, and a company of aircraft. Blue's commander was
General Stachiewicz, the director of the Military Science
Section in Warsaw. The main body of his force was grouped to
the south of the line from Warsaw to the Bug river. Group
Stachiewicz was assembled in the vicinity of Makow. Patrols
had sighted enemy forces north of the Bug in the vicinity of
Ostrow. Blue's assignment was to cross the Narew and to
harass the enemy concentration near Ostrow.
     Playing "Red" was the 18th Infantry Division, plus
various attached units: one tank battalion, one pioneer
(bridging) section, plus two companies of aircraft. Besides
these forces, Red would receive reinforcements consisting of
the 28th Infantry Division and the 2nd Cavalry Division from
Warsaw. The commander of this force was General Orlicz-
Dreszer, commander of the 2nd Cavalry Division. Group Dreszer
was assembled in the vicinity of Ostrow. Red's task was to
advance on Rozan, cross the Narew, and destroy the enemy
assembled around Makow. It was assumed that all bridges of
the Narew had been destroyed.
     The situation thus postulated an attack by the Soviet
army, ironically called the "Red army," which had advanced up
to the Narew just north of Warsaw. The Blue force contained a
large contingent of cavalry, whose task was to disturb Red's
crossing of the Narew and if need be to drive Red back over
the river. At first, Blue's cavalry was completely successful
in crushing Red's bridgeheads on the left bank of the Narew.
After the arrival of Red's reinforcements, however, Red successfully crossed the river at Rozan. Red's reinforcing cavalry division played an especially important role in the river
crossing.
     In his report on this exercise, Rauscher mentioned that
the general opinion of those present was that the Polish
infantry was relatively well trained according to modern principles. The quality of the infantry, he declared, showed most
of all the influence of the French military mission. The
personnel were extraordinarily efficient and stoic. The
spirit of all the troops, but particularly that of the
cavalry, was very high. The artillery, however, left much to
be desired in terms of tactics and training. The cooperation
between infantry and artillery, he stated, was totally
lacking.
     This lengthy report also described the leadership situa-
tion within the Polish army. Rydz-Smigly had done well in
formulating the maneuver problem. The decisions of the
leaders of both groups and their subordinates, however, came
under sharp criticism. Most impressive had been the decision
of the officers not to rest at night, but to use the cover of
darkness for large troop movements. Least impressive had been

the relationship between artillery and the infantry. Artillery liaison officers were only occasionally assigned to the infantry regiments, and none at all were assigned to the battalions, where they would have been most useful. It appeared that the Polish commanders had no conception of the importance of artillery-infantry cooperation. The German official told of one particular episode in which a Red infantry division formed into march column on an observed road. The commander of this unit knew of enemy positions some four kilometers ahead in a wooded area, and so decided to send ahead as the advance guard an infantry regiment with two batteries attached. He sent them forward, however, in a tight formation with no cover. The column received heavy fire. Its supporting artillery, still in limbered formation, galloped backward without attempting to silence the enemy guns. The result was that the infantry regiment suffered heavy casualties before it could deploy.

According to Rauscher, the individual infantry units from battalion on down had functioned well. The attacks followed modern principles, were deeply echeloned, and took good advantage of cover. Only several members of each group were visible in the advance. The infantry, at least, laid great stress on the "emptiness of the battlefield" as the key to victory and employed camouflage cleverly. The men stuck branches in their helmets and sought to hide themselves from aircraft even during their rest periods. Tactically, the infantry companies formed up into "task forces," semi-independent groups of all arms designed for specific missions. These groups were weaker than they should have been, however, since each company possessed only one or two light machine guns instead of the planned six. The Poles, it has been noted, suffered from a severe shortage of machine guns, which the large order from Belgium had not yet begun to solve. It was significant that the Polish forces attempted no indirect, unsighted machine-gun fire during this maneuver. Indirect fire from machine guns formed the basis of German infantry tactics, and the Reichswehr found that it was valuable in suppressing fire from hidden defensive positions. As it was, the Polish infantry was highly vulnerable in the advance, since its own machine guns had to stop firing. The Poles had begun to recognize this weakness, and the military school in Torun had just recently instituted a course in indirect machine-gun fire. The final weakness of the Polish infantry, according to the German report, was the lack of radios amongst the troops. The principal means of communication between the units remained the telephone, which the war had shown was a highly vulnerable method of transmitting messages. Again, this would have put Polish troops at a severe disadvantage to the Germans, who had begun to experiment with radios during their own maneuvers. The discussion of the infantry finished with a compliment to the men: "Especially noteworthy was the good attitude of the troops, even after long marches and other exertions."

The cavalry units distinguished themselves during the 1928 maneuver. According to the German report, "The attitude and the achievements of the individual riders and horses were extraordinary." The attack of Red's three cavalry regiments against one Blue infantry regiment, which took place immediately after a strenuous night march, had taken Blue by surprise. According to the military obervers present, the cavalry had also performed well in dismounted combat, had shown fine spirit, and had displayed a high level of technical skill in the numerous crossings of the Narew which it had made. Most interesting, however, was the backward state of mechanization in the Polish cavalry. In Germany, Seeckt saw a future for cavalry only in close cooperation with mechanized and motorized units. In the Polish army, however,

> modern means of battle, such as armored cars, are not favored by the cavalry leaders. The mission of the Red cavalry would have been achieved in a much easier fashion if the Red commander had not left his armored cars unused in the rear.

In the Reichswehr, a cavalry commander who ignored his mechanized assets would probably have been relieved of command.
    The military observers present were most vocal in criticizing the Polish artillery. In general, the criticism was raised that the artillery fought only for itself and did not worry at all about its sister arms. The problems were not only of doctrine, however, for the German report mentioned also that the technical aspects of the artillery left much to be desired. The artillery failed to distinguish itself either by the rate or accuracy of its fire. Rauscher's report mentioned several specific criticisms:

> Changes of position occurred seldom. Where batteries stood in the morning, there they stood in the evening. The artillery made no use of camouflage. The artillery regiments possessed only six instead of the planned nine batteries. The horse artillery battalions had only two instead of three batteries. Each battery, instead of four guns, had only two. The official explanation for this was the lack of horses. There were no tractors present for the heavy artillery.

Only the horse artillery batteries escaped criticism. They rode well and performed several river crossings. They shot "very seldom," however.
    In conclusion, the report discussed the technical arms of the Polish army. Although the pioneers had performed efficiently in building bridges over the Narew, the other technical troops left a great deal to be desired. The activity of the fliers was very disappointing, since they limited themselves to long-range reconnaissance. They performed no bombing. There were no air-to-air battles. Armor saw no action at all, but was kept twenty kilometers behind the front in reserve. Also, the armored cars were of little value, due to the bad roads. Finally, gas discipline had been poor. In several cases, small detonators of tear gas were used to represent poison gas. The troops required a long time to don their gas masks.[55]
    The problems identified in the maneuver of 1928, above all the poor quality of the artillery and the technical troops, were the same deficiencies which had plagued the Polish army since before Pilsudski's seizure of power. Although the infantry and cavalry had performed well, the lack of infantry-artillery cooperation would have doomed the Poles to high casualties if the bullets had been real. Also

noteworthy was the total lack of interest displayed by the
Poles in the use of tanks and armored cars, which stood in
sharp contrast to the German maneuvers in East Prussia during
1925.   All in all, the performance of the Polish army in 1928
showed that it was totally inferior to the German army in a
qualitative sense.

There were no such grand maneuvers during 1929, since the
Polish government ordered the cancellation of large-scale
exercises for financial reasons.   Instead, maneuvers of
smaller units were scheduled, which, although cheaper, lacked
the advantage of promoting inter-unit cooperation.   At least
three such smaller maneuvers took place: in Galicia, in the
northeastern part of Poland, and in Upper Silesia.[56] The
Silesian exercise involved the 23rd Infantry Division, and was
the subject of a long report from Richard Du Moulin, the
German military attache in Warsaw and a retired colonel.   It
was evident that the Polish army was still experiencing problems in its modernization.   Of particular interest is the
simplicity of the maneuvers attempted during the exercise, a
fact which the German minister attributed to poor leadership:

> When orders were given out, it was apparent that
> they dealt only with broad concepts, not particu-
> lars.   Above all, it was noticeable that the orders
> contained no regulations for liaison, either with
> neighboring troops or subordinate units.   It
> appeared that this was done, not to encourage inde-
> pendent thought in lower-ranking officers, but
> because there was a general lack of organizational
> talent.   Still, no serious problems resulted because
> of the simplicity of the orders given to the troops.
>   In the defense, there were four battalions in
> the front line.   A strong force of five battalions
> and five batteries was held in reserve for a
> counterstroke.   It is interesting, however, that the
> reserve batteries never did in fact see action.   The
> attacks proceeded frontally.   Envelopments were not
> attempted.   It is a principle in the Polish army
> that the urge to move forward is the most important
> quality in a soldier.   It is also undeniable that
> the personnel have great elan.   In remarkable
> measure, the troops possessed the urge to advance.
> Unfortunately, neither the generals nor the officers
> understood how to channel this enthusiasm in the
> right direction, nor did they know how to conduct a
> methodical advance according to the modern
> principles of fire and movement.

Again, the infantry received praise for its march discipline and spirit, while the artillery failed the test of
modern warfare, particularly in terms of cooperation with the
infantry:

> The cooperation of the infantry and artillery still
> left much to be desired, even though the 23rd
> Infantry Division contains some of the best troops
> in the Polish army.   In one case, three batteries
> received orders to unite their fire on one point.
> Immediately after this short fire had ceased, the
> infantry was to attack.   The fire actually proceeded

successfully.   From the moment the firing stopped,
however, it was twenty minutes until the infantry
moved forward.[57]

All in all, the maneuver of 1929 of the 23rd Infantry
Division was a more impressive showing than the exercise of
the previous year.   But the 23rd Division, it must be remembered, was something of an elite formation within the Polish
army.   Further, the maneuver orders were so simple, featuring
a frontal assault upon an enemy infantry force, that good
results were to be expected.   The presence of a large number
of foreign military attaches, moreover, indicated that the
true goal of the maneuver was in the field of public relations.

As in 1929, the year 1930 saw no large maneuvers of two
to three divisions apiece, but rather smaller exercises
featuring one to two divisions.   The major exercise of the
year took place in northeastern Poland, near Slonim and
Baranowiczi.   The forces attached to each side were as follows. The Blue force consisted of the 29th Infantry Division,
the Suwalki Cavalry Brigade, one battalion of border guards,
one squadron of mounted border guards for use as divisional
cavalry, one armored car squadron, and one section of aircraft.   Red's force was the 20th Infantry Division, the
Baranowiczi Cavalry Brigade, one battalion of mounted border
guards, one section of aircraft, one tank company, one squadron of mounted border guards for use as divisional cavalry,
one group of Carden-Lloyd two-man tanks, and one bridging
train.

By 1930, these maneuvers seemed to yield the same results
year after year.   Minister Rauscher wrote that "the general
impression of the military attaches present was that although
the tactical leadership of the lower ranking officers showed
progress, there could still be no talk of a 'modernization of
the Polish army.'"   To Rauscher, the Polish army seemed to
resemble the old Russian army during the World War, surely an
unflattering observation.   Unlike the 1929 maneuver, these
forces were not at all "elite," and their performance showed
it.   There was also little evidence of tactical wisdom.   The
forces were spread far too thin (nine battalions per sixteen
kilometers) to attack or defend effectively.   There was no
concentration of force at the decisive spot, so that the
infantry assaults possessed only the weak force of an
advancing line.   "At no place," wrote Rauscher, "were the
troops assembled in decisive strength."   In the defense, the
Poles relied upon obsolete principles: the most visible high
ground was seized and held with no regard for camouflage or
protection.   One Polish general, questioned on this point,
responded that "it is more important to have a favorable
firing position than it is to keep out of sight."   Rauscher
praised the spirit of the infantry, but stressed that often,
high morale and tactical wisdom did not go hand in hand.
Polish soldiers, he maintained, went about their business with
such single-mindedness that they seemed to ignore any subsidiary tasks which arose.   As a result, they sometimes gave
the impression of being clumsy.   In addition, the equipment of
the troops was so diverse as to be ridiculous.   Within
individual units, soldiers had different uniforms, rifles, and
bayonets.

As usual, the cavalry performed well during this maneuver. Even more than in the past maneuvers, it became evident that the cavalry was the most efficient arm in the Polish army. Especially noteworthy was its stress upon dismounted combat. Rauscher wrote, "The horse is seen as a means of transport but not of battle. Attacks were not made from the saddle. Rather, the troopers assiduously dismounted and fought on foot." Yet even the cavalry possessed certain deficiencies, particularly in its leadership. The attacks made by the cavalry during the 1930 maneuver were frontal assaults, with little thought apparently given to exploiting the mobility of the horse soldiers through the use of flanking actions. Indeed, in the course of a two-day struggle, the four cavalry regiments of the Baranowiczi Brigade failed totally to force back a defending force of only two cavalry regiments.

By far the worst showing was provided by the artillery and the mechanized forces, which, in Rauscher's words, "had made the least progress along the road to modernization." The artillery did not cooperate with the infantry companies and, more seriously, never changed position. The maneuver did have some tanks, but their effectiveness was indicated by the following report:

> The Red forces sent ten tanks up to the front line during a night march. The deployment continued in the morning, however, in completely open terrain without any protection. The tanks then received the order to break through the enemy line. They went over to the attack, in a single line, straight as a rod. There were two groups of five tanks, without any deployment into echelon. About 100-150 meters to the rear followed an infantry battalion. The tanks had orders to drive 1 1/2km past the enemy line and assemble there. They proceeded in a straight line, without paying any attention to events to their right or left. In one place, the attack came to misfortune, since the tanks drove into a swamp whose presence had not been announced before the maneuver.[58]

It is evident, then, that the Poles had not yet assembled what could reasonably be called a modern army. The cavalry and infantry were relatively well trained and equipped, even if their tactical doctrine was outmoded. The attributes which define modernity in warfare, effective artillery and mechanized forces, however, were still lacking. The reason for Poland's military inadequacy remained as it had been before: the state simply could not afford the expenditures necessary to improve these arms.

The winter maneuver of 1931 took place near Smorgau, southeast of Wilno, and was an indication that the Poles were beginning to realize that their strength lay not in modern technology, but in the quality of their foot soldiers and cavalry. The maneuver concentrated on the use of infantry in winter conditions. No use was made of tanks, and aircraft played only a minor role. Stripped down to the bare essentials, the Polish army gave a good accounting of itself in this mock battle.

The hostile force, designated Red, was concentrated near Molodeczno and had orders to march on Wilno, where the friendly Blue force had concentrated. The foreign observers present were most impressed with the use of ski troops by the Blue force. The skiers had only a two- to three-week tactical training course behind them. But they moved over the terrain very adroitly and moved forward in their firing line especially quickly. The machine guns were fastened to small sleds and were drawn by two skiers. The ski troops were equipped with snow smocks and sleighs. In advancing through the streets, the ski troops were occasionally drawn by the riders of the border patrol. In this manner, the forces achieved a rate of march of about ten kilometers per hour, at least on paths where the snow was stamped down.

The regular infantry, however, found the going a bit rougher. The Red infantry had not been equipped with skis and possessed only several ski patrols. As a result, it had to overcome the greatest difficulties due to the deep snow. The men often sank up to their waists. One could therefore not expect the infantry to operate at its regular efficiency. The poor weather, it was noted, caused a tendency amongst the troops to huddle together in closed columns and to forego the intelligent use of terrain. Still, the observers' final judgment was favorable to the Polish forces: "The troops accomplished the most important missions assigned to them in an outstanding manner. They proved themselves to be extraordinarily tenacious and frugal. At the closing review, the men appeared in very good form.[59]

What conclusions can we draw from these maneuvers? First, the traditional arms of the Polish army, that is, the cavalry and the infantry, were effective forces. They were hardy, well conditioned, and had high morale. Those technical arms which we usually consider to be the hallmarks of a modern army, artillery, air forces, and mechanized units, lagged behind the infantry and cavalry both in terms of the quality of their equipment and the effectiveness of their training. Second, unlike the German army, with its affinity for infiltration tactics, the Poles did not use their maneuvers to conduct tactical experiments. During the Polish maneuvers, the troops attacked to the front after a suitable preparatory bombardment. The cavalry tried envelopments only rarely; the infantry tried them not at all. There is one record in 1930 of an armored breakthrough being attempted but this attempt failed when the tanks promptly drove into a swamp. The new tactical possibilities opened to ground armies by the growth of air power remained unexplored by the Polish army during this period. In 1930, the Poles were at least fifteen years behind their neighbors in military development. Third, the location of the maneuvers and the situations postulated during the exercises indicated clearly that the Poles looked to the Soviet Union and Lithuania as their primary enemies. The favorite location for these maneuvers, particularly after Pilsudski's coup, was the Wilno region. The staging of military exercises near Wilno served two purposes: they warned the Lithuanians to end their agitation over their lost city, and they prepared troops to fight in a likely theater of war should the Red Army invade Poland. As we have seen, the Poles did hold maneuvers in Upper Silesia and the Corridor. These exercises, however, were aberrations in the general pattern of Polish maneuvers in the eastern regions, and usually occurred

as a direct response to some crisis in German-Polish
relations. It is significant that the last great Polish
maneuver before 1933 occurred at Rowno and once more had as
its assumption a Soviet attack on Poland's eastern
territories.

The stress which Pilsudski's government placed on the
danger from the east was evident also in the Polish wargames
of the period. Instructors of the French military mission had
introduced Polish officers to wargaming in the early 1920s as
part of the regular course work in military science.[60] Soon
after Pilsudski's return to power, he established a yearly
double wargame in which hand-picked participants gamed an
operational and a tactical situation. Pilsudski excluded all
foreign officers, even the French, from these games, which
took place in the offices of the General Inspectorate.
Military intelligence records indicate that the majority of
the games dealt with eastern scenarios, that is, war with the
Soviet Union or Lithuania. The 1928 game, for instance,
postulated a Polish-Lithuanian war, although Poland also had
to deploy large forces on its borders with Germany and the
Soviet Union. Likewise, the game of 1931 concerned the Soviet
Union. This game was the subject of a report by an official
of the German legation in Warsaw. His report indicated that
the wargame was directed against Russia. The prevention of a
German attack while the army fought the Russians was left to
the Polish diplomats.[61]

The next month, the legation received further information
on the wargame situation:

> The basis for the wargame was that Poland and
> Romania went to war with the Soviet Union during the
> summer. The Polish army was drawn up along the
> border, and had adopted a defensive stance. The
> Romanian army defended the line of the Pruth River.
> The Soviet Army launched an offensive towards Kowel,
> crossed the line of the Styr River, and was engaged
> in further advances. Polish reserves stood around
> Strij and Lublin. Marshal Pilsudski ordered the
> Polish commander, General Orlicz-Dreszer, to master
> the situation through a counterattack. Dreszer
> decided on a counterblow from Galicia, using the
> united forces of the Romanian army and the southern
> Polish army.
>
> Pilsudski declared during the post-game analy-
> sis that Dreszer's decision was incorrect.
> Pilsudski stated that a flank attack proceeding in a
> southeastern direction from the Wilno region was the
> correct decision. Since the battle was supposed to
> have taken place in the summer, Pilsudski stated
> that, in his opinion, the Pripet marshes offered no
> serious obstacle to the accomplishment of his
> plan.[62]

The wargames, then, were further evidence that Poland's
war plans were directed against the Soviet Union. The Germans
were well aware of the Polish army's concern with its eastern
frontier. Two documents from the winter of 1929-30 show
conclusively that the Germans knew they had nothing to fear
from the Poles. The first was a report from Richard Du
Moulin, the German military attache to Warsaw after 1928. The

leadership of the _Reichswehr_ had asked Du Moulin to draw up a report on Poland's plans for war with Germany. He found two difficulties in gathering information for this report. First, of course, the matter was one of strictest secrecy. Second, and more surprisingly to Du Moulin, public opinion in Poland considered a war against Germany so unlikely that there was almost no discussion of the form such a war might take.

Still, Du Moulin recognized several possibilities for Polish behavior in the event of a war against Germany. He realized that his information might be merely impressionistic. Hence, he did not follow the usual procedure in the German military of investigating each possible contingency (two-front war for Poland, two-front war for Germany, and so on). Instead he relied upon what he called a "thoroughly unsystematic" presentation of the military situation.

The basis for Poland's military planning against Germany, he stated, was that the Polish army felt altogether inferior to the _Reichswehr_. He had seen this feeling expressed on many occasions, and it was a sentiment shared by all the foreign attaches present. Polish feelings of inferiority were based on the industrial capabilities of the two nations as well as on the superior quality of the German army compared to the Polish. The Polish military was aware of military developments in Germany, and it appeared to Du Moulin that the experience of disarming German soldiers in Warsaw after the war had been all but removed from Polish memory. The Poles' consciousness of their own inferiority made it difficult for them to plan for a great offensive against Gemany during any future war in which French aid was not certain. The other attaches to whom Du Moulin spoke agreed that there was little chance of a great Polish offensive against Germany. The chances of success were just too small as long as Poland was not sure that the _Reichswehr_'s main strength would be tied up elsewhere.

Still, according to the attache, "It is an entirely different question whether Poland would conduct itself in a purely defensive manner in case of a war with Germany." He believed that to assume a passive stance on the part of the Poles would be a dangerous underestimation of the Polish national character. The Poles had told him repeatedly that, in a future war, the army would need early successes in order to uphold civilian morale. Du Moulin was not entirely convinced of the logic of this argument. The one war which Poland had fought in modern times seemed to prove the opposite. Only after the total collapse of the Polish forces facing the Bolsheviks did the Poles create a force which was capable of defeating the Red Army. Still, it appeared to the military attache that the ruling circles in Poland would stress the necessity of an early success against the Germans. The logical place to look for this type of moral victory, he stated, was East Prussia. While the Poles did not consider an invasion of East Prussia simple, neither did they consider it impossible. A recent wargame, in which a Polish invasion of the province had failed ignominiously, had shown the Poles that small forces would not do for this venture. Du Moulin stressed that the failure would not deter the Poles from marching on Königsberg, but would only force them to assemble a larger force for the operation.

In addition to an invasion of East Prussia, operations to secure Poznan and Polish Pomerania were quite likely. Du

Moulin was unsure, however, if these would be offensive, that is, whether they would include a drive in the direction of Stettin.   At any rate, operations in Poznan and Pomerania would fit in well with a generally defensive strategy.   A drive into German Pomerania would increase the separation of East Prussia from the Reich as well as widen Poland's access to the sea.

The attache ended by summarizing Poland's limited aims in the event of a war with Germany:

> All of these observations lead to the conclusion that, besides the maintenance of the defensive as its central idea, the Polish army may quite possibly conduct small tactical advances against East Prussia and even Pomerania. In the long run, it is expected that Poland's feelings of inferiority against Germany are so strong that the Poles will look for success only where our resistance is weakest.

The plans for war with the Soviet Union, he maintained, were much more ambitious.   He was astounded to find that the danger of a renewed war with the Red Army was "bagatellisiert." Du Moulin found the opinion widespread that the Soviet Union was not in a position to make war on Poland. If war should come, Du Moulin found no pessimism on the part of the Poles, who considered their soldiers far superior to the Bolsheviks.   He was unable to establish whether these feelings of superiority derived from the great Polish victories of 1920 or from the achievements of the Polish Legion on the western front.   At any rate, he stated, Polish confidence against the Red Army would be evident in Polish operational plans, which would probably involve a great offensive north of the Pripet Marshes.[63]

The second document sent to the German Foreign Office during the winter of 1929-30 was a report from Rauscher on "The Spirit and Military Ability of the Officers and Personnel of the Polish Army." After years of paying close attention to the material aspects of the Polish army, Rauscher chose to examine its human side.   Here he found the army's greatest strength to be its soldiers, and its greatest weakness its officers. "The picture will show," he wrote, "that ten years of work has created a noteworthy army, in the modern sense of the word." Still, the Polish leadership had to overcome grave difficulties "in order to make this army a battleworthy instrument."

He began his report with an analysis of the troops.   He found that they possessed many good soldierly qualities, but criticized the short, two-year term of service as insufficient time to develop these qualities.   Moreover, the experimentation by the army with new technical means of warfare meant that the amount which the soldier had to learn during his short training period had increased.   Rauscher also noted the differing conceptions of drill and discipline in the German and Polish armies, which he felt was another disadvantage for the Poles.   Finally, he discussed the problem of the ethnic minorities within the Polish army, and warned Berlin not to place too much emphasis on the possibility of the army's dissolution:

The yearly contingent of recruits in Poland is made up, as you well know, from racially different elements. The military inclination of those recruits from purely Polish areas is by nature good. All of the military attaches present confirm this observation, as it is identical with the experiences of the armies of the partitioning powers. Just as in the former German army, the Polish soldiers in the Habsburg and Russian armies were generally capable, if we understand this word to include perseverance, courage, contentedness, and obedience.

The task of educating the Polish recruit into a capable modern soldier within the short term of service causes difficulties. In the old German and Austrian armies, the observation was made that the Polish soldier comprehended things more slowly than his German comrades-in-arms. This meant that more drill and energy had to be used in the Pole's training than in that of the German soldier. As the best officers in the world, operating with a long term of service, had difficulty in training these men, Poland naturally has even more problems now.

It is known that the infantry only serves 16-18 months, and is then granted leave. During this short training period, the Poles now attempt to school their slow-learning troops in many more technical things than was formerly the case. The only possible way to achieve this is at the cost of basic training. To reconcile these competing interests, the Poles have begun to emphasize youth training, so that recruits entering the army will already understand the basic principles of military affairs.

It is obvious that to solve these problems, the Poles could institute a strict drill system, in order to quickly gain control of the men. This however has not been the case. Poland has not adopted the method, tested in the German army, of parade march drill, but has adopted instead the French system, which stresses a looser hand with the men. This system would perhaps work with an independently thinking, culturally developed people, but as the educator of Polish peasants it causes extraordinary difficulties.

It is difficult to say how far national sentiment within the minorities has affected the military ability of the army. This, however, is a matter of great concern to the Polish leaders. The high command attempts to give elements friendly to the state the upper hand by the careful mixing of minority contingents with all-Polish units. As a result, there are many companies in which 30-40 men are members of one of the minorities. One should not place too many hopes in this situation, for it would be wrong to think that any member of a Slavic minority will take matters into his own hands as long as he is stationed far from home and in totally unfamiliar surroundings. It should also be mentioned that the technical arms, including the artillery, are manned strictly by Poles.

Rauscher then turned to the officer corps. Here, his verdict was that Poland would never possess a first-class officer corps, even if some of the officers were personally brave. The class of officers was not homogeneous, as it was in the German army. Instead, men who had trained in many different systems were thrown together. In addition, Rauscher pointed out that the poor social and economic position of the officers prevented them from developing a powerful esprit de corps. Finally, he criticized the technical knowledge of the officers, declaring that they had too much interest in political affairs at the expense of the study of war.

Rauscher reserved his harshest judgment, however, for the Polish High Command. He declared that the deficiencies of the higher leadership were "even more problematic" for the army. He was intensely critical of Pilsudski's performance as supreme commander, particularly for the marshal's failure to implement his often sound ideas. To make matters worse, Pilsudski's entourage consisted largely of sycophants. There were several able officers, notably General Rydz-Smigly, but Rauscher was sure that they would not have a free hand in an emergency:

> The personality of Marshal Pilsudski is well known. His military capabilities are viewed with skepticism not only by his political opponents, but also by the foreign officers, if the military problem to be solved is beyond the abilities of a divisional commander. It can not be denied that he has many good ideas, but he is not the man to carry them out. Besides, the condition of his health is so variable that there are times when he is totally apathetic and uninterested. When his health is good, he is such a passionate soldier that he reserves to himself the smallest decisions. His entourage would not dare to pass over an order of the day given out by the "old man." Almost all of these men, even the most famous generals, seem to live in fear of Pilsudski.

Rauscher finished with an indictment of Poland's military leaders, which also gave an interesting impression of how the Polish army would have fared in a war against the Reichswehr:

> From the maneuvers and the other rare occasions which allowed me to make an impression, the inaccuracy of the orders was always a matter of sharp criticism from the foreign attaches. In fact, the capability of quick and precise organization does not belong among the Polish virtues. Whoever has stood watching for hours as units march past in parade, and continually bump into each other because of imprecise orders, has an idea of how this army would function in wartime, when even larger units have to make even more complicated maneuvers.[64]

The Polish army during the interwar period was unable to solve its most pressing problems. The artillery did not possess the modern weapons it required, and was also not trained in the techniques of modern warfare. Cooperation with the infantry was especially poor. The army made little

progress toward mechanization. Although the Poles possessed a
fair number of tanks, they were mostly obsolete French Renault
models.   In   addition,   as the maneuvers showed,   the   Polish
leadership   failed   to formulate any doctrine for the   use   of
mechanized forces.   Although Poland made some progress   after
1926 in creating a domestic arms industry, the state was still
dependent for most of its arms on foreign countries,   particularly France. Yet the economic problems which beset the world
also   prevented   Poland   from purchasing the modern   arms   its
forces   required.   Throughout this period,   items verging   on
obsolescence,   such   as   the old   French   75mm   gun,   remained
standard issue in the Polish army.
     Aside   from   purely   material problems,   the   Polish   army
suffered   from poor organization.   The problem was,   in part,
the legacy of the partitions,   since the Polish army contained
officers, men, and equipment from the three imperial armies as
well   as from the Polish Legion.   Within certain   units,   one
could find different uniforms,   weaponry, and ammunition.   The
Polish army,   in short,   remained a quartermaster's nightmare.
During   a war,   of course,   the non-standardization of   Polish
equipment   would have led to severe   logistical   difficulties.
Other   organizational problems stemmed from doctrinal disputes
within the army.   The Poles were unable to decide how to   use
their   cavalry most effectively.   Basically,   the problem was
one of concentration versus dispersion.   Hence,   after   1926,
there   were   two disruptive cavalry reorganizations   in   quick
succession.   The   first   reorganization   created   cavalry
divisions;   the second reversed the process and recreated brigades.   Likewise,   the Poles could not decide whether armored
units   should   be   part   of   the   cavalry   formations,   largely
because the army had no doctrine for the use of armored units.
     The   failures of the Polish army during this period   were
largely   the   fault of Jozef Pilsudski.   He seized   power   at
least   partially   in   order to rescue   the   army   from   chaos.
Although he undoubtedly did some good in modernizing the army,
particularly   in   recognizing   the need for a   domestic   arms
industry,   he made other costly mistakes.   The purge of former
Austrian   officers   and their replacement by Pilsudski's   loyal
supporters   removed   many   able,   experienced   officers   from
service.   Observers   at   the   time remarked that   loyalty   to
Pilsudski,   not   military   talent,   had   become   the   primary
criterion for advancement in the Polish army.   Pilsudski also
failed   to improve in any significant fashion the training   of
his   officers and men.   The reports on Polish army   maneuvers
indicate   that,   despite   the   praiseworthy   qualities   of
individual   soldiers,   the   Polish   army was in a   very   sorry
condition.   Again,   these   problems were   organizational   and
doctrinal as well as material: artillery failed to   support
the   infantry;   tanks rested far behind the line or   blundered
into   swamps;   air power failed to intervene at all in   ground
battles.   As   supreme   commander and head of state,   Pilsudski
had no excuse for failing to solve any of these problems.   The
implications   of his failure would become truly apparent   only
at the hands of the Wehrmacht in 1939.   Yet even in comparison
to   the   Reichswehr of 1930,   the Polish army   was   hopelessly
inferior, a fact of which the Germans were well aware.

NOTES

1.   Ministry of the Interior to the Foreign Office, 22
April 1921, Berlin, Akten des auswärtigen Amtes (Records of
the German Foreign Ministry),   hereafter AA, reel 3758, serial
K190,   frames   K035   244-247.   In   shorthand   notation,
AA/3758/K190/K035 244-247.
2.   The interrogation of this anonymous deserter is contained in AA/3758/K190/K035 296-298.
3.   Truppenamt to Foreign Office, 15 September 1921,
Berlin, AA/3758/K190/K035 251. This document was also sent to
the Prussian Ministry of the Interior.
4.   Unsigned memorandum, 17 September 1921, Berlin,
AA/3758/K190/K035 252-253.
5.   Reichswehr Ministry to Foreign Office, 4 October
1921, Berlin, AA/3758/K190/K035 289-290.
6.   Königsberg Police Director to Foreign Office, 2 June
1923, Königsberg, AA/3758/K190/K035 430.
7.   Stobbe to Herbert Dirksen, Foreign Office, 26 June
1922, Posen, AA/ 3758/K190/K035 368-374.
8.   Commissioner for the Maintenance of Public Order to
Foreign Office, 10 December 1924, Berlin, AA/3758/K190/K035
614.
9.   Mayer to Foreign Office, 9 January 1925, Paris,
AA/3758/K190/K035 619.
10.   Rauscher to Foreign Office, 9 January 1925, Warsaw,
AA/3758/K190/K035 620.
11.   For the issue of the "eastern Locarno" treaty, see
Christian Höltje, Die Weimarer Republik und das Ostlocarno
Problem, 1919-1934 (Würzburg: Holzner-Verlag, 1958). For the
treatment of the Polish delegation at Locarno, see Harald von
Riekhoff,   German-Polish Relations,   1918-1933 (Baltimore:
Johns Hopkins Press, 1971), pp. 121-131.
12.   Commissioner for the Maintenance of Public Order to
Foreign Minister Joseph Wirth, 5 April 1922, Berlin,
AA/3758/K190/K035 344-345.
13.   Prussian Minister of the Interior to Foreign Office,
23 February 1925, Berlin, AA/3758/K190/K035 664.
14.   Prussian Minister of the Interior to Foreign Office,
6 March 1925, Berlin, AA/3758/K190/K035 665-666.
15.   Prussian Minister of the Interior to Foreign Office,
4 February 1925, Berlin, AA/3758/K190/K035 648-653.
16.   Stobbe to Foreign Office, 7 February 1924, Posen,
AA/3758/K190/K035 562-564.
17.   Dirksen to Foreign Office, 19 April 1924, Danzig,
AA/3758/K190/K035 578.
18.   Dirksen to Foreign Office, 9 February 1925, Danzig,
AA/3759/K190/K035 655-658.
19.   See, for instance, the telegram from Minister
Rauscher to Foreign Office, 1 April 1925, Warsaw,
AA/3758/K190/K035 672. See also K035 675.
20.   Rauscher to Foreign Office, 22 August 1925, Warsaw,
AA/3759/K190/K035 800-803. For the French reaction to these
maneuvers, see also K035 804.
21.   German Commissioner to the Arbitration Court in
Upper Silesia to Foreign Office, 22 September 1925, Breslau,
AA/3759/K190/K035 833-834.
22.   Rauscher to Foreign Office, 24 December 1925,
Berlin, AA/3759/K190/K035 842.

23.   Mayer to Foreign Office, 5 June 1926, Paris,
AA/3759/K190/K035 846.
24.   Rauscher to Foreign Office, 11 January 1926, Warsaw,
AA/3759/K190/K035 848.
25.   German Ambassador to Foreign Office, 29 January
1926, Washington, AA/3759/K190/K035 852.
26.   Memorandum signed by Erich Zechlin, Chief of Polish
Section (IV Po) in the Eastern Department of the Foreign
Office, 16 March 1926, Berlin, AA/ 3759/K190/K035 861.
27.   See the Monthly Reports on the Polish Army from the
Lithuanian Intelligence Service in AA/3758-3760/K190/K035 302-
314, 316-320, 321-328, 329-334, 335-342, 347-355, 381-388,
402-407, 418-420, 445-450.
28.   Richard Watt, Bitter Glory: Poland and Its Fate,
1918-1939 (New York: Simon & Schuster, 1979), p. 220.
29.   Erich Wallroth, Chief of the Eastern Department (IV)
of the German Foreign Office, to Rauscher, Berlin, 12 March
1925, AA/3758/K190/K035 661-663.
30.   Rauscher to Foreign Office, 21 May 1926, Warsaw,
AA/3759/K190/K035 876-879.
31.   Rauscher to Foreign Office, 6 August 1926, Warsaw,
AA/3759/K190/K035 934-935.
32.   Rauscher to Foreign Office, 10 May 1926, Warsaw,
AA/3759/K190/K036 302.
33.   Rauscher to Foreign Office, 8 August 1928, Warsaw,
AA/3759/K190/K036 261-262.
34.   Rauscher to Foreign Office, 10 May 1929, Warsaw,
AA/3759/K190/K037 300-307.
35.   Unsigned, German Legation to Foreign Office, 16
November 1927, Warsaw, AA/3759/K190/K036 450-451.
36.   Rauscher to Foreign Office, 10 November 1928,
Warsaw, AA/3759/K190/K036 216-217.
37.   Rauscher to Foreign Office, 22 March 1930, Warsaw,
AA/3760/K190/K036 450-451.
38.   Rauscher to Foreign Office, 7 March 1929, Warsaw,
AA/3759/K190/K036 271-272.
39.   Rintelen to Foreign Office, 15 August 1929, Warsaw,
AA/3759/K190/K036 348.
40.   Rintelen to Foreign Office, 1 September 1931,
Warsaw, AA/3760/K190/K036 525.
41.   Moltke to Foreign Office, 25 November 1931, Warsaw,
AA/3760/K190/K036 248-250. K036 248-250.
42.   Unsigned, German Legation to Foreign Office, 27
October 1932, Warsaw, AA/3760/K190/K037 068-069.
43.   Rintelen to Foreign Office, 17 February 1932,
Warsaw, AA/3760/K190/K036 839-840.
44.   German Legation to Foreign Office, 6 April 1932,
Warsaw, AA/3759/K190/K036 038-043.
45.   Dirksen to Foreign Office, 28 July 1932, Warsaw,
AA/3760/K190/K036 883-884.
46.   Rintelen to Foreign Office, 28 July 1932, Warsaw,
AA/3760/K190/K037 043.
47.   Rauscher to Foreign Office, 3 March 1927, Warsaw,
AA/3759/K190/K037 007.
48.   Rauscher to Foreign Office, 26 September 1930,
Warsaw, AA/3760/K190/K036 547-548.
49.   Rintelen to Foreign Office, 2 April 1931, Warsaw,
AA/3760/K190/K036 656-669.
50.   Dirksen to Foreign Office, 18 November 1931, Warsaw,
AA/3760/K190/K036 762-763.

51.   Rauscher to Foreign Office, 23 July 1926, Warsaw, AA/3759/K190/K035 911-915.
52.   Rauscher to Foreign Office, 14 March 1929, Warsaw, AA/3759/K190/K036 274-275; Rintelen to Foreign Office, 23 May 1929, Warsaw, AA/3759/K190/K036 313-314.
53.   Rauscher to Foreign Office, 3 July 1930, Warsaw, AA/3760/K190/K036 687-690.
54.   Rauscher to Foreign Office, 31 October 1928, Warsaw, AA/3759/K190/K036 200-203.
55.   Rauscher to Foreign Office, 2 November 1928, Warsaw, AA/3759/K190/K036 205-210.
56.   Rintelen to Foreign Office, 15 August 1929, Warsaw, AA/3759/K190/K036 351-352.
57.   Du Moulin to Foreign Office, 5 October 1929, Warsaw, AA/3759/K190/K036 361-367.
58.   Rauscher to Foreign Office, 7 October 1930, Warsaw, AA/3760/K190/K036 551-557.
59.   Unsigned, German Legation to Foreign Office, 6 March 1931, Warsaw, AA/3760/K190/K036 624-631.
60.   Unsigned, German Legation to Foreign Office, 24 November 1928, Warsaw, AA/ 3759/K190/K036 221-222.
61.   German Consul to Foreign Office, 17 June 1931, Thorn, AA/3760/K190/K036 684.   See also Dirksen to Foreign Office, 26 June 1931, Warsaw, AA/3760/K190/K036 700-701.
62.   Moltke to Foreign Office, 10 July 1931, Warsaw, AA/3760/K190/K036 711-712
63.   Du Moulin to Forster, 27 December 1929, Warsaw, AA/3760/K190/K036 418-423.
64.   Rauscher to Foreign Office, 8 January 1930, Warsaw, AA/3760/K190/K036 425-434.

4
The Era of Planning:
The German Army and Navy during the Groener Era, 1927-1933

The period from 1926 to 1933 was an era in which German naval and land forces planned seriously for a war with Poland. The previous period, dominated by Hans von Seeckt and his very agreeable civilian defense minister Otto Gessler, was a time in which the task of rebuilding the army absorbed all of the attention of the High Command. As we have seen, Seeckt's leadership stressed tactical developments. While the troops received the training for a possible war against Poland, notably in the maneuvers of the 1st Infantry Division in 1925, it was clear that the development of strategic and operational plans for such a conflict received little attention. After 1926, new leadership came to the fore. Both Seeckt and Gessler had to resign as a result of political scandals.[1] With the fall of these two officials, responsibility for German military planning fell into the hands of a new generation of German officers. The key figures were General Wilhelm Groener, defense minister from 1928 to 1932, and General Kurt von Schleicher, one of Groener's closest personal friends and head of the political bureau (Ministeramt) of the Defense Ministry. These new men possessed personalities far different than Seeckt's, less ingenious, to be sure, but also less tied to the past, and therefore less inclined to take a romantic view of military affairs. A "new realism" was evident among Germany's military leaders, a fact quite noticeable to all the foreign military attaches in Germany. The development of more detailed contingency plans for war followed from the more sensible--as they viewed it--outlook of the new leaders. This new course included cooperation with the civilian government and industry to prepare the armed forces for war; regular and numerous maneuvers, including the largest held during the Weimar era; staff wargames, which investigated in detail the military and political possibilities of a German-Polish war; redeployment of the German eastern forces into more militarily defensible garrisons in contrast to the dispersion of the Seeckt period; the assignment of a military attache to Poland; a much greater emphasis on naval strategy and planning; and perhaps most importantly, the development of plans to expand the army dramatically in case of war. At the same time, the new leaders preserved and expanded much of the Seeckt legacy: the reliance on fortifications and irregular border defense units to aid and supplement the regular forces;

the stress upon tactical mobility as the army's most important
attribute; and the nurturing of the offensive spirit within
the army. In fact, it was Seeckt's success in forming a high-
quality force which permitted his successors the luxury of
concentrating on war planning.[2]
     Schleicher's first contribution to the question   of
national defense in general and the Polish question in particular came in 1927, while he was still only a colonel.   In
October of that year, at the request of Defense Minister
Gessler, Schleicher prepared an essay for Foreign Minister
Gustav Stresemann.   The subject of the essay was the Landesschutz, a term meaning national defense in its broadest context, which had first come into usage among German officers in
the Seeckt era.   In Schleicher's words, "National defense
includes the defense of the Reich's borders as well as the
protection of the lives and property of the population from
enemy attacks or acts of violence on land, sea, or air."
Schleicher separated national defense from purely operational
military measures, which sought victory over the enemy forces
only on the field of battle.   In his concept of national
defense, the whole nation--government, industry, and the
civilian population--had to devote itself to the war effort.
He advised that Germany prepare for war during peacetime so
that the state could overcome the great disadvantages which it
would carry into any war. In the end, his goal was political.
In case of an enemy attack, Germany must be strong enough to
bring the issue before the League of Nations: "The goal of
our preparations is to be ready, in case of a hostile attack
on land, sea, or air, to prevent a fait accompli which could
prejudice a decision of the League of Nations or another
international court of arbitration." To that end, he listed
his recommendations for both the military and the civilian
leadership: preparation of antiaircraft defenses (including
protection of the civilian population against poison gas);
preparations for the evacuation of the border regions in case
of war; recruitment of a border defense force to protect the
borders against enemy assault; preparations for the transfor-
mation of the peacetime army into a field army under the
protection of the border defense forces; preparation by the
civilian officials of supply sources for personnel, materiel,
and reinforcements in cooperation with the military; and the
protection of stores of weapons, munitions, and army equipment. Given the wide scope of his recommendations, Schleicher
concluded that the "preparations could be undertaken only with
the participation and active help of the authorities of the
state, and not by the armed forces alone."
     Of Schleicher's suggestions for military preparations,
his recommendation for the defense of the borders by an
irregular defense force was of the greatest significance to
German-Polish military relations.   We have seen already how
defense forces came into existence outside of army control in
East Prussia in 1920 and Upper Silesia in 1921.   Schleicher
wanted to expand, reorganize, and standardize these forces so
that they would become a supplement to the army rather than a
potential rival.   By 1927, there already existed a firm
foundation of military preparations in almost every province
in Germany.[3]   It is evident that the preparations in the
eastern territories had already proceeded to a point where any
Polish attack would have met with significant opposition from
extramilitary forces.   The two most vulnerable   areas,

Pomerania and East Prussia, were at the highest level of readiness, while the Berlin region was still in need of a border defense force. In keeping with his concept of a comprehensive national defense, Schleicher included sports schools and groups in the military preparations as well as private stores of weapons. In the view of the colonel, these preparations were necessary, since "border defense only makes sense if it be prepared for action." He continued:

> Border defense must be organized in peacetime, its leaders must be assigned to their units, its men must be trained in the use of their weapons. It is the same for the peacetime army, which depends upon replacement stocks to fight a war. Since the war, Germany's trained reserves have shrunk from year to year. Therefore, we depend only on former members of the armed forces for reserves and replacements. In this situation, military preparation and training amongst the civilian population is an urgent necessity.[4]

Schleicher recommended above all the cooperation of the army and the civilian government to achieve his program. Only with the help of civilian officials, at both the federal and provincial level, could the Reichswehr fulfill the tasks allotted to it in the Versailles treaty. In Schleicher's view, these tasks included the protection of the borders and the prevention of a Polish fait accompli; there must be no "German Wilno."

Commenting on Schleicher's essay, Colonel Werner von Fritsch, chief of the Truppenamt's Army Section, stated that the question of border defense was applicable only to the east:

> There is no question of military preparations in the west. There we have to rely upon the security guarantee of the Locarno Treaty. The actions are in essence applicable only in the east. We should create a security that can, as far as possible, prevent the occurrence of a fait accompli on the eastern border, and win time in case of a war.[5]

Of course, Fritsch recognized that any new border defenses, whether in the west or the east, were violations of the Versailles treaty, so they would have to proceed in secrecy. His goal was to erect a border defense for all of the eastern provinces similar to that which already existed in East Prussia.

The arguments of the army officers failed to convince the Foreign Office of the desirability of defensive preparations in the east. In a memorandum to the defense minister, Gerhard Köpke of the Foreign Office wrote that the army's plans for active preparations had to be cut back, since Germany should do nothing in its present powerless condition to arouse the suspicions of the Allies. At the same time, Köpke recognized the need for some defensive measures in the east:

> We share the worries of the Defense Ministry regarding the sudden creation of a fait accompli on the eastern border, and we cannot and do not want to

accept the responsibility for a policy in which the
government twiddles its thumbs in the face of such a
danger.   The fact that we cannot be active without
breaking the Versailles Treaty does not disturb the
Foreign Office.   We must, however, limit the necessary preparations for national defense so that
Germany's vital interests are not endangered. These
preparations should not risk everything.[6]

The Foreign Office's position on national defense was not
satisfactory to the army.   In late 1927, the Defense Ministry
invited officials of the Foreign Ministry to an operational
wargame.   The goal of the game was to investigate a "politically conceivable conflict."[7]   More importantly, army
officials intended to demonstrate that defensive preparations,
particularly the establishment of border defense formations,
were necessary.   On 20 December, Colonel Werner von Blomberg
of the Truppenamt met with officials of the Foreign Office to
explain to them the political and military situation for the
game.   In the course of year X, an arbitrary year, but one
with the military force levels of 1927, relations between
Germany and Poland became so tense that a strong anti-German
movement came into existence in Poland, with the toleration
and support of the Polish government.   Germany raised
objections in Warsaw to this anti-German propaganda, and when
it obtained no satisfaction, turned its complaints to the
League of Nations. Toward the end of the month, the situation
in Poland reached a crisis.   At the beginning of October, it
was clear that the Polish government was thinking about the
use of force against Germany.   The government's intention was
to seize East Prussia without a declaration of war or mobilization.   To support this action, a general attack against
Germany was planned.   Poland concentrated its forces, which
had been expanded by postponing scheduled discharges, in three
groups: one on the East Prussian border, the second in the
Corridor, and the third southwest of Poznan, with orders to
attack into Silesia between Breslau and Glogau.   The advance
guard was made up of irregulars. The German government had to
decide, in light of its weak forces, whether to sacrifice East
Prussia and retreat behind the Oder or to defend East Prussia
and the entire eastern border.   It decided to fight for East
Prussia.   It should be mentioned that the war situation
omitted any German consideration of France or Polish consideration of Russia.   Instead, the scenario assumed that
German relations with France were good and that Russia's
domestic political struggles were so serious that it represented no threat to Poland.   Thus the game postulated a war
with Poland alone, a situation which Dirk Forster of the
Foreign Office labeled "extraordinarily favorable."[8]
The game took place in the hall of the Defense Ministry
on Königin Augustastrasse.   The purpose of the game was to
persuade the government to proceed with defensive preparations
in the east.   In this case, the army attempted to secure
governmental agreement by scaring civilian officials with an
apocalyptic version of a war in the east.   The Blue force
represented Germany, the Red, Poland. At the beginning of the
game, both sides received the following chronology of the
political events preceeding the outbreak of the war between
the two states.   In the summer of 1927, negotiations between
German and Poland over an unnamed issue foundered.   The result

was anti-German propaganda in Poland. In September, with tensions running high, the German government presented its case before the League, and advised that body of the possibility of an eastern conflict. When it received no answer, the government again appealed to the League for quick action. On 20 September, the League decided to form a commission to study the problem. This commission began its work in October. But on the night of 30 September, Polish insurgents invaded East Prussia. Allenstein was bombarded from the air.

In response, the German government decided on several measures. First, it imposed a military state of emergency upon the entire Reich. Second, it gave permission to East Prussian authorities to form a volunteer border defense force in the eastern areas. The use of these troops was not to occur immediately, but required the approval of the government. Third, it ordered the German minister in Warsaw to demand an explanation from the Polish government about the attack against East Prussia. Fourth, it brought a formal protest to the League about the East Prussian border violations. The government sought to resolve the conflict peacefully and only to take military measures if steps three and four failed.

On 1 October, the order went out to form a border defense in East Prussia. At the same time, the minister in Warsaw wired that his attempt had failed. The Polish government refused to accept responsibility for a popular movement of the Polish people. It claimed that it was no longer able to influence popular opinion. The consequences were attributable to the intransigent German attitude during the negotiations. Late that evening, the chief of the Army Command announced that regular Polish cavalry were assembling on the East Prussian frontier and that he expected that it would be used against East Prussia. At this point, the German government decided to appoint a Chef der Wehrmacht, responsible for the defense of the state. It ordered the deployment of all available forces--including the marines--for the defense of East Prussia and the preparation of an accelerated mobilization for the army and the navy. Finally, it decreed the formation of more divisions in the interior of the Reich.

In the early morning of 2 October, Red sea forces tried to block the harbor of Pillau. At the same time, Red launched heavy bombing attacks against Pillau. Red had thereby opened active hostilities. The assembly of all available forces was ordered in East Prussia. In the eastern areas of the Reich, the formation of a military border defense force began. In the afternoon, the German government received a note from the president of the League informing it that he was seeking to avoid hostilities and a resolution of this conflict by force. He had summoned the League council to an immediate meeting. By 1700 hours that evening, the chief of the Army Command received orders from the Chef der Wehrmacht to "continue the measures you have already introduced. Enemy forces which have crossed the border are to be thrown back. It is important to establish whether and where active enemy troops are participating. Our own forces are not to cross the border." But on 3-4 October, regular Polish troops invaded East Prussia. As a result, on the evening of 5 October, in the absence of any League action, the German government announced that "since regular Polish troops have crossed the German border, the

German leadership is no longer concerned with limiting the conduct of the fight to German territory."[9]

As the game proceeded, it was evident that the army was trying to prove its point with regard to Germany's alleged helplessness in the east. By the end of October 1927, all of East Prussia with the exception of Königsberg had come into the possession of the Polish occupation forces. After battles with the German border forces and a hefty counterattack on the Oder by the German army, the Polish army had occupied all of Silesia and Pomerania. Both belligerents had respected Danzig's neutrality. At this time, Germany requested action by the League. Finally, the League forced Poland to cease hostilities. A temporary demarcation line was established. In East Prussia, the line ran southwest along the axis Brandenburg-Uderwangen-Tapiau-River Deime. The bridges over the Deime were considered destroyed. In the Reich proper, the line ran along the Oder between the Baltic Sea and the bend in the river south of Fürstenburg, then south along the Görlitzer Neisse. The Oder bridges along the demarcation line were destroyed. The bridges over the Görlitzer Neisse were undamaged. This description of a Polish occupation of Germany up to the Oder-Neisse line, at the time a "worst-case" scenario, would turn out to be rather prophetic after 1945.

The game continued after the cease-fire. In the winter of 1927-28, the Russian government had succeeded in strengthening the anti-Polish feeling in the country to the point where a war with Poland was possible. After weeks of war preparations, the Russians invaded Poland at the beginning of April 1928. The Romanians immediately entered the war on the side of Poland. On 8 April, German-Polish negotiations in Geneva were broken off. The sharp English-French conflict, which had come to light during the negotiations, had become milder because of the Russian attack. In the French press, an active agitation in Poland's favor was noticeable. The other states bordering on Germany, except for Belgium, had all declared neutrality. On 9 April, it became known in Germany that the Russians had won a great victory over the Polish First Army at Baranowiczi. The next day, the Russians demanded that Germany enter the war immediately. If Germany refused, the Russians stated that they alone would decide Poland's fate.[10]

At this point, the chief of the armed forces informed the government that the army's buildup had progressed far enough to permit an attack upon Poland. In order to provide a good chance of success, however, all forces had to be free to deal only with Poland. It became the task of the political leadership to prevent other states, especially France and Britain, from attacking Germany. Wooing Britain was especially important since Germany's war economy had to rely on seaborne imports. In a memorandum to the Foreign Office, the defense minister inquired "under which conditions was it possible for Germany to participate in a war against Poland, without France and England becoming involved." The Foreign Office was unequivocal in stating that it considered the chances slim of treating the Polish question in isolation: "We advise the Defense Minister that a situation whereby Germany and Russia conduct a war against Poland, without France and England becoming involved, is politically unthinkable."[11] The Foreign Office was skeptical about other aspects of the army's wargame. In particular, it claimed that a Russian attack on

Poland was unlikely. At the same time, Russian aid in the form of propaganda and troop movements on Poland's eastern frontier was likely, which would have the positive effect of tying up a large part of Poland's forces. The Foreign Office also claimed that the army had overrated Poland's war-making capability:

> We can reckon with a weakening of Poland's offensive strength through domestic political events. The unwillingness of the national minorities to flock to the colors will slow the Polish mobilization. Reliable troops will be needed just to carry out mobilization. Also, acts of terror and sabotage (destruction of bridges, plots against military trains or military leaders) are to be expected. Finally, even if it does not occur in the first days after mobilization, we can reckon with the likelihood of a Ukrainian uprising, which can command 40,000-60,000 irregulars in eastern Galicia. This will probably tie up a considerable portion of Poland's mobile forces.[12]

In sum, the Foreign Office felt that the most effective action which Germany could take was an appeal to the League of Nations. If Germany appealed for the cessation of hostilities, and if Poland refused, then the League might be persuaded to begin economic sanctions against Poland. While this would probably not force Poland to cease operations against Germany, it would, in the eyes of the Foreign Office, be a German political victory over Poland.

The wargame of 1928 was important for three reasons. First, it indicated that the army High Command had abandoned the aloof stance toward political questions it had adopted prior to 1926. The active participation of civilian officials at an army exercise would have been unthinkable while Seeckt was commander. At the same time, the army invited officials from the Foreign Office to take part in the military exercises planned for every regiment of the army during the summer.[13] Under Seeckt, maneuvers had taken place in the presence of only one civilian official, Defense Minister Gessler. Second, although the civilian participants had some doubts about the wargame's realism, the government did allow defensive preparations along the eastern border. Third, it was clear that Germany's new military leadership was turning its gaze to the future, when Germany would once more be a great power and the Versailles restrictions would no longer control the Reichswehr. As demonstrated in the wargame situation, the army leadership was sufficiently realistic to acknowledge Germany's powerlessness in the current situation. At the same time, however, it was recognized that in the future, a rearmed Germany would have the opportunity to reverse the territorial settlement. In the wargame situation, Germany's opportunity came as the result of cooperation with the Soviet Union against Poland. We have ample testimony that most German officers considered the lands lost to Poland to be a legitimate cause for war.[14] During the period after 1928, the leadership of the army began to plan for such a war. This is not to say that Germany intended to attack Poland; most of the wargames and maneuvers of the period postulated a Polish attack and placed German forces on the defensive. These exercises did contain the seed for an eventual campaign of liberation in the east. In this sense, it may be said that the leadership of the Reichswehr after 1926 was more interested in strategic questions than Seeckt had been.[15] Although the army still practiced tactics during its maneuvers, and experiments with air power and mechanization continued, the eyes of the army leadership were on the larger questions of national defense, geopolitics, and foreign policy.

The ability of the army to concentrate on strategy while maintaining its tactical expertise was a credit to General Wilhelm Groener, defense minister from 1928 to 1932. Groener's career prior to his appointment as Defense Minister had indicated that he was not the stereotypical narrow-minded general. In particular, his role in the abdication of the Kaiser and the signing of the Versailles treaty demonstrated that he had a strong interest in politics, without the romantic outlook of many former imperial officers. At the same time, his credentials as a military man were impeccable. Groener had been head of the railway section of the General Staff during the first years of the war, and in that capacity was responsible for the complex task of deploying German forces in the west. In 1917, he received a field assignment as commander of the 33rd Infantry Division in France. In 1918, he traveled east to assume to the post of chief of staff to the Kiev Army Group. In November of that year, he succeeded General Erich Ludendorff as first quartermaster general. It was in that capacity that he advised the Kaiser to abdicate, a role which won him the hostility of a significant body of his fellow officers. In addition, as we have seen, it was he who advised the government to sign the Versailles treaty in the summer of 1919. He had previously held one post in the Weimar Republic, minister of communications, which enabled him to put to civilian use his considerable expertise with regard to railroads. After his resignation from this post in 1923, he had turned to his first love, writing military history. His major works, Feldherr wider Willen, about the younger Helmuth von Moltke, and Das Testament des Grafen Schlieffens, were both concerned with the relationship between the supreme command and the army in the field. He was a great admirer of Schlieffen, but his portrayal of Moltke's unfortunate role in the early days of the First World War was brutal.[16] He was also an essayist of some note, and he wrote widely about the effects of the new technology upon warfare.

The broader view which Groener brought to military affairs was evident as early as April 1928, when he ordered the dispatch of an unofficial military attache to Poland. Before 1928, German military intelligence relied upon officials of the legation in Warsaw as well as upon the intelligence services of the Baltic states. Groener was unsatisfied with the intelligence he had about the Polish military and thought that the transfer of an officer to Warsaw would result in more reliable and timely information. Erich Zechlin described Groener's opinions on the subject:

> The dispatch of a Polish military attache to Berlin has raised the question of whether a German attache ought to be sent to Warsaw. He felt that an attache had no worth outside of Warsaw. Poland was the single land, he declared, that interested us

militarily. Foreign Minister Stresemann was also
not unsympathetic to the notion. Groener saw no
problems in sending an attache to Warsaw. He would
even be satisfied if an inactive officer with no
connection to the Reichswehr were attached to the
legation as counsel or secretary. That would
satisfy him fully, and would be of great worth to
the Defense Ministry, since the intelligence supplied by the agents was not sufficient.[17]

By May 1928, Groener had decided on Richard Du Moulin as the
military attache to Warsaw. Groener felt that to send a
regular officer to Poland might appear provocative to the
Allies, so Du Moulin was an ideal choice. He was a former
officer with a broad knowledge of military affairs. In order
to prepare Du Moulin for his task, Groener assigned him to the
Defense Ministry for three months; in addition, the future
attache participated in the army exercises at Döberitz and the
maneuvers of the 1st Infantry Division in East Prussia.[18] The
attache arrived in Warsaw in September, and he quickly became
Groener's most trusted source of information on Polish
military affairs. As we have already seen, he was especially
helpful in informing Berlin about Polish war plans, a subject
about which the Germans previously had received little
information.

Further evidence of Groener's broader view was the
emphasis he placed upon naval affairs. Seeckt had little
interest in naval questions; he felt that Germany's destiny
lay with its army. Under Groener, naval planning began to
assume a major place in German military circles. Almost
immediately upon the assumption of his office, Groener became
embroiled in the Panzerkreuzer affair, and questions of naval
policy continued to play an important role throughout his
tenure as minister.

The navy which Groener desired to see play a larger role
in German defense was certainly not an awe-inspiring fleet
when he entered office. The Versailles treaty had reduced the
German navy to 15,000 men, including 1,500 officers and war-
rant officers, and the number of ships to six old battleships
in commission and two in reserve, six cruisers in commission
and two in reserve, twelve destroyers, and twelve torpedo
boats. New ships constructed were not to exceed the following
tonnages: armored ships, 10,000 tons; light cruisers, 6,000
tons; destroyers, 800 tons. By 1927, only four battleships,
the Elsass, Hessen, Schleswig-Holstein, and Hannover, were in
commission. Out of the eight cruisers in the fleet after the
war, only five remained in commission by 1927. These were the
Emden, Berlin, Hamburg, Amazone, and Nymphe.[19] The navy had
no submarines or aircraft. Luckily for the Germans, however,
the Polish "fleet" facing them in the Baltic consisted only of
a small assortment of destroyers, old torpedo boats,
submarines, and light patrol craft.

In 1928, the navy decided to build a new type of armored
cruiser, or Panzerkreuzer, which would represent a significant
step forward in German naval technology. The new design was
fast and heavily armed. In order to meet the Versailles
tonnage restrictions, the designer sacrificed armor in favor
of guns. The armored cruiser was thus sufficiently quick to
hunt down anything afloat, even much smaller ships. It was
powerful enough to defeat enemy cruisers in combat, but fast

enough to run away from most enemy battleships.   In addition,
construction of this new ship would mean German domination of
the Baltic Sea, at least against Poland alone.   The only
problem with the armored cruiser was its enormous cost.   The
debate over financing Panzerschiff A, as the first ship in the
series was called, came to dominate the proceedings of the
Reichstag during the spring of 1928.   The parties of the Left
were against funding the ship, declaring it to be a waste of
Germany's scarce resources as well as a threat to peace.   In
fact, Groener pointed out, the construction of the ship would
give new life to Germany's depressed shipbuilding industry.
To Groener, the economic question was not the decisive factor
in building the ship.   Instead, he viewed the new cruiser as a
major component of his new naval strategy toward Poland.
    In November 1928, Groener drafted a long memorandum on
the need to build the Panzerschiff.   He began by asking four
basic questions: What are the likely possibilities of conflict for the armed forces? Which tasks will the navy have to
fulfill?   Will these tasks be easier to carry out after
building the armored cruiser?   Are there any further reasons
for building the ship?   Recently, he observed, the armored
cruiser had become a matter for public debate, and political
maneuvering had only served to confuse the public. It was now
time to rescue the cruiser question from the resulting "fog of
opinions" and discuss the matter clearly.
    Groener then drew a gloomy but realistic picture of
Germany's military situation, referring in definite terms to
the situation in the east:

> We may entertain no thoughts of a great war.   It is
> impossible for Germany to conduct one as long as the
> Versailles Treaty has disarmed us.   Even an isolated
> war with a small state is unthinkable for us today.
> We would soon have to reckon with the entry of the
> Great Powers according to the numerous treaties and
> alliances.   Slogans such as "better a grave than a
> slave," however, must be rejected by any reasonable
> man.   The belief that a great people is free to
> choose its own decline is senseless.   Even the
> freely chosen death of the individual makes sense
> only if it serves the greater good. . . .
>   The German armed forces, however, are insuffi-
> cient to fulfill their mission.   Ought we therefore
> to abolish them?   To the foreign states who yearn
> for German territory, the presence of the German
> army presents a risk, while the weaknesses of the
> army present a temptation.   The states who would
> seek to tear away parts of our territory must reckon
> with the risk of failure.   They have to fight our
> well-trained professional army and run the danger of
> suffering heavy losses or even failing altogether.
> On the other side of the coin, helplessness is a
> temptation to such attacks.   Would not the Pole by
> now have seized the much-coveted territory of East
> Prussia, if he had not any armed force to fear?   It
> might be said, "A German Wilno is no longer pos-
> sible.   The Reich is united and once again powerful;
> no neighbor would dare to disturb us."   Whoever says
> this confuses cause and effect.   If our borders are

really secure, it is because the state has rebuilt
its means of power, the army.

Groener then stated two possible cases in which Germany
might become embroiled in a war: defense against a sudden
coup de main or the protection of German neutrality in a
conflict between foreign powers. The navy would have an
important role to play in each of the scenarios. In the first
case, Groener saw the strong possiblity of a Polish coup
against East Prussia. The crucial battles of this campaign,
of course, would be land battles, which Germany would have to
fight under the following three disadvantages: the enemy
would possess superior force; any attempt by German forces to
break through the Corridor would fail; East Prussia would very
shortly face a crisis of supply, especially in munitions.
In Groener's opinion, only the navy could help to offset
these disadvantages, particularly the problem of supplying
East Prussia. The shipment of replacement personnel and munitions was only possible by sea. Moreover, the navy had other
tasks should the Poles invade East Prussia. Groener summarized the mission of the navy as conducting and protecting
vital sea transport, fighting battles for the coastal areas,
and protecting land forces against hostile sea power. This
would free the land army from worrying about its flank and
rear and free coastal artillery for use in other areas.
The second case was a war between foreign powers which
threatened German neutrality. This would present the navy
with two tasks: protecting German home waters and preventing
the use of German ports by a belligerent power. If Germany
should nevertheless have to enter the war, then the navy would
have the crucial task of transporting raw materials from
Scandinavia.
Having outlined the navy's mission during a future conflict, Groener then turned to the question of whether building
the armored cruiser would allow the navy to accomplish its
mission more efficiently:

The fleet can only accomplish its mission in Case I
if it dominates Poland in the Baltic. This is today
the case against the forces which Poland possesses.
It will not be possible against the Polish fleet
with which we may have to reckon in the future.
Poland is today strengthening its fleet in two
ways. The construction of modern destroyers and
submarines is proceeding in foreign shipyards. The
second method of strengthening its naval forces is
by a treaty with France. In this agreement, France
has promised to support Poland in a war by dispatch-
ing a cruiser squadron to the Baltic. This squadron
can fly the Polish flag, so that France does not
have to enter the war. We are at the moment
inferior to any such fleet.

Groener then discussed the means by which Germany could
redress the naval imbalance which it was likely to find in the
Baltic. He believed that a modern warship had to possess the
quickness to cooperate tactically with cruisers and to do
battle with enemy battleships. At the same time, it needed
the firepower to battle both cruisers and ships of the line.
Finally, a warship should be as secure as possible against

attacks from submarines or aircraft. The present German fleet
of pre-World War I vessels, he argued, had none of these
qualities.   The new type of "pocket battleship," however, was
both quick and powerful enough to destroy any ship of equal
size or smaller.   Again, Groener left no doubt against whom
the new ship was intended:

> It remains to be seen whether Poland, through the
> use of submarines and battleships, can overcome the
> superiority of our new armored cruiser.   The effect
> of submarines is limited.   Their use in the Baltic
> has a practical limit--the shallow depth of the
> water.   The danger for German transports will be
> less if an armored cruiser accompanies them.   They
> can then make the crossing from Swinemünde to Pillau
> by day, and they will therefore be safe from the
> most dangerous submarine tactic, the night attack.
> At the end of the last war, it must be noted,
> methods of defense against the submarine had to a
> great degree overcome the threat of submarine
> attack.   The pocket battleship also has the ability
> to fight the battleship.   The probability of large
> battleships entering the Baltic is small.   Poland
> has neither docks nor repair facilities for battle-
> ships.   The cost of building these from scratch
> would be enormous.[20]

In a speech before the Reichstag on the armored cruiser,
Groener summarized the ship s significance to Germany: first,
it increased the strength of Germany's land forces by freeing
them from concern about their seaward flank;   second,   the new
ship would give Germany freedom of action in the Baltic.
Groener was a man who took history seriously, and in his view,
history had shown conclusively the importance of a strong
naval presence.   It was Germany's deficiency in this vital
aspect of military power, he thought, that had lost the war,
and Germany must never enter another war without a powerful
navy.[21]   Groener's arguments eventually prevailed, and the
Reichstag approved the construction of two pocket battleships.
The first of these, the Deutschland, was launched on 19 May
1931.
Before Groener's arrival on the scene, the navy had
concentrated on defending the Baltic Sea in case of a war.
The strategic maneuver of 1923, for instance, had tested the
navy's ability to defend the Baltic from a French incursion
or, failing that, to bottle up the French in the western
Baltic.   The maneuver of 1924 was similar in nature.   The navy
received the mission of maintaining sea communications with
East Prussia by sailing to meet the French in the narrow sea
areas of the western Baltic and there destroying the enemy in
a decisive fleet battle.   The navy hypothesized four situations in which a naval battle with the French might be possible: a Polish invasion of Pomerania; a war with France in
which the threatening attitude of the Soviet Union kept the
Poles at bay; a general European war with France and Poland
allied against Germany and the Soviet Union; and war between
the Soviet Union, on the one hand, and Poland and the Baltic
states on the other.   In all of these situations, the naval
command realized that the fleet which France could send into
the Baltic was superior to what the Germans could muster.   In

all of these situations, the navy ignored the prominent naval power, Great Britain, by leaving it to the Foreign Office to keep Britain out of any conflict.[22]

The naval wargame of 1927 showed that the navy was beginning to look beyond the Baltic to operations in the North Sea in the event of a war. The game assumed that a war had broken out between France and Italy, and that Poland entered on the side of France, Germany on the side of Italy. During the prewar period, both France and Italy had sent ships to the Baltic and Poland had occupied Danzig. The western Mediterranean was, therefore, the main theater of war. The Baltic and the North Sea were subsidiary theaters, although the North Sea was of particular significance to Germany because of the need to protect German commercial shipping there. Naval action in the Baltic centered around the Danziger Bucht, while German forces in the North Sea met with little success. The chief operations in the Mediterranean were the transport of native troops from North Africa to France and the Italian attempt to interdict this transport.[23]

As with the army wargame of the same year, the Foreign Office was critical of the navy game. At the close of the proceedings, the chief of the naval High Command, Admiral Hans Zenker, declared that the goal of the exercise was to lead the navy out of the narrow constraints placed on it by the Treaty of Versailles and once again to consider its role in a great European war. "Correspondingly," wrote Dirk Forster, "a certain optimism about Germany's importance as a maritime power appeared in the operations." As to the political basis for the game, Forster stated that "in the interests of maritime operations, the navy has constructed a scenario which it knows scarcely corresponds to reality." On the one hand, he was pleased with the willingness of the navy to consider the political realities and subordinate itself to the Foreign Office in political affairs. On the other hand, he noted that the navy overestimated Italy's potential as an ally and seemed to assume French hostility in all cases. These two assumptions had led to the unlikely situation of French-Italian naval battles in the Baltic as well as German operations against France in the North Sea.[24]

The fall maneuver of 1928 was a further indication that the German navy had begun to devise a strategy for the Baltic, provided it had the ships. The goal of the maneuver was to investigate "the possibilities of securing the sea lanes over which we receive our food and materiel, and cutting off the enemy from theirs," in the words of Admiral Erich Raeder. In particular, the maneuver stressed the maintenance of communications between the Reich and East Prussia and the destruction of any enemy who threatened them. The background situation was a Blue (German) war with Gold (France and Poland), which broke out after a short period of tension. The Poles had immediately seized Danzig, and Gold naval forces had broken into the Baltic. These forces included three battleships, two cruisers, and several destroyers. In an early engagement Gold destroyers had sunk a Blue battleship, though not without considerable losses to the attacking force. Blue forces had blocked the Polish port of Gdynia and hindered Gold's use of Danzig by laying mines in the Danziger Bucht. On land, Gold forces had invaded East Prussia. Blue hoped to conduct a delaying defense, but this strategy depended on the arrival of men and materiel from the Reich. Gold's entry into the Baltic, however, had forced Blue to halt all transport to East Prussia. Meanwhile, the Blue fleet had assembled at Swinemünde. This force was equal in size to the Gold fleet; that is, it contained three battleships and two cruisers.

From the beginning of the maneuver, lack of access to Gdynia crippled Gold's operations. Gold's orders stated that due to doubtful repair facilities in the Baltic, Gold should shun decisive fleet encounters except under favorable circumstances. Gold was also unable to accomplish its primary mission, seizure of the East Prussian port of Pillau, as long as there was the possibility of suffering damage which Gold would be unable to repair outside of Gdynia. In fact, without Gdynia, the maintenance of the Gold fleet depended on the Gold army seizing Pillau. The Gold fleet commander decided to keep his forces intact for later use and sailed to the northeast to keep distance between his own and the Blue fleet. His main concern now became fuel, since Gdynia was his main refueling station. In response, Blue sailed to the western entrance to the Baltic, preventing Gold from exiting the sea. Cut off from communications with its home base and lacking supply and repair facilities in the Baltic, the Gold fleet would soon be ripe for destruction by Blue. This favorable strategic situation disappeared, however, with Denmark's entry into the war on the side of Gold. A naval battle ensued. Gold, with its lifeline to the west reopened, was victorious.[25]

Admiral Raeder's closing observations on the maneuver stressed the importance of barring enemy naval forces from Gdynia. In any likely future war, the German navy would have to fight both France and Poland. The first Schwerpunkt would be the Baltic Sea, where the navy would have the dual mission of destroying the Polish fleet and preventing the French from establishing themselves. The means to both of these ends was to close the port of Gdynia, an act that would create refueling problems for the French. If it could be done quickly, he hinted, it might even deter the French fleet from entering the Baltic. Raeder felt that, because of the weak state of Germany's land forces, the responsibility for operations against Gdynia was the navy's. "A coup de main against Gdynia by land forces is not possible," he wrote, "as long as the Polish army is one of the strongest on the continent." Raeder believed that the navy was sufficiently strong at the present time to carry out the operation, but that this favorable situation would soon change. Poland had created "a significant port from nothing" in the past five years. The next few years would surely bring improvement to Gdynia's defenses. Improved defenses would make a direct attack on the port too risky for Germany's limited naval resources. In that case, the operation would have to rely on blockships or bombing attacks.[26]

The maneuver of 1928 was a significant departure from previous exercises. The maneuvers and wargames of 1923, 1924, and 1927 centered on a passive defense of the Baltic Sea, while favorable international situations helped the navy to overcome its weaknesses. The maneuver of 1928, however, dispensed with any help from the Foreign Office, postulated a situation in which German strength in the Baltic equalled that of the French, and featured a bold stroke which permitted Germany to tip the naval balance in its favor. The implied goal of this more active policy was to free naval forces for operations against the French in the North Sea. Before the navy could turn to the west,   however,   it would have to close Gdynia.

The Truppenamt ordered the first detailed study of a naval conflict with Poland,   entitled "Study Gdynia," in June 1928.   As the name indicated, the purpose of the study was to consider the feasibility of a strike upon the Polish Baltic port.   The attack was to be a sudden blow, made either during peacetime   or   as a counter to a Polish attack upon Germany. The Truppenamt gave responsibility for planning the strike to the Baltic Naval Department,   in cooperation with the army authorities in Defense District II in Stettin.   At first, the Truppenamt did not exclude the possibility that regular or irregular land forces might participate in the operation. Therefore, it ordered operational studies from both the army and the navy.[27]

The Poles had built Gdynia in the early 1920s because of concern over their access to the Baltic.   Although the Treaty of Versailles guaranteed Poland the use of Danzig's port facilities, Poland had found this arrangement unsatisfactory in the national emergency of 1920.   In that year, with the Red Army advancing upon Warsaw, German dock workers in Danzig had gone out on strike and refused to unload shipments of war materiel sent from the west to aid the Poles.   There was no guarantee against a repeat of this occurrence should Poland once more go to war,   especially since Germany was a potential adversary.   It is understandable that Poland saw the construc- tion of alternate port facilities on the Baltic as a pressing need.   Work on Gdynia began in 1921 and the port was in opera- tion   by   1923.   Commercial   traffic   through Gdynia   soon surpassed that of Danzig.   Besides its importance as a com- mercial center, Gdynia was also significant in military terms. Not only did it give Poland access to the sea and to the vital imports of raw materials and manufactured goods which the nation required,   but it was also useful as a naval strong- point.   The Poles realized Gdynia's importance and had equipped it with heavy guns and air cover.

For the German navy, the strategic benefit of a strike on Gdynia was plain.   Elimination of Gdynia meant victory at sea for the Germans,   assuming that Danzig remained out of Polish hands.   In operational terms, the Truppenamt designated three goals for German planners: destruction of Gdynia's port facilities; destruction of the seaplane stations at Puck and Reva and the air base at Rahmel; and the destruction of land and sea batteries, including the heavy batteries on the fortress of Hel.   The Truppenamt viewed the first operational goal as the most important.   An attack on Gdynia with the limited goal of removing the coastal batteries and the air- fields would not be worth the cost.   From the beginning,   the Defense Ministry attempted to limit operational planning for Study Gdynia to the elimination of the port.   The ministry stated further that the operation required forces large enough to overcome all Polish resistance within twenty-four hours. The purpose was to limit the political repercussions as well as to present Poland with a fait accompli before Polish mobilization was complete.

The task did not appear easy.   The navy,   which received primary responsibility for the project, was hesitant at first. In accordance with Gdynia's strategic importance as the center of Polish maritime activity, the Poles had fortified the port. In 1928,   German naval intelligence identified five heavy

batteries, capable of plunging or flat-trajectory fire, as
well as an unknown number of antiaircraft batteries, in the
region surrounding Gdynia. There were two or three heavy
batteries in the fortress of Hel, as well as a railroad
battery inside Gdynia itself. In 1928 the French delivered
some eighteen heavy artillery gun tubes to Gdynia, which made
it likely that the Poles would soon erect new batteries there.
The port was also well mined and was under the air umbrella of
Polish air units operating from the fields at Puck, Rewa, and
Rahmel. German Fleet Commander Oldekop believed that an
attack upon Gdynia would be ill-advised, since it would tie up
all available German naval forces and keep them from more
important tasks, such as sealing off the Baltic to the French
navy. In addition, the navy would have other tasks to perform, including denying the use of Danzig to the Polish navy,
the destruction of the Polish surface fleet, and the defense
of the East Prussian naval base at Pillau. Besides, he saw
the possibility of heavy losses to the German fleet which it
could not afford. For these reasons, he stated that an attack
on Gdynia must come from the land.[28]

Oldekop's suggestion was unacceptable to the Defense
Ministry, which envisioned using only small contingents of
land forces for the operation. These would be mainly demolition experts and commandos. The ministry based its insistence
on naval action against Gdynia upon a different assessment of
Gdynia's defenses than Oldekop had used. According to the
Truppenamt, there were in Gdynia and environs the following
forces: one marine company, one coastal battery, and one
railroad battery. A marine battalion had recently arrived in
the port, but it appeared that the purpose of this 900-man
force was to fill empty billets on the ships in the harbor,
rather than to act as a land defense force. In addition,
there were air bases at Puck, Rewa, and Rahmel. None of these
bases had sufficient military personnel to form an effective
defense. The headquarters of the 8th Cavalry Brigade was at
Starogard, but the only field units in Starogard were the 2nd
Jäger Battalion and the 2nd Cavalry Regiment. There was
another Jäger battalion, the 1st, at Chojnice and an infantry
battalion, the 2nd of the 69th Infantry Regiment, at Mewe.
While the Poles had planned for some time to strengthen their
forces in the Corridor to six Jäger battalions, four cavalry
regiments, one horse artillery battery, one antiaircraft battery, and two armored battalions, this reinforcement had not
yet occurred. The Polish forces, led by the truck-mobile
Jägers, could react within eighteen hours of a German attack.
According to German intelligence, the Jäger battalion at
Chojnice had received orders to take up a defensive position
from Chojnice to Kamin immediately after the outbreak of
hostilities between Germany and Poland. This force would
therefore be in a position to upset the twenty-four-hour
timetable which the Germans planned to follow. In addition to
the regular forces, there were also some ten battalions of
irregular border defense forces near Gdynia. These were
formed around the cadres of the peacetime border police. In
the event of mobilization, the Germans expected the Poles to
form two distinct groups, one at Kartuszy of six battalions
and one at Chojnice of four battalions. Each border defense
battalion contained about 350 men, organized into three or
four companies. Finally, the Poles had available at Puck and
Neustadt a battalion-sized force of irregulars. All told, the

Poles could call on 10,000 men for the defense of Gdynia.
This was far more than the Germans could assemble for an
attack on the port.

The terrain around Gdynia also made the Defense Ministry
wary of ordering a land attack. The region is basically flat,
although there are occasional rises in elevation. There are
woods with thick undergrowth around the city, impassable to
all but small bodies of infantry. Few good roads existed at
the time, those from Lauenburg to Gdynia being the exception.
Lateral east-west roads, that is, those which an attacking
German force would have to use, were in bad condition.
Movement of large bodies of troops off the roads would be
impossible. Small roadblocks by Polish Jägers or cavalry
detachments could therefore hinder the operation seriously.
The one advantage offered by the terrain was that German
forces would be able to camouflage themselves against Polish
air attacks, but this was not sufficient to offset the many
disadvantages an attacker would have to bear. Like the manpower balance in the region, the terrain made it unlikely that
land forces could achieve the quick decision favored by the
Defense Ministry.[29]

The disinclination of the Truppenamt to use land forces
received further reinforcement from the officers of Defense
District II in Stettin. The Defense Ministry had ordered the
staff officers at Stettin to draw up plans for an attack on
Gdynia in June 1928. In keeping with the requirements of a
quick, bold operation, Defense District II's plan gave responsibility for seizing Gdynia to active troops already stationed
near the Corridor. These forces consisted of about three
battalions of infantry, one cavalry regiment, and assorted
marine garrison troops. They were to receive small reinforcements to form three advancing columns. The middle column had
the main task of seizing Gdynia; it would march to its
objective via Neustadt. As the minimum strength for this
column, the plan called for two infantry battalions, made more
mobile by bicycles, motorcycles, and trucks and receiving fire
support from infantry guns; one reconnaissance battalion, with
a squadron of armored cars; two artillery batteries; pioneer
units; communications troops; and marine demolition units.
The mission of the southern column was to protect the flank of
the main column. It was to consist of one mobile infantry
battalion, one artillery battery, one platoon of armored cars,
and pioneer troops. The northern column would have as its
objectives the air base at Puck and the fortifications at Hel.
Its strength was equal to the southern column, minus the
armored cars.

The task of protecting the southern flank of the main
column was crucial to the mission, since keeping Polish
reinforcements out of Gdynia was a prerequisite for success.
To help the southern column in its task of sealing off the
Corridor, Defense District II planned to destroy railroads,
roads, and communications in the Corridor prior to the attack
through the use of agents and saboteurs. In addition, noisy
concentrations of border defense units in the area would help
to draw off Polish reserves heading for Gdynia. Because of
the poor quality of these irregular forces, German planners
had no intention to use them in the advance. Finally,
Germany's meager air assets would keep watch over the southern
approaches to the Corridor.[30]

Defense District II's plan convinced the Defense Ministry that a land drive on Gdynia would not work. Hence, it was a catalyst in the Truppenamt's final decision to opt for a naval attack. In a study drawn up on 30 January 1930 and sent to the Baltic Naval Department and Defense District II, the Truppenamt explained its decision. Gdynia was sure to be well defended from the land side, and would probably receive reinforcements if war threatened. It would take German forces at least thirty-six hours to reach their objective by land if there was no opposition from Polish border guards, and forty-eight to sixty hours if opposition did occur. If regular Polish forces resisted the German advance, the delay would extend indefinitely. The Defense Ministry estimated that it would take land forces several days, at least, to destroy Gdynia's port facilities, and declared that there were insufficient forces for a simultaneous advance on Gdynia by three columns. In addition, the ministry believed that German forces would be unable to prevent the Poles from reinforcing Gdynia. The regiments of the 8th Cavalry Brigade and other forces garrisoned on the lower Vistula would soon arrive on the scene. In all, these forces included five infantry regiments, two Jäger battalions, four cavalry regiments, and two light artillery regiments. These would outnumber the two infantry regiments, one pioneer battalion, one cavalry regiment, and two light artillery regiments which were all the units the Germans could spare for the operation. The mobility of the Polish cavalry brigade, in particular, would render futile any attempt by the southern German column to seal off the Corridor. The result would be a bloody battle for Gdynia. The Truppenamt estimated that this would result in the destruction of two-thirds of the 2nd Infantry Division, which would effectively remove the division from further action. In the opinion of the Defense Ministry, there were four prerequisites for a successful land-based attack. These were the following: no reinforcement of the Polish forces in the Corridor during peacetime; no fortifications on Gdynia's landward side; immediate launching of the attack at the outset of war; and no concentration of Polish forces in the Corridor before the operation began. The Defense Ministry stated that this was a very unlikely combination, but that if even one were missing, a land attack on Gdynia would be hopeless. If all the conditions were met, the success of the operation was still doubtful. The Poles could rush enough troops into the area that the result would be a street battle for the port. This would wear down the German forces and delay the demolition work. It was even possible that the Germans would be expelled from the city. Finally, the Truppenamt objected to the diversion of army units to what it considered a sideshow at Gdynia when Polish units were capable of marching into Pomerania and Brandenburg and threatening the heart of the Reich. For all of these reasons, the Defense Ministry ordered planning for a land operation by Defense District II to cease.[31]

The navy seems to have accepted its mission with new confidence after 1930. In a new strategic study drawn up in the spring of 1931, the navy refuted the gloomy assessment which Oldekop had delivered in 1928. The new study analyzed Gdynia's defenses in some detail, as well as the probable Polish reactions to a German attack on the port. Its conclusions were favorable to a German attack. Gdynia was not

heavily defended. Polish naval units in the area, particularly the surface forces, were insignificant. The only danger
from this quarter was that Polish destroyers would harass
German minesweepers sent to clear mines from the Danziger
Bucht. The Germans were also concerned about Polish
submarines in the area. The study noted the lack of strong
artillery in and around Gdynia, although this deficiency was
correctable in a short time. Again, the minesweepers would
need protection, since they were vulnerable even to light
artillery. Any landing of troops would also have to take the
defender's artillery into account. The naval command warned
that the Poles would rush every piece of artillery they had
into Gdynia, since they recognized the importance of the port.
The mine defenses in the Danziger Bucht were of decisive
importance to naval operations. In this area, the navy
declared that its mine defense and minesweeping assets were
more than adequate to deal with Polish mine belts, especially
since the Polish navy lacked expertise in this area. The
study cautioned that France would probably supply Poland with
materiel and that the Polish navy would throw every vessel it
had into minelaying operations. The result, predicted the
naval command, would be a double belt of mines in front of
Gdynia.
The greatest danger to the mission was the Polish air
force. The Germans had to rely solely on passive antiaircraft
defenses, since they had no combat aircraft of their own. The
presence of the Polish air force precluded much chance of
surprise by the Germans and represented a serious threat to
the German navy's light surface forces. Polish warplanes
would be operating close to their bases, and the narrowness of
the sea area would restrict German maneuverability to a great
degree. Air attacks on German shipping also had the potential
to hinder the navy's primary mission--shelling the port.
German naval leaders had confidence in their antiaircraft, but
recognized that the most effective defense against a Polish
air attack would be warplanes of their own.[32]
The navy also discussed possible Polish reaction to Study
Gdynia, now called Study East. The Poles, it stated, would
very likely undertake operations in the Baltic designed to
relieve Gdynia by drawing off German forces committed there.
The first of these relief operations would be to threaten the
German port and naval base at Pillau in East Prussia. The
Poles had many options available to them. They could attack
Pillau by using light craft operating from the Danzig region,
or send blockships to close Pillau altogether. The Poles
might also mine Pillau harbor, but this seemed less likely in
the light of Poland's lack of minelaying craft. Finally, the
Poles might attack Pillau from the air. The navy declared,
however, that Polish operations against Pillau would only
upset the Gdynia operation if the Germans took longer than
anticipated in closing the Polish port. As a counter to the
Polish threat to Pillau, the navy suggested that if tensions
rose between Germany and Poland which could lead to war,
Pillau should be fortified immediately. These defense
measures were to include antiaircraft positions, an auxiliary
minesweeping force, supply depots, and security forces to
guard against sabotage.
Another possibility was that the Poles would occupy
Danzig. The Germans were aware that a Polish occupation of
Danzig would offset the advantages gained by the attack on

Gdynia.   Committing German forces to defend Danzig, however, would embroil Germany in a difficult legal problem, since the free city was under the protection of the League.   In addition, Danzig was tied to Poland by treaty in matters of defense.   The politically minded officers of the German navy feared being labeled aggressors in a future war; hence, Danzig was more or less absent from German naval planning.

In general terms, the German navy felt that its Polish counterpart would not remain passive in the event of war. Despite Poland's naval weakness, Polish destroyers, torpedo boats, and submarines would probably operate aggressively outside of the Danziger Bucht, laying mines and threatening German strongpoints.   In fact, the German naval leadership suggested the suspension of all merchant shipping in the Baltic for the duration of Study East, which would free German naval units from having to protect commercial traffic.   In addition, the Germans expected Polish air attacks, with Pillau, Swinemünde, Königsberg, and the aerodrome at Nest as the most likely targets.[33]

The navy plan for operations against Gdynia contained four steps: shelling the port, clearing mines, landing troops, and destroying the port.   Like the Defense Ministry, the navy stressed speed in preparation and execution of Study East: "Only if we catch Poland early in its preparations will the attack succeed," stated one naval strategist in 1931. Therefore, the navy formed a task force, sufficient in size and strength, and equipped with on-board munitions, to carry out the mission.   The goal was to have light forces before Gdynia within hours of the outbreak of hostilities.   These light forces had three tasks: the location and removal of minefields; the prevention of a break out by Polish naval units in Gdynia harbor; and the protection of the larger German units to follow. This task force was to consist of two cruisers, two torpedo flotillas with flak guns, and mine boats.   The force would base its activities on intelligence received from German reconnaissance aircraft which would fly their missions during the tense prewar period.   This air activity, since it was being carried out by unarmed planes, would have to cease when the war actually started.

Within twenty-four hours of the arrival of the light task force, heavy units including four battleships would arrive at Gdynia.   One cruiser would operate against Puck to hinder use of the airfield there.   Three of the four battleships would shell targets in the harbor from a range of eight thousand to nine thousand meters, while the fourth would repel attacks by Polish forces sailing toward Gdynia.   Under the protection of the battleships' heavy guns, the minesweepers would go in to clear a path for the light ships and landing vessels.   After disembarking, the troops would destroy anything in the port which had survived the bombardment. To protect the demolition workers from a Polish counterattack, the navy demanded a land force. This force would need heavy armaments, since the Poles would have machine guns, mortars, and howitzers.   The land battle, not surprisingly, received only a cursory treatment in the navy plan.   Following demolition, the German forces would re-embark and leave the area.   The final stage of the operation involved mining the harbor and sinking blockships to close Gdynia permanently.[34]

In a second operational study, in 1932, the navy expanded on its demand for land forces.   Study East was important for political reasons, to demonstrate to the world Germany's determination to defend itself, and to make potentially friendly powers more inclined to intervene on the German side. Psychological reasons also played a part; Study East would strengthen the morale of the army and the civilian population. The navy further declared that it recognized its own primary responsibility for the operation.   A prerequisite for success was the penetration of the belt of mines the Poles would lay from Hel to the mouth of the Vistula.   Naval units would have to accomplish their minesweeping task under the guns of Hel. Two options existed to silence these guns.   The first, bombardment by the heavy guns of German warships, was of doubtful efficacy since naval guns historically had a difficult time silencing fortresses.   The second option was to disembark land forces to destroy the guns.   The navy possessed marine landing parties for such operations, but the study of 1932 claimed that marines were unsuited to an operation against Hel because of the sandy, dune-like terrain on the beaches.   Instead of marines, one regular infantry battalion was required.   The army had been conducting experiments in amphibious landings for years, so this new demand did not present any threat to the execution of Study East.

A naval wargame of 1932 demonstrated the confidence which navy planners had in their ability to defeat the Polish navy and control the Baltic Sea.   The situation for the wargame assumed a favorable international situation for Germany which enabled the German navy to turn and face the French in the west after disposing of the Poles.   The wargame proceeded along the following lines.   In a two-front war against a Red eastern power (Poland) and a Gold western power (France, Belgium), Blue (Germany) was forced to obtain raw materials, food, and goods from overseas.   These imports were necessary both for the conduct of the war and for the civilian population.

In recognition of the necessity of Blue's imports, Gold set its fleet along the sea approaches to Blue.   Red was essentially cut off from the sea by Blue's operations.   Blue's goals in the wargame were to analyze German naval policy up to 1938, to practice switching the gravity of naval operations from east to west after the destruction of the eastern enemy, to determine the most effective methods of protecting German ships against French attacks, and to test the tactical and strategic use of the Panzerschiff against offensive French moves.

The game situation began on 1 September 1938.   An unnamed crisis had led to serious political tension between Blue and Red.   War broke out on 3 September. On 1 September, the naval command ordered the expansion of the navy, which was carried out by 3 September.   All of the armed forces received orders to mobilize on 3 September.   The navy received orders to carry out operations against Red immediately.   On the first mobilization day (4 September), the Blue fleet carried out its attack on Gdynia, with the result that the Red naval strongpoint was blocked for any further use.   Red's surface ships were in large part destroyed.   Small Red surface forces and submarines lay damaged in Danzig.   Nothing was known of the remainder of Red's submarines.   The air base at Puck was destroyed, but Red had not lost large numbers of planes.   The Blue fleet did not suffer great losses in these operations, although some ships were damaged, and Blue used large

quantities of fuel and munitions. Swinemünde suffered several
bombing attacks by Red warplanes, as did Blue's cities and
industries.   There   was   no   significant   military damage,
however.

Since the beginning of the war, twenty-five to thirty
steamers had arrived in Blue's North Sea ports loaded with
coal   from England.   Blue expected large quantities of
manufactured and goods and weapons to arrive shortly from the
United States.   Because of the danger of Gold entering the
war, the American ships were diverted north of the British
Isles.   Traffic between the North Sea ports and Finland had
been heavy. Steamers had brought in ore, wood, and food.

Blue now had to reckon with Gold's imminent entry into
the war in support of Red. Since 3 September, Gold had called
up its reserves and assembled its troops on its eastern
border.   Gold's naval forces were still in their ports, in
peacetime organization, but were ready to sail. Blue expected
Gold's land forces to seize the Ruhr coal fields three to five
days after Gold's entry into the war. Meanwhile, Russia and
Lithuania had called up part of their reserves and appeared
ready to attack Red at any moment.

England, the United States, the Netherlands, and the
Nordic states were neutral. They showed a benevolent attitude
toward Blue, however, allowing Blue to import raw materials,
food, and goods. They had, to this end, given Blue extensive
credits. The neutrality of the Free City of Danzig had so far
not been violated.   Rounding out the neutrals' picture, there
was strong tension between France and Italy.   The remaining
Mediterranean and southeastern European states were neutral.
However, French pressure had forced them to block the shipment
of weapons or materiel to Germany.

By the afternoon of 5 September, border battles raged in
East Prussia.   In Upper Silesia, Red had occupied the
industrial and coal-producing areas.   In the Polish Corridor,
there had only been small movements of troops and material.
According to reports, Red had assembled a large part of its
army on its eastern and northern borders. Meanwhile, the Blue
fleet stood ready north of the Danziger Bucht.

This was an extraordinarily favorable situation for
Germany. The attitude of Russia and Lithuania allowed Germany
to limit itself to the forces necessary for border security in
the East.   The Blue army was deployed in the West.   Here,
Blue's leaders intended to avoid any decisive battle.   At the
same time, Blue searched frantically for sources of arms and
possible allies.   In view of the threat to the western coal
and industrial area, Blue had to import coal, raw materials,
and food to a large degree.   These were arriving on neutral
shipping.   Meanwhile, France was effectively checkmated at
sea. According to operational orders used in the game:

> It is to be expected that Gold, because of the
> threatening situation in the Mediterranean and the
> need to protect its troop transports from North
> Africa, will send its heavy forces and part of its
> light forces to the Mediterranean. However, Gold
> has a strong interest in cutting off Blue's sup-
> plies.   Therefore, at the outbreak of a war, Gold
> will probably commit to action light naval forces in
> the English Channel, North Sea, and Skagerrak.
> Because of the destruction of Red's strongpoint in

the Baltic (Gdynia), the commitment of Gold surface
forces into the Baltic is improbable.[35]

The wargame of 1932 showed that the navy was far ahead of
the army in planning for an actual war with Poland. Although
this hypothetical conflict contained a number of doubtful
assumptions, particularly with regard to British neutrality,
it also showed the navy's devotion to the idea of an attack on
Gdynia at the beginning of hostilities. Only after the
neutralization of the Polish naval presence in the Baltic
would the navy turn west to oppose the French. The navy's
aggressive planning outstripped that of the army, which
thought of tactical offensives against the Poles only in the
context of an overall defensive strategy. To be fair to the
army, it was inferior in size to Poland's land forces, while
Germany's navy was larger than Poland's. German land planning
had to be more cautious than German naval planning, for to
commit the army to a premature offensive against Poland could
well have resulted in a crushing defeat. The navy's offensive
stance also reflected General Groener's philosophy of naval
strength as an important component in national defense. As
Studie Ost demonstrated, the German navy was unwilling to
limit itself to the role of a coastal defense force, but was
looking ahead to the future when Germany would once more be a
Great Power. In this sense, the German navy was far ahead of
its Polish counterpart, which due to its small size and lack
of modern equipment was unable to play a significant role in
Polish war planning.

Despite his interest in naval affairs, Groener was first
and foremost a soldier, and he also devoted a great deal of
his energy to studying the effect of technology upon war. In
late 1928, he wrote a long article, entitled "Thoughts about
the Development of War." In his view, it was the great impact
of technology upon warfare which had been the most important
lesson of the war. Despite the provisions of the Versailles
treaty which forbade Germany to possess the new instruments of
war, Groener's discussion of modern weaponry, mechanization,
and air power was an indication that, on the theoretical level
at least, the Reichswehr was very much a modern army. In this
respect, the German forces were very much superior to the
Polish army, which possessed modern weapons but did not seem
to have developed any doctrine for their use.

In this article, Groener left no doubt of his agreement
with Seeckt that cavalry was still an effective arm. Like
Seeckt, Groener called for cavalry's modernization rather than
its abolition. While the value of cavalry was disputed by
many, "the experience of the war does not seem to call for the
abolition of mounted troops." Indeed, at the war's beginning,
Germany had cause to regret that it did not have more cavalry.
Naturally, he felt, cavalry tactics must change. Cavalry must
be trained in the use of modern weapons: "We need 'modern
Hussars,' which I picture as a sort of machine gun corps. To
what degree cavalry will be motorized will only be established
in the next decade."

Groener saw the future of warfare in the mobility of the
tank rather than the mobility of the horse. "Tanks may fight
either in support, in the manner of cavalry, or as independent
forces," he wrote. Like the tank theorists in England,
France, and the United States, he differentiated tanks by
mission. For a war of movement, Groener wanted three types of

tanks.   Small   tanks would have a weight of two to five tons.
Their   range on or off the road should be between   twenty   and
fifty   kilometers.   Their   mission   was   reconnaissance   and
security.   Light   tanks would have a weight of five to   seven
tons.   Their range should be between fifteen and forty kilometers.   Their mission was to support infantry and cavalry in
battle   or to attack   independently.   Finally,   medium   tanks
would   have   a weight of seven to fifteen tons.   Their   range
should   be between fifteen and forty kilometers,   their mission
the   same as that of the light tank.   For a war of   position,
Groener   thought a heavy tank,   weighing between   fifteen   and
seventy tons,   was necessary.   Its range,   however,   only had to
be eight to twenty-five kilometers,   since its objective would
rarely lie beyond the enemy trench line.   Its mission would be
to clear a path through fortified hostile positions over which
friendly infantry could pass.[36]
     In one sense,   Groener's fascination with the new weapons
of   war   was   a disadvantage for someone   entrusted   with   the
direction   of an infantry-cavalry force.   The danger   existed
that   Groener   was   planning for a war   which   the   Versailles
restrictions   would   not permit the Reichswehr to fight.   In
another sense,   however,   Groener's interest in   mechanization
and   tank   warfare was a great advantage for the German   army,
especially   in   comparison with   the   Poles.   Under   Groener,
German   armored theorists were permitted to conduct   exercises
and   experiments equalled only in Great   Britain.   Certainly,
the Poles performed no such comparable studies.   Polish tanks,
as   we   have seen,   were semi-obsolete,   and the small   Polish
budget   would   permit   no thorough   overhaul   of   the   armored
forces.   As Germany had no tanks,   a large number of   junior
officers,   among them the young Heinz Guderian,   were permitted
the   luxury of letting their minds roam freely about the possibilities open to modern mechanized armies.   The joint German-
Soviet tank school at Kazan in the Soviet Union,   which opened
in   1930,   supplemented   the   theoretical work being   done   in
Germany.   It is no exaggeration to say that Groener sowed the
seeds   of   Blitzkrieg during his tenure as   defense   minister.
Seeckt's   emphasis   upon mobility was   the   foundation,   but
Groener   brought the Reichswehr into the mechanized   era.   In
this   sense,   it   was Groener who was   the   truly   significant
figure for German-Polish military relations.   Despite Seeckt's
oft-repeated phrases about "destroying Poland,"   it was Groener
who designed an army capable of doing so.
     One   of   Groener's   most   important   accomplishments   as
defense   minister   was the redeployment of the German forces in
Defense District III,   that is,   around Berlin and Silesia, in
August 1928.   As we have seen in chapter 2, the deployment of
forces   in   the   east displayed a   preference   for   dispersion
rather than concentration.   The reason for this,   in Seeckt's
eyes,   was   to reassure the jittery civilian population   by
making   sure   that no part of Germany's eastern   regions   went
without   some military protection.   Groener refused to accept
this rationale.   He preferred to base his military   decisions
upon   purely military reasoning.   He saw several deficiencies
in the current deployment:

     The   previous deployment of the troops in the   gar-
     risons,   which resulted from the forced reduction of
     the   army from 750,000 to only 100,000 men and from
     the   postwar situation,   is not suitable and   should

not therefore be permanent. Numerous battalions, sections, and cavalry regiments are split up amongst several garrisons. This fragmentation is not, in the long run, bearable. For military reasons, therefore, a concentration of troops and a reduction in the number of garrisons is unconditionally necessary. Further, the entire force posture on the eastern border must undergo a definite change, which will also make changes necessary in the interior of the country. Giving up a number of garrisons is unavoidable. These towns share the fate of so many others which have lost their garrisons as a result of the peace treaty.[37]

In a memorandum of August 1928, when the new deployments were just beginning (see table 4.1),[38] Groener described the basis upon which he made his decision:

Smaller units than a battalion of infantry or a section of artillery should not receive their own garrison. The cavalry regiments should be split up into at most two garrisons. We will strive in so far as it is possible to assemble the different arms (infantry, cavalry, artillery) in the same garrison. At the same time, we must take care to ensure the best conditions for training. Strategically, we will follow the principle of pulling away from the borders. This has already started in the area which would be most seriously threatened in the event of an emergency, East Prussia. The concentration of forces is taking place there with the agreement of local officials. The other Defense Districts should follow as the financial situation allows. It is the decision of the Defense Ministry that the reorganization of Defense District III be finished by 1930.[39]

An examination of the new deployments indicates that Groener succeeded in concentrating Germany's forces in Defense District III. The new garrisons were located in the interior of the country, while the border towns of Militsch, Namslau, Züllichau, Leobschütz, and Lüben lost their garrisons. These new garrisons were much more appropriate for an army which was, as we have seen, planning to fight a war of maneuver. In their old garrisons, the separated units of the Reichswehr risked being overrun in the first wave of a Polish invasion. The 7th Cavalry Regiment, for instance, which had formerly been split up along the Polish border at Lüben, Breslau, and Oels, even had had one of its squadrons in distant Potsdam. Although the presence of these squadrons was soothing psychologically to the citizens of the border towns, the number of troops was too small and the distance between the squadrons too great for the regiment to have any hope of contesting a Polish advance into Silesia. After the new deployment, four squadrons and the regimental staff had Breslau as their garrison, while the remaining two squadrons were placed at Oels. The 8th Cavalry Regiment had been split up among five garrisons in a forward deployment extremely close to the Polish border. This unit was now pulled back and placed in the two garrisons of Ohlau and Brieg. The squadrons in these two

towns were placed favorably to guard the eastern approaches to
Breslau and were close enough to cooperate with each other.
The deployments of the 10th and 11th Cavalry Regiments showed
a similar emphasis on concentration and interior placement.
The deployment center for the 10th Regiment was at Sprottau,
that for the 11th Regiment at Oppeln to the southeast.
Silesia now possessed a "spine" of concentrated cavalry
forces, equally ready to face enemy forces advancing from the
north or south.
     The deployment of the three regiments of the 3rd Infantry
Division at Neisse, Glogau, and Potsdam was also beneficial,
since these forces were now capable of concerted action as
regiments rather than as scattered companies. While it cannot
be said that Silesia was now safe from any enemy attack,
Groener had done the correct thing in attempting to deploy his
limited forces more sensibly. He had insisted on the new
deployments despite the outcry from local officials in the
border regions, who claimed that to remove the Reichswehr from
their towns would render them helpless against the Poles.
More tradition-bound officers had also objected to the abolition of some of the oldest garrisons in the German army. The
reorganization of the eastern garrisons showed that Groener
was a truly modern soldier, unaffected by the romantic outlook
typical of former imperial officers.
     It would be a mistake, however, to deny the continuity
which existed between Groener's policies and Seeckt's. This
continuity is plain in the matter of the eastern fortifications. Like Seeckt, Groener felt that some degree of fortification in the east was necessary to the security of the
border, which was far too long for the limited number of
troops to defend. To Groener, fortifications were an
important part of the Landesschutz, and he intended to expand
them. He did not have to be as clever as Seeckt had been in
hiding them, since the Interallied Control Commission, which
had tried to halt any German attempts to fortify the border,
had left the country in 1925. In March 1929, Groener wrote a
letter to Stresemann stating his intention to build new fortifications on the Oder:

> At a cabinet meeting of 18 October 1928, which dealt
> with the question of national defense, I revealed my
> intention to strengthen the especially vulnerable
> part of the Oder River's left bank. I intend to
> proceed with peacetime construction between the
> mouth of the Oder at Katzbach and Tschicherzig,
> where the Polish border approaches to within 20-30
> kilometers of the river. Now that the preparations
> have proceeded far enough that they approach comple-
> tion, I can reveal that we are talking about 25
> concrete bunkers for the immediate defense of the
> river line.[40]

Like Seeckt, Groener was not overly optimistic about the value
of fortifications in modern war. However, the intelligence
which he had received about the Polish army convinced him that
the fortifications could hinder a Polish advance into Germany.
In particular, the sad state of the Polish artillery, great
quantities of which would be necessary to reduce the new
German bunkers on the Oder, indicated to Groener that the
construction of new fortifications would be useful.

Table 4.1
Redeployment of German Forces, 1928

Unit	Previous Garrison	New Garrison
7th Cavalry Regiment	Breslau	Breslau
1st Squadron	Breslau	Breslau
2nd Squadron	Breslau	Breslau
3rd Squadron	Oels	Oels
4th Squadron	Lüben	Oels
5th Squadron	Breslau	Breslau
6th Squadron	Potsdam	Breslau
8th Cavalry Regiment	Oels	Brieg
1st Squadron	Militsch	Brieg
2nd Squadron	Ohlau	Ohlau
3rd Squadron	Militsch	Brieg
4th Squadron	Namslau	Ohlau
5th Squadron	Breslau	Brieg
10th Cavalry Regiment	Züllichau	Sprottau
1st Squadron	Torgau	Lüben
2nd Squadron	Lüben	Lüben
3rd Squadron	Züllichau	Sprottau
4th Squadron	Züllichau	Sprottau
5th Squadron	Züllichau	Sprottau
11th Cavalry Regiment	Neustadt	Oppeln
1st Squadron	Torgau	Oppeln
2nd Squadron	Leobschütz	Oppeln
3rd Squadron	Neustadt	Neustadt
4th Squadron	Neustadt	Neustadt
5th Squadron	Ohlau	Oppeln
3rd Cavalry Regiment	Rathenow	Stendal
2nd Squadron	Rathenow	Rathenow
5th Squadron	Rathenow	Rathenow
4th Cavalry Regiment		
2nd Squadron	Perleberg	Perleberg
4th Squadron	Perleberg	Perleberg
6th Squadron	Potsdam	Breslau

Unit	Previous Garrison	New Garrison
3rd Artillery Regiment		
5th Battalion	Sagan	Sagan
(Horse Artillery)		
14th Battery	Sprottau	Sagan
15th Battery	Sprottau	Sagan
16th Battery	Sagan	Sagan
7th Infantry Regiment		
1st Battalion	Neisse	Neisse
1st Company	Oppeln	Neisse
2nd Company	Oppeln	Neisse
3rd Company	Neisse	Neisse
4th Company	Neisse	Neisse
13th Company	Glatz	Schweidnitz
8th Infantry Regiment		
2nd Battalion	Liegnitz	Glogau
5th Company	Glogau	Glogau
6th Company	Glogau	Glogau
7th Company	Liegnitz	Glogau
8th Company	Liegnitz	Glogau
14th Company	Lüben	Liegnitz
15th Company	Lüben	Liegnitz
16th Company	Lüben	Liegnitz
9th Infantry Regiment		
2nd Battalion	Berlin	Potsdam
5th Company	Berlin	Potsdam
6th Company	Potsdam	Potsdam
7th Company	Potsdam	Potsdam
8th Company	Berlin	Potsdam

As during the Seeckt period, the Poles objected to the renewed construction activity in eastern Germany. Yet Polish attention continued to be directed against East Prussia rather than to the Oder district.[41] The Poles worried about the threat of a German offensive from East Prussia. To Warsaw, the maneuvers and fortification activity within Germany's detached province were an indication that the <u>Reichswehr</u> was plotting to use East Prussia as a base of operations against Poland. An article in the <u>Kurjer Warszawski</u> in late 1932 declared:

> There have been recent movements of troops in East Prussia on a much larger scale than in past years at this season. Large detachments of all arms have been marching throughout the whole province. Heavily loaded trucks have been transporting some kinds of loads to the frontier garrisons. There are rumors that military barracks are being constructed in the midst of the forest and supplied with food and ammunition. Uneasiness is further increased by information of increased activity on the field fortifications in the Heilsberg triangle. Large detachments of all arms have been seen on the road to Ortelsburg with red bands on their helmets indicating two-sided maneuvers. Troops were concentrated near Neidenburg and were quartered in the villages along the highway between Willenberg and Jedwabno. All this made the impression of large maneuvers along the Polish frontier which had not been announced in the press.[42]

One Western officer who visited East Prussia at the time declared that he had seen the construction of a "fortified triangle" in the area Königsberg-Heilsberg-Elbing for the purpose of forming a "point d'appui" or base of operations in East Prussia. He noted, however, that Polish accusations about the Heilsberg triangle were

> written so as to give the idea to a person who is not familiar with the geography of East Prussia or who does not look up the locations of the towns named that the fortifications are along the Polish frontier and that there were large numbers of troops engaged in the maneuvers. But if one analyzes the article in question, Heilsberg is about 80 kilometers from the nearest point on the Polish frontier. The two towns Willenberg and Jedwabno are but 22 kilometers apart and not very many troops could be quartered in the villages between the two.

In addition, he labelled as false the Polish claims about new German border fortifications:

> On the question of fortifications of the Polish-East Prussian frontier, I have not been able to discover any signs of any new works on either side. The Polish fortifications at Grudziadz and Torun on the other hand are entirely out of repair and in no state for use in case of war. In fact they have every outward appearance of having been abandoned

for defense purposes.   The casemates, storerooms,
batteries, etc. are all being used as living quarters for officers.[43]

It was plain that the Germans did not intend to rely upon the
fortifications alone to protect their border.   Just as Seeckt
was an apostle of mobility, while at the same time building
fixed fortifications, so too were the leaders who succeeded
him.   The maneuvers of the post-1926 period emphasized maneuver, concentration, and the spirit of the offensive.   At the
same time, they came to examine even more explicitly the
possibility of a German-Polish war.
The first eastern maneuver after Seeckt's resignation was
a relatively minor affair, and was of interest primarily for
tactical rather than strategic reasons.   The maneuver, which
took place during Spring 1927, occurred at the Döberitz
training ground in Defense District II.   The maneuver problem
was very much in the Seecktian mold, an analysis of the possibility of a cavalry brigade (Red) stopping or delaying the
advance of a regiment of infantry (Blue).   The American military attache was present and wrote the following report:

> The cavalry commander had the intention of delaying
> the march of the infantry regiment on Döberitz by
> sending only a small force for the delaying action
> in its front, chiefly with machine guns, and sending
> the mass of the brigade in two columns on the flanks
> to draw off the infantry in a false direction. This
> policy was successful only in part: the infantry
> battalion allowed itself to be drawn off to the
> eastward but thereafter continued northward as a
> flank guard.   The other cavalry column itself got
> lost and apparently had no effect on the movements
> of the Blues.   The problem was commented on in the
> critique by the commander of the Berlin garrison who
> directed the maneuver and afterwards by General
> Heye, Chief of the Reichswehr, and Herr Gessler,
> Minister of Defense, who were both present at the
> maneuver.

The emphasis on flanking action in the maneuver was reminiscent of the Seeckt era, and showed that under General Wilhelm
Heye, the army was continuing Seeckt's military policies.
At the Döberitz maneuver, the attacking force (Blue)
represented the 1st Infantry Division and the reinforced 2nd
Infantry Regiment.   The Blue force was advancing in a northerly direction, pursuing a Red force which it had evidently
routed some days before.   Red had already crossed the Havel
River and was retreating in a northerly direction.   While the
location of this maneuver west of the Havel placed it outside
of the probable theater of operations in a German-Polish war,
the types of forces engaged in the mock battle were representative of the German and Polish armies.   The Red force
probably represented the German army, since all previous
maneuvers had portrayed the Germans on the defensive.
However, if the Red force actually was meant to represent the
Germans, then the assignment of forces was curious. Usually,
the "Polish" forces in the maneuvers contained the cavalry
units.   In the Döberitz maneuver, however, the "German" force
possessed the cavalry.   This maneuver situation was

delightfully ambiguous, and it gave the troops of the Reichswehr equal training in either attack or defense. It is, indeed, possible to view this maneuver as an examination of the Polish cavalry's ability to hinder an advance by German infantry. Here, then, we see the first tentative shift toward a strategy of offensive war against Poland.

The American attache present was not as interested in the implications of the maneuver for German strategy against Poland as he was in a single tactical point, however:

> Germany is forbidden under the treaty to have machine guns in cavalry units. An interesting feature of this maneuver was that this proviso of the Peace Treaty was gotten around by the attaching to each of the cavalry regiments of a machine gun company from another infantry regiment not participating in the maneuver. It has been previously noted that the Germans have two types of machine gun companies. In both types the weapons are carried on limbers and caissons, but, in one type these are drawn by two horses and in the other type by four horses with the entire personnel mounted. The machine gun companies attached to the cavalry regiment were of the latter type which leads to the supposition that this type of machine gun company is intended for operation with the cavalry and that when the restrictions of the peace treaty in this matter are removed, the cavalry regiments will each have a machine gun troop of this type.[44]

The investment of so much firepower in the cavalry units indicated that in 1928 the officers of the Reichswehr still held on to Seeckt's belief in the continued usefulness of horse soldiers. It was only in later maneuvers that mechanized and motorized forces came to play a larger role. Even then, the cavalry remained important; with three out of its ten divisions forced to remain mounted by Allied fiat, the army could follow no other policy. But in the years after Groener's entry into the Defense Ministry, mechanized auxiliary forces--trucks, armored cars, and tanks--supported the cavalry and increased its effectiveness.

We are fortunate to have detailed reports of the major maneuvers of the Groener period. These reports lend support to a characterization of the Groener era as a time in which the German army began its process of modernization. While the basic tenet of German military strategy remained the encirclement of advancing enemy forces, it is evident that the army command intended in the future to achieve such encirclements with a mixture of mechanized forces and cavalry.

The first major eastern maneuver of the Groener period was the exercise of the 1st Infantry Division in East Prussia which took place from 3 September to 8 September 1928. Like the 1925 maneuvers, the situations were demanding and complex, and showed the superiority of the Reichswehr compared to the Polish army. Again, as in 1925, the most noticeable characteristic of the 1928 maneuvers was their stress on envelopment and encirclement of the enemy forces. In contrast to the Polish maneuvers, which throughout this period were mainly rehearsals for frontal assaults, the Germans strove constantly to drive in the flank of the enemy army.

The maneuvers took place in the Masurian Lakes country, south of Goldap. The American military attache, Edward Carpenter, described the terrain in the following manner:

> From the military standpoint, the maneuver terain, which is undulating, dune-like, largely wooded but lacking considerable elevations, offers many diffi-culties in the conduct of combat and particularly makes the artilleryman's task far from easy, especially when it comes to the selection of obser-vation posts. On the field and communicating roads, it is often not easy for vehicles to get forward. The quartering of the troops in distant quarters is a problem and requires careful consideration by the Maneuver Direction in the arrangement of the exer-cises. The fact that the crops had, for the most part, not yet been harvested at times forced the troops to forego deployment and development, as they would have done under actual war conditions.

The terrain turned out to be the dominating factor in the exercise, since the situation emphasized tactical rather than strategic movements. The 1925 maneuvers had an enemy corps marching into East Prussia, and the exercise was intended to instruct German officers in the movement of large bodies of troops. In the 1928 maneuver, however,

> It was not the purpose of these maneuvers to train the higher and middle commanders in the solution of large operative and tactical problems. Their scope was too small for that. But they brought for the lower commanders and the troop leaders a wealth of decisions such as only warfare of movement can offer in such variety. This variety, combined with the difficulty of "commanding into the uncertain," to use a German expression, makes great demands upon commanders and troops, and was demonstrated repeatedly in the maneuvers.[45]

The maneuver of 3-4 September took place between Widminnen and Marggrabowa. The object of the maneuver was a meeting engagement, the breaking off of the combat, and the transition to a delaying action. The initial situation had Blue's 2nd Army, with its front facing northeast, engaged in an inconclusive battle with a Red force, just to the northwest of Lyck. Blue's north wing (II Army Corps) stood on the southern shore of Lake Uleffke. The defile at Alt-Jucha was protected by Blue's reserve forces.[46] The Red 1st Army, with its front toward the southwest, was engaged in severe defensive battles. Red's right wing (I Army Corps) was on the southwestern point of Lake Laszmiaden. Blue sought to achieve a decision with its new forces (I Army Corps, including the 1st and 2nd Infantry Divisions) advancing from Nikolaiken. The plan called for these divisions to cross between the lakes on Red's right flank and to swoop down on Red's rear. Red's principal unit in the area was the 1st Cavalry Regiment, located behind Lake Haaszner near Grunheyde on the Marggrabowa-Angerburg railway. Red's reinforcements were arriving from Goldap. By 2 September, elements of the reinforcing Red 1st Division had reached Marggrabowa.[47]

On the evening of 2 September, upon the receipt of news that the enemy would soon be reinforced, both Blue and Red decided not to await the completion of their own concentrations, but to attack with the forces at hand. By that evening, two-thirds of Blue's 1st Infantry Division had concentrated west of Widminnen. Together with the attached 2nd Cavalry Regiment, this unit received orders to advance on 3 September via Pietraschen toward the Haaszner River. The units of the Red 1st Division, which had arrived in the evening of 2 September together with the Red 1st Cavalry Regiment, received orders to prevent the advance of the Blue force through the defile between Lakes Gablick and Sonntag. The combat situation of the maneuver thus took place well to the northwest of the main forces which were engaged at Lyck. The struggle around Widminnen and Pietraschen was of decisive importance, since the victor would be able to march on the open flank and rear of the hostile main body.

Red's cavalry force reached the defile before Blue's units could pass through it. The Red horsemen deployed on a broad, thin front between the lakes. Blue's attacking force consisted of the 2nd Cavalry Regiment, followed by two infantry columns deployed side by side. These units were supplemented by an artillery battery, an armored car platoon, and a machine-gun company. Aided by these forces, Blue gradually pressed the Reds back toward the east. At noon, the Blue 3rd Infantry Regiment almost succeeded in pushing through to Pietraschen; by this time, the one remaining squadron of the Red 1st Cavalry Regiment still offering resistance had been almost destroyed. The arrival of elements of Red's 1st Infantry Division stabilized the situation somewhat. A detachment of Blue cavalry, meanwhile, had carried out a skillful flank march to the north of Lake Gablick. It had broken through the meager Red forces in the area and threatened Red's right flank around Kowalewsken.

At 1300 hours on 3 September, there was a break in the exercise so that the troops could eat their dinner. It was assumed that the Blue forces had succeeded in forcing the Reds back to the Haaszner River in the Grunheyde-Wessolowen sector. According to the new orders, Blue was to keep its attack moving and achieve a decisive result over Red. Red, for its part, was ordered to retreat to the northeast and make a stand on the line Mesuhren-Griesen, to the southeast of Lake Haaszner.

When the battle reopened later that afternoon, Blue discovered that Red had left only patrols to watch over the Haaszner crossings and had destroyed all the bridges. Blue's soldiers had to build temporary foot bridges to facilitate their crossing of the Haaszner. In addition, Blue possessed a number of small collapsible boats, the forerunners of the Sturmboote on which the Wehrmacht crossed the Meuse in 1940. The crossing was made under cover of darkness on a wide front with relatively weak forces. Immediately after crossing, the pioneer troops accompanying Blue began to construct two all-purpose bridges, one of which used the collapsible boats as supports. Blue's forces formed up on the east bank of the Haaszner, with the artillery finally making the crossing at 0430 hours on 4 September. By 0800 hours, the Blue force had launched its attack on a broad front toward Mesuhren to the north, against Red's right flank. The attack was preceded by a concentrated artillery barrage and made good headway. As

Blue's line now faced to the north, however, remnants of Red's 1st Cavalry Regiment at Chelchen seized the opportunity to march on Blue's unprotected flank and rear. Thus matters stood at the close of the exercise.

The maneuver of 3-4 September was a good example of the German army's devotion to the tactics of envelopment. Indeed, the entire two-day battle was a series of attempts by one side to flank the other. The battle around Pietraschen and the lake defile might at first appear as a frontal assault, but the fact that the battle occurred at all was a result of Blue's attempt to attack the flank of Red's main body near Lyck. During the attack on Pietraschen, Blue's cavalry marched around Lake Gablick and attacked Red's right flank. Finally, the assault by what was left of Red's 1st Cavalry Regiment against Blue's right flank after Blue had swung its axis of attack to the north, although it lacked force due to Red's weakened condition, was a classic flanking maneuver. The German troops carried out all of these difficult maneuvers with great skill. Colonel Carpenter wrote:

> The exercise of September 3-4 offered situations that were instructive in the cooperation of infantry with attached cavalry and that were by no means easy for the commanders concerned. This was especially true on the first day. The problem required putting in the infantry at the place where the cavalry was already fighting and then successfully withdrawing the latter for further employment elsewhere. This requires timely establishment of contact by the commander of the detachment with the commander of its cavalry, which is already forward and engaged in combat.[48]

After a one-day rest, during which time the German hosts took their foreign guests on a tour of the nearby battlefield of Tannenberg--the German army's most perfect encirclement battle--the maneuvers began again with an exercise consisting of a Red withdrawal under cavalry cover. After the Blue force had pursued the Reds, the situation was reversed. During the last two days of the maneuver, Blue would retreat and Red would attack and pursue.

The area of the maneuver of 6-8 September was north of the terrain employed in the first exercise. The main area of operations was the terrain between Marggrabowa and Goldap. The problem consisted of an engagement on the first day, pursuit of a retreating enemy on the second day, and an attack against an enemy occupying a defensive position behind the river Goldap.

The initial situation had the right wing of a Red army advancing in a northwesterly direction. This detachment included two-thirds of the Red 1st Infantry Division, and on 5 September it had pushed Blue forces back to the line Griesen-Salleschen, along the Angerburg-Marggrabowa highway. The Red division's 3rd Infantry Regiment reached Olschöwen, while the 1st Red Cavalry Brigade reached Marggrabowa. Blue reinforcements, including the 1st Infantry Brigade, were concentrated at Rogahlen, to the southwest of Goldap. The mission of Blue's 1st Brigade was to advance to the south in a night march through Gollubien, to the east of the line Goldap-Marggrabowa. Its purpose was to aid the main Blue body locked

in combat at Griesen.   Blue's marching orders detailed   the
following forces:[49]

> In the lead was the 1st Reconnaissance Detachment
> (3rd Squadron,   1st Cavalry Regiment) with the
> Machine Gun Platoon (3rd Battalion, 2nd Infantry
> Regiment); 1/2 of the 6th Battery, 1st Artillery
> Regiment; 1 light horse-drawn radio squad (2nd
> Company, 1st Signal Detachment); and an Armored Car
> Platoon.
>   The Advance Guard consisted of the 2nd Bat-
> talion, 1st Infantry Regiment; a Platoon of light
> trench mortars (1st Infantry Regiment); elements of
> the 3rd Squadron, 1st Cavalry Regiment; the 1st
> Battery,   1st Artillery Regiment;   and the 2nd
> Company, 1st Signal Detachment.
>   The Main Body consisted of elements from the
> 3rd Squadron, 1st Cavalry Regiment; 1 Company (3rd
> Battalion, 1st Infantry Regiment); the Staff of the
> 1st Reserve Brigade; the 3rd Battalion, 1st Infantry
> Regiment; a Trench Mortar Company from the 1st
> Infantry Regiment; an Infantry Gun Company (1st
> Infantry Regiment); the 3rd Battalion, 2nd Infantry
> Regiment; the 2nd Battalion, 1st Artillery Regiment;
> the 1st Battalion, 1st Artillery Battery; the 1st
> Battalion, 2nd Infantry Regiment; the 2nd Battalion,
> 2nd Infantry Regiment; a Trench Mortar Company and
> Infantry Gun Company (2nd Infantry Regiment); the
> 2nd Company, 1st Pioneer Battalion; Motorized Units
> (2nd Company, 1st Signal Detachment); and a Smoke
> Platoon.

This was surely the most modern force yet to appear in a
German military exercise.   Of particular interest was the
armored car-cavalry combination in the lead, supported by the
firepower of machine guns and artillery.   The presence of a
radio squad complemented this detachment's firepower by giving
it the ability to move independently.
     Red's 1st Division and 1st Cavalry Brigade, meanwhile,
received orders to continue the attack in the direction of
Wensöwen and Grabowen.   At the same time, a Red armored car
platoon went ahead of the main force to determine Blue's
strength along the Czychen-Sokolken-Kowahlen road.   The purpose of Red's maneuver was to prevent the Blue enemy
reportedly concentrating around Rogahlen from intervening to
the south.
     The morning of 6 September found both forces advancing
upon the same objectives, Wensöwen, Barannen, and Kowahlen.
The battles were therefore small meeting engagements, in which
the decision went to whomever reinforced first.   The stakes
were high, however.   If Blue were successful in its march on
Barannen, it could tip the scales decisively in the battle of
the main bodies at Griesen and Salleschen.   Likewise, Red
success in its drive on Kowahlen would place it behind and to
the left of Blue's main body.   Once more, as so often in the
German maneuvers, the exercise became a struggle for the
enemy's flank.   Perhaps most interestingly, the march of
Blue's 1st Brigade toward Barannen had placed the town of
Marggrabowa on its left flank.   The Red cavalry gathering in
Marggrabowa would therefore have a target of opportunity,

should the cavalry commander seize the moment. In order to protect itself from this threat, the Blue 1st Brigade detailed two "defense groups" from the 1st Reconnaissance Detachment to its flank.

The American attache was extremely interested in the problems of flank security posed by the exercises. With reference to the Blue march on Barannen, he wrote:

> On the Blue side the detached defensive may be said to have accomplished their mission, but, on the other hand, the Blues have had to keep one battalion available against the Red cavalry in addition to those two reinforced companies. One and a half out of a total of five battalions, a very considerable part, were thus tied up by the cavalry, an illustration of how troublesome is its mere appearance on the flank.[50]

After several inconclusive attacks by both sides, the maneuver was interrupted for lunch. When the battle resumed, the Red force had received reinforcements to boost its strength to five infantry battalions; the Blues, meanwhile, were reduced to one infantry regiment (the 2nd) and one cavalry regiment (the 1st). Blue's forces were now much inferior, and their new orders called for a disengagement, delaying action, and retreat to the north, behind the Goldap River on both sides of Jukneitschen. By 7 September, the Blue force had accomplished its mission. The disengagement had been accomplished by detailing a smoke company to Kleine Blandau and deceiving the Red force into believing that Blue's troops were retreating to the West.[51] Once over the Goldap, Blue's cavalry secured all the crossings between Morathen and Gross Jahnen, while the engineers began work on building entrenchments along the west bank of the river.

On 8 September, Red's forces received orders to cross the Goldap at Morathen. To aid in this crossing, Red received the 1st Battalion of the 1st Heavy Artillery Regiment. Actually, the Goldap itself was no real obstacle. Stretches of the river south of Morathen were shallow enough to be forded. Still, Blue held the high ground near the town of Audinischen and had strengthened its defense line across the Goldap. Red led off the attack with a thirty-minute barrage of supporting fire, and began the river crossing at 0730 hours, 8 September. Once again, as in the crossing on 6 September, Red's forces used inflatable assault boats, which, an observer noted, "offered the enemy an excellent target." Once across the river, however, Red's superior forces were able to storm the Audinischker Hills and seize the dominant position in the area.

Although Colonel Carpenter was very impressed overall with the troops he observed, he criticized the river crossing:

> It is difficult to decide in a peacetime exercise whether the attack across the Goldap would have succeeded in real warfare. Surely it would have been more protracted. It appears to me that the attack formation that was decided upon, in which a grip was taken on the whole front with equally strong forces, was faulty. A concentration at a point, decided upon after reconnaissance as best

suited for this purpose, in connection with feints at other points and omission of certain sectors of the front, would perhaps have given a better prospect of success.[52]

Carpenter was correct in his opinion. Greater concentration of firepower at a strategically decisive point would surely have won the Goldap at a lesser price, had the bullets been real.

The East Prussian maneuvers of 1928 demonstrated conclusively that, in terms of organization, armament, training, and leadership, the Reichswehr remained far ahead of its Polish counterpart. In comparison to the poor performance of Polish formations during contemporary maneuvers--a poor performance attested to by both the Poles and their foreign guests alike--the Reichswehr showed in 1928 that it could still lay claim to the title of the finest army in the world. Carpenter was especially impressed with the foot soldiers, and he described his opinion of them in the following manner:

> In the East Prussian maneuvers great exertions were consciously demanded of commanders and troops by the Direction. Both showed themselves equal to the hardships brought about by the combat action running day and night and by the high daily march requirements. Those who saw the attack of the East Prussian regiments against the Audinischker hills on the last day of the maneuver and subsequently reviewed the march formations of the homeward bound units could not tell from their appearance that they had been three days and two nights on their feet.

In many ways, this one-week exercise in East Prussia demonstrated the degree to which the Reichswehr was modernizing. In appearance, for instance, the infantry appeared in their new coats with the open, turned-down collars. In addition, the troops wore for the first time their new brimmed field caps, which, according to the American attache, "resembled the old Austrian field cap." In appearance, at least, 1928 was the year in which the army ceased resembling the old imperial army and started looking like the post-1935 Wehrmacht. The cavalry showed that it, too, had entered the modern era. Once more, Carpenter's description is valuable: "For the first time the cavalry appeared without any lances. I am informed that they have been definitely and permanently placed in the discard." In addition, the use of armored cars to aid the cavalry increased the pace of battle greatly: "These were employed in groups of three, with the cavalry and in independent raids. Tactically they were operated at high speed, were kept moving and proceeded one behind the other at distances of 200 yards."

In fact, Carpenter noted that the high mobility of the German forces was in danger of rendering its armaments obsolete:

> The heavy machine guns lacked mobility for the task frequently assigned them, namely, support of the infantry in the most advanced echelons. It was stated by a senior infantry commander that the employment of the heavy machine guns was not, in his

opinion, up to the standard reached at the close of the war. He stated that it was in danger of being put out of business by the mobile and active light trench mortar of the enemy. The German heavy machine gun is heavier and clumsier than most. The light trench mortar to which my informant referred was probably a mortar similar to the light and mobile weapon upon which the Germans have done much development work and which I understand is ready to be put into quantity production to replace their present mortar whenever necessity requires or opportunity permits.

Of course, students of the Second World War will recognize the reference here to the 81mm mortar, with which German expertise became almost legendary.

In fact, Carpenter's only complaint about the Reichswehr reflected as much upon the American army as upon the German:

One night the bivouac method of resting during the night was practiced for all units. It was evident that the troops were inexperienced in it. It took them a very long time to pitch their shelter tents, which are made up of individual sections into large tents to hold a half company or even a company. They were clumsy in getting their fires going and food prepared and cooked. In fact, they were amateurs at this business as compared to American troops. Their camps were quite disorderly and looked very uncomfortable.[53]

Whatever its level of expertise in bivouacking, the Reichswehr left little doubt during the maneuvers of its ability to fight.

Apart from its consistent striving for quality, we know today that by 1930 the Reichswehr had a plan to expand itself to 21 infantry divisions in case of a war. The purpose of this plan was to put the army on a wartime footing, in case the government decided that an enemy invasion was imminent. The germ of this expansion plan was Seeckt's recommendation, in January 1921, to treble the number of infantry divisions from 7 to 21 in the event of an emergency. The new plans of expanding the army received the title of "Aufstellungsplan," or A-Plan. German planners wished to avoid the term "Mobil- machung," which might alarm the Allies.[54] Still, the A-Plan called for a peacetime mobilization of sorts. The purpose was to amass enough trained reserves, ammunition, and strategic materials to be able to field, by March 1933, 16 fully equipped divisions, 5 skeletal divisions, and 3 1/2 cavalry divisions. According to the chief of the Army Command, it was a matter of producing "some 350,000 rifles, 12,000 light and heavy machine guns, 400 trench mortars, and 600 light and 75 heavy guns." The A-Plan went into effect on 1 April 1930, and it has been estimated that by 1933, Germany possessed some 65 percent of the stocks required for an army of 21 infantry divisions.[55]

These preparatory measures for mobilization indicated the great economic advantage which Germany held over its eastern neighbor. During most of the interwar period, Poland had to conduct its military policy under severe financial

constraints.   Lack of money forced a reduction in the size of
the Polish army, from 500,000 men in the years immediately
following the war with Soviet Russia to about 270,000 men in
1933.   Often, the Poles had to release soldiers from the last
six months of their two year-term of service in order to save
money.   Lack of funding made the Polish army conduct its
maneuvers under less than ideal conditions when they were
conducted at all.   Finally, an underdeveloped industrial base
made it more difficult for the Polish army to procure the
modern weaponry it required.   During the same period, the
small size of the Reichswehr was a blessing for Germany in
financial terms.   Rather than reducing its size, as in Poland,
the army's leaders were by 1930 planning to expand it to
roughly the size of the Polish army.   Germany's highly
developed industries worked closely with the army throughout
the 1920s and early 1930s.   Although the army sometimes had
problems procuring funds for maneuvers from the Reichstag, the
exercises were, as we have seen, much more complex and larger
than those of the Polish army.   Quite simply, Germany was more
able, in even the worst of economic times, to field, train,
and equip an army of 100,000 men than Poland was able to
support an army three times as large.   In 1930,   the Polish
General Staff analyzed the German military budget, and came to
the conclusion that Germany had the most expensive army in the
world on a cost-per-man basis.[56]
    The Reichswehr showed that this money was well spent
during the fall maneuvers of 1930.   These were the largest
maneuvers held since the war, and every division in the army
participated to some extent.   Among the German officials
present were Groener, Schleicher, Heye, and the aged President
Paul von Hindenburg.   Every foreign military attache in
Germany received an invitation, with the exception of the
Polish, French, and Belgian.   The scene of the exercise was
Franconia, and the situation called for a superior Red
(French) force to invade from the Rhine frontier, push back
the Blue (German) armies, and advance into central Germany.
We need not concern ourselves with the details of this maneu-
ver, since it occurred in the west, but the reactions of those
present illustrated once more the modernization and high
quality of the German army.   In an article in the Berlin
newspaper Tempo, one observer wrote:

> The great Hindenburg maneuvers of this year are
> ended.   The last night and today have, as the
> preceding days, again been marked by unusual demands
> both on the leaders and the men.   This continuous
> burdening of the units with great physical exertions
> caused by the alternating fights in attack and
> defense, and the long marches by day and by night,
> has been a test of the human material of all grades
> in our Reichswehr, both in a physical and spiritual
> respect.   They were sometimes far greater than those
> to which the troops were put in the prewar times and
> are hardly required as matter of fact in any other
> European army.
>   The last day of the maneuvers in Upper
> Franconia has offered a further opportunity to ob-
> serve the combat training of the units.   The self-
> reliance and confidence with which almost every
> soldier advanced during the course of an attack or

stood in a defensive combat, his knowledge of his
task, and the manner in which he carried it out,
astonished even those who from their knowledge of
the German army are accustomed to regard the extraordinary performances as something self-evident. To
the many foreign officers who attended the maneuvers
it must have been a surprise to discover that these
troops may be tackled only by a really superior
enemy.

Once more, the modernization of the cavalry was evident
to all present. Hindenburg remarked after the maneuver that

> while the role of the cavalry had changed, its
> importance as an arm had not lessened. While it had
> been hard for some cavalrymen to reconcile them-
> selves to giving up the lance as a weapon and there-
> by accept a change in cavalry fighting tactics, he
> felt that by developing new tactics the cavalry
> could make itself a more useful arm than it had ever
> been before.

Tempo's journalist agreed on the continued importance of
cavalry, but was also a bit bewildered by the onrush of
modernity:

> In the cavalry one sees a change of the times.
> After the fancy uniform the lances also disappeared
> a few years ago. There exists no parade formation
> proper in the modern cavalry. But a parade is
> nowadays one of the few occasions where one can
> really ride. In lieu of the line of lances of the
> former times straight as a chalk line, one now sees
> a pace of riding past the reviewing stand which
> takes the breath away. In about twenty minutes, six
> cavalry regiments and two horse artillery battalions
> have dashed past, and the parade is over.[57]

The assistant American military attache, Major P. W.
Evans, was also present at the 1930 maneuvers, and was
likewise impressed with the modern nature of the army, despite
its deficiencies in tanks and aircraft:

> The transportation of the 5th Division was quite
> modern and up to date. The standard truck of the
> division was not unlike our Liberty truck, and is
> rated at 3 1/2 tons. The staff cars were of recent
> models and high speed. Those that I saw were mostly
> Horch and Mercedes-Benz. The motorcycle detachment
> at division headquarters was made up of 18 men with
> solo machines. These men were well-selected and
> highly trained. They were thoroughly familiar with
> the officers and organization of the division. They
> could read maps and act intelligently under almost
> any circumstances.
>   Although there were no air corps forces con-
> nected with this maneuver, all officers and men
> behaved exactly as though they were operating under
> wartime conditions in which the enemy aerial obser-
> vation was very alert. Great pains were taken by

everyone to keep motor transport under cover from
aerial observation. I did not see any driver leave
his car or motorcycle in an exposed place any longer
than was necessary to load or unload passengers.
Camouflage nets were spread over the artillery
pieces when they were in the open, and in many
instances I have seen enlisted men pulling brush and
grass over their vehicles, without instructions,
with a view to concealing them.

In accordance with the Versailles treaty, the
Germans are not allowed any tanks. They had a full
quota of dummy tanks with the 5th Division. These
tanks were made by constructing tin covers over
light automobiles. In the distance, they looked
very much like tanks.[58]

The last maneuvers held under the Weimar Republic, which
took place from 19 to 22 September 1932, showed a deepening
interest in mechanization. The exercises took place in the
vicinity of Frankfurt on the Oder. For the first time, these
maneuvers dealt with a large-scale Polish offensive against
Germany's highly vulnerable Oder front. The timing of this
maneuver was political; it occurred on the eve of the League
of Nations disarmament talks, at which Germany hoped to regain
the right to equality of armaments. Hence, it was to
Germany's interest to portray Berlin's vulnerability to a
lightning strike by Polish cavalry. Yet, to label this
maneuver a "propaganda exercise," as one historian has done,
is an oversimplification.[59] Whatever its political implications, the 1932 maneuver's primary purpose was military: to
train both the Red and Blue forces in the techniques of mobile
attack and defense. There was much hard fighting. Claims
that the Red (Polish) cavalry was allowed to cross the Oder
too easily for propaganda purposes run contrary to the actual
facts of the maneuver.

As in 1930, the 1932 exercises took place in front of a
great number of German and foreign military observers,
including Commander Mikhail Tukhachevsky of the Red Army.
Again, the French, Polish, and Belgian military attaches were
excluded. The exercise consisted of a rapid passage by Red
cavalry through the Blue (German) lines, covered by a seizure
of an Oder bridgehead by a motorized reconnaissance detachment. No attempt was made to copy Polish cavalry organization. According to the American military attache, Lieutenant
Colonel Jacob Wuest, the maneuver analyzed two basic problems:

1.   The employment of experimental organizations of
the infantry and cavalry divisions which were being
tried out for the first time in large operations,
and in which the main point of departure was the use
of a highly mobile reconnaissance battalion which
formed an integral part of the divisions.
2.   The technique used in crossing large bodies of
troops over a wide and rapidly flowing stream.[60]

The troops involved were the 3rd Infantry Division for Blue
and the 1st and 2nd Cavalry Divisions for Red. The commanding
officers were some of the most talented officers serving in
the east: Lieutenant General Gerd von Rundstedt for Blue;
Lieutenant General Fedor von Bock for Red; Major General

Werner   von Fritsch for Red's 1st Cavalry Division;   and Major
General Erwin von Kleist for Red's 2nd Cavalry Division.
      The "mobile reconnaissance battalion" of which Wuest
wrote, and the testing of which was a key factor in the maneuver, consisted of the following units:[61] one battalion headquarters; one signal platoon (mounted);   one armored car
platoon (four cars); one antitank platoon (two 37mm guns); one
bicycle company (three platoons); one machine gun troop (four
heavy machine guns);   and one cavalry troop.   Because of the
treaty restrictions, the antitank platoon contained no actual
guns,   but rather wooden dummies mounted on actual gun
carriages.
      The organization of the Red cavalry corps is particularly
interesting.   The corps combined horse and motorized units,
the combination of which Seeckt had spoken in the early 1920s,
and which had been tried on a small scale in the 1928 maneuvers (see table 4.2).   Now, however, the Reichswehr was
experimenting with a highly mobile corps-sized formation.[62]
This motorized cavalry corps, despite its largely theoretical
nature, was far ahead of the Poles in terms of the employment
of cavalry, despite the traditional Polish interest in this
arm.   The organization of the corps showed the intention of
the Germans to mix horse and motorized units.
      The situation investigated in the maneuver of 1932 was
the following.   Early in September 1932, the Blue territory
(Germany) was invaded by strong Red (Polish) forces along its
eastern frontier.   By the middle of September, there were two
main battle fronts: one in Pomerania and one in Silesia.
These two fronts were separated by the Oder-Warthe salient.
In Silesia, the Red forces succeeded in forcing passage of the
Oder.   The Blues were in retreat toward Liegnitz and Sprottau.
The Silesian Blue army's north wing was located at Naumburg on
the Bober River.   In Pomerania, Blue's forces were drawn up in
a defensive position along the line Friedberg-Arnswalde-Labes,
facing the superior Red 1st Army.   The Oder-Warthe salient was
so far free of troops, although small units of frontier
customs guards were stationed on the border.[63]
      The situation for Blue was that the 3rd Infantry Divi-
sion, acting as the army reserve of the Blue 1st Army, was
advancing from Angermünde, to the north of the Oder-Havel
canal, at the rate of forty kilometers a day.   By 18
September, it had reached Neudamm, to the north of the Warthe
River.   The division's command post was at Küstrin.   At the
same time, the Blue 2nd Division was on the move by rail; by
18 September, elements of the division had been deployed along
the Küstrin-Vietz road.   The 2nd Division's Reconnaissance
Battalion was also located at Vietz.   Blue's Oder bridges at
Frankfurt and Fürstenberg were protected by small detachments,
and were also prepared for demolition.   The Oder bridges at
Tschicherzig and Crossen had been destroyed.
      The situation for Red was that the Red 2nd Army
(headquarters, Poznan), which consisted of the I Cavalry Corps
and I Army Corps, was advancing in the direction of the Blue
frontier.   By 18 September, two-thirds of the 1st and 2nd Red
Infantry Divisions had reached the border between Birnbaum and
Bentschen, while the 3rd Infantry Division was to the rear at
Pinne.   The motorized units of the I Cavalry Corps had, after
a one-day march of forty-five kilometers, reached the area
Bentschen-Köbnitz, on the border.   The rest of the cavalry
corps formed up to the rear.   Red possessed powerful air

Table 4.2
Red 1st Cavalry Corps, 1932

Cavalry Corps Headquarters
        1 signal troop (motorized)
        1 motorcycle section (messengers)
        1 observation squadron (6 planes, represented by flags)

Antiaircraft Artillery Battalion (motorized)
        1 battalion headquarters
        1 signal platoon
        3 batteries 77mm guns (12 guns)
        1 battery 37mm guns (16 guns)
        1 searchlight company
        1 battalion ammunition train

Heavy artillery battalion (motorized)
        1 battalion headquarters
        1 signal platoon
        2 batteries 105mm light howitzers (8 guns)
        1 battery 105mm guns (4 guns)

1st Cavalry Division

    Division headquarters
            1 motorcycle section (messengers)
            1 engineer company (motorized)
            1 signal company (partially motorized)
            1 antitank company (motorized)

    1 reconnaissnace battalion (motorized)
            1 battalion headquarters
            1 signal platoon
            1 armored car company (unarmed), 3 platoons of 4
              cars each
            1 armored car company (armed), 3 platoons of 4 cars
              each, each car armed with one or more small guns
              (30 to 50mm)
            2 motorcycle rifle companies

    4 cavalry regiments, each consisting of
            1 regimental headquarters
            1 regimental signal platoon
            1 platoon 37mm antitank guns
            1 trench mortar platoon
            1 machine-gun troop (heavy machine guns)
            1 regimental ammunition column (motorized)
            4 cavalry troops

    1 horse artillery battalion
            1 battalion headquarters
            1 signal platoon
            3 batteries 77mm guns
            1 battery 105mm howitzers
            1 battalion ammunition train (motorized)

1st Cavalry Division, continued

    1 bicycle battalion
        1 bicycle battalion headquarters
        1 signal platoon
        1 antitank platoon
        1 trench mortar platoon (2 mortars)
        1 machine gun company
        3 bicycle companies, with same arms as the rifle
        company

2nd Cavalry Division

    Division headquarters
        1 motorcycle section (messengers)
        1 signal troop (partially motorized)
        1 engineer company (motorized)
        1 antitank company (motorized)

    1 reconnaissance battalion
        1 battalion headquarters
        1 signal platoon
        2 armored car companies (armed), 12 cars each
        1 motorcycle rifle company

    2 cavalry brigades, each consisting of
        1 brigade headquarters
        1 signal platoon
        2 cavalry regiments, each organized the same as the
            regiments of the 1st Cavalry Division

    1 horse artillery battalion, organized the same as the
            artillery of the 1st Cavalry Division

    1 motorcycle battalion
        1 battalion headquarters
        1 signal platoon
        3 motorcycle companies (there was no machine gun
          company in this battalion as each motorcycle
          company was equipped with 3 heavy machine guns
          and 9 light machine guns).

forces; its bombers had successfully bombed the Oder bridges at Küstrin.

At the opening of the maneuver, the Blue Pomeranian army detected the Polish buildup west of Poznan. The Blue 2nd Division, recently arrived at Küstrin, received orders to set out for Schwerin on the Warthe; Blue's 3rd Division was ordered from Küstrin through Reppen to Sternberg. The purpose of these maneuvers was to halt the threatened Red march on Frankfurt. Meanwhile, however, Red's 2nd Army had crossed the border early on 19 September and directed its infantry toward Schwerin and Meseritz. The cavalry corps crossed the German border on the left of the infantry, near Bentschen. Red's plan was to seize the Oder on both sides at Frankfurt and then turn to deal with either the Blue Pomeranian or Silesian armies.

The 19th of September was used by both sides for reconnaissance and maneuver. Blue's 2nd Reconnaissance Battalion moved from Vietz to Lagow; the 3rd Reconnaissance Battalion moved toward Sternberg, while the motorized engineer unit attached to it constructed roadblocks to motor vehicles beyond Reppen. Red's cavalry corps received orders to advance and cross the Oder as far as Seelow-Müllrose-Guben. During the day, there were small clashes between the opposing reconnaissance forces. In the course of these, Red's 2nd Motorized Reconnaissance Battalion, with the help of a motorcycle rifle battalion, crossed the Oder south of Fürstenberg. Blue's river guard then destroyed the Fürstenberg bridge. On the north wing of the Red cavalry corps, the 3rd Cavalry Regiment almost completely destroyed the Blue 2nd Reconnaissance Battalion at Lagow.

"What worries the leaders must have had in the evening," commented General Kurt von Hammerstein, the chief of the army High Command. This was especially true for the Blue commanders. Blue was in danger of being bypassed and flanked by the swift Red advance. Still, Blue commander Rundstedt decided on a general advance toward Sternberg to take the pressure off of Blue's Pomeranian army. Red's cavalry commander, General Bock, had learned of Rundstedt's plans when his forces captured a copy of Blue's divisional order; he therefore decided to defeat the new enemy in the Oder-Warthe bend before attempting to cross the Oder. By now, Red's high command had decided to turn on the Blue Pomeranian army first; consequently, it ordered Bock to seize Küstrin and advance into Pomerania from the south.

Early on 20 September, Blue's forces received orders to halt their advance on Sternberg due to Red's overwhelming strength and the danger of encirclement. Instead, Blue's 2nd and 3rd Divisions were to take up a defensive position in front of Küstrin. Meanwhile, the Red cavalry had begun to advance through Sternberg to Reppen. Its orders were not to attack Küstrin directly, but to cross the Oder south of Frankfurt, roll up the Blue river defense, and seize Küstrin from the rear. The Blue forces intended to make their principal stand on the Oder-Neisse line; two new divisions had been ordered to the Fürstenberg area, but these would not arrive until 22 September. Luckily for Blue, Red's forces were now mired in confusion as the complexities of making a major river crossing became apparent. General Hammerstein commented:

During the preparation and the carrying out of the
crossing of the Oder by the Red Cavalry such intense
confusion had arisen in issuing the orders, in their
transmission, and in the bringing up of the troops,
that not only the crossing of the river was delayed
by many hours, but in addition large numbers of the
troops were unduly moved about and subjected to
fatigue.   I must with all emphasis declare that the
crossing did not reach the expectations which I had,
after the many exercises in river crossing practiced
during the past summer.[64]

Due to these problems, Red's two cavalry divisions did
not cross the Oder until noon of 21 September. The crossing,
which took place at Fürstenberg, went unopposed, since Blue's
infantry was drawn up in a semicircle south and east of
Küstrin.   In response to Red's appearance on the west bank of
the Oder, Blue ordered two regiments of infantry south to
Bresen, where they were to seize the high ground.   Once the
Blue commander had learned of Red's strength, however--by now
two whole divisions of cavalry--he ordered these regiments
back to their starting line in the woods south of Frankfurt.
At this time, Red, which had underestimated the trouble of
crossing the Oder-Spree Canal, paused in its advance on
Küstrin.   It was apparent that Blue's reserve forces were
approaching from the direction of Berlin, and now it was Red
which saw its flanks threatened.   This was the general situation when the maneuver ended.   Red had successfully crossed
the Oder, but had failed to defeat Blue's forces decisively.
In the view of Hammerstein, the maneuver had studied
several basic problems: the initiation and carrying out of
motorized reconnaissance;   the combination of motor and horse;
the knowledge of the capabilities of motors; and the knowledge
of their limitations.   He viewed the maneuver as a test of the
Reichswehr's expertise in motorized warfare, and he was
basically, though not unreservedly, happy with the results:
"The dash of the newly formed motorized units, even though the
tactical conception was sometimes wrong, is deserving of
commendation."
The American military attache, Colonel Jacob Wuest, was
highly impressed with what he had seen in 1932.   His report
left little doubt that the emphasis placed on mobility and
physical toughness had a good effect on the Reichswehr. "The
length of the marches," he wrote, "was dictated only by the
requirements of their missions." The cavalry was particularly
impressive in this regard; some units covered three hundred
kilometers in just three days.   All the troops stood the test
well:

They appeared in good physical condition.   Upon the
conclusion of the maneuvers there were no unusual
signs of fatigue either among the officers or men.
This is due to two main reasons: the German soldier
is young, carefully selected and still in the prime
of his life when his service is completed; the
present maneuvers were the culmination of the summer
season of progressive field exercises and the troops
were at the top notch of their training.

Behind this physical toughness, Wuest saw the hand of a wise and humane training, based on discipline, but tempered by respect for the individual:

> The general impression one receives of the present German Army is that it is an army of young men. It is a well disciplined army, probably as well so as before the war, although the means of securing discipline in the present army have undergone a change. There are no longer stories of brow-beaten recruits and rough handling in the squad rooms. The volunteer soldier is a thinking individual with a sense of freedom of action arising from good team training. His responses are those that come from intelligent leadership based upon a proper inculcation of individual responsibility of the members of the team. He is no longer machine made, but is a hand-worked product of carefully selected stock.

Wuest was just as impressed by the quality of officers in the Reichswehr, particularly in comparison to the officers of the American army:

> The officer is serious minded and keen; as a rule he is quiet, with a natural sense of dignity, the maintenance of which he is careful to preserve, and is at pains at all times to maintain the prestige of his class. All whom I have come in contact with were well informed on their work which they regard as a duty highly ordained and therefore scrupulously to be performed. They keep themselves physically fit, probably not so much because they like it, but because present day Germany needs the best that is in them. Financial pressure enforces simple living upon them and the gaieties of social life no longer make demands upon their time. They have become a class of careful students of their professions which they follow with a seriousness not known in our Army.[65]

While Wuest preferred to stress the traditional qualities of the soldiers he had observed, the 1932 maneuver was most impressive for its modernity. Each unit which took part in this maneuver possessed motorized elements to some degree. The Blue infantry divisions contained motorized reconnaissance units; the Red cavalry force was motorized to an even greater degree, with motorcycles, trucks, and armored cars all present.[66] More importantly, the 1932 maneuver demonstrated that the Reichswehr was beginning to devise operational and tactical methods to employ these new, highly mobile forces. Red's initial plan on 19 September "to attack the Blue forces fighting on the Oder deep in the flank and rear" was the essence of what would come to be known as Blitzkrieg tactics.

During the period from 1926 to 1933, the German armed forces forged even further ahead of the Polish forces than in the years of Seeckt's leadership. The "new realism" of the leaders during this period enabled the German army to begin more serious planning for a conflict with Poland. For the first time, the army cooperated with the civilian government, especially the Foreign Office, in determining military policy.

The key event in army-government planning was the joint wargame of 1927.   This game convinced the government that it
needed to work with the army in developing border defense
formations for the eastern regions.   The army's new doctrine
of Landesschutz included all aspects of German society--
government, industry, the civilian population, and the armed
forces--in Germany's military posture.   With the active
cooperation of German industry, the army developed plans to
triple its size at the outbreak of hostilities.   As the Weimar
Republic headed toward collapse, the Reichswehr came once more
to resemble the army of a great power.
     Much of the credit for the success of the armed forces
goes to General Groener.   Groener saw the concept of national
defense in broader terms than Seeckt.   Under his leadership,
the navy again became an intrinsic part of Germany's armed
forces.   Although the navy remained small in size, Groener
upgraded its weaponry through the construction of the Panzerschiff.   Armed with this new vessel, the navy was able to plan
confidently for a war with Poland, which possessed an even
smaller and much more poorly equipped fleet.   The navy's plan
called for a lightning strike against Poland's only Baltic
port, Gdynia, featuring bombardment and the landing of demolition teams.   German naval superiority over Poland allowed the
navy to plan more aggressively than the army, which had to
adopt a more defensive attitude.   The naval wargame of 1930,
Study East, contained evidence of the navy's confident attitude toward Poland.
     Groener also improved the army's position with regard to
Poland.   He appointed the first German military attache to
Warsaw, which increased the amount of information available on
the Polish army.   His interest in technology and warfare meant
that the German army increased its experimentation with motorization to the point where an entire motorized cavalry corps
appeared in the 1932 maneuver.   Groener also dealt with the
dispersion of the German forces in the east.   His new deployments concentrated the eastern regiments and increased their
readiness for war.   While many of his policies represented a
break with the previous leadership, he also retained Seeckt's
policies in some areas.   Fortifications continued to play a
role in Germany's eastern defenses, with new bunkers appearing
along the Oder River.   Like Seeckt, however, Groener depended
upon the high mobility and tactical expertise of his army more
than on fixed fortifications.   The principal maneuvers of the
period, in 1928, 1930, and 1932, showed that the German army
still relied upon the strategy of counterattacking the flank
of any invading army.   The difficulty of the maneuvers and the
exertions which they demanded of the men indicated the high
level of training which each soldier received.   Indeed, the
Reichswehr was the most expensive professional army, man for
man, in the world.   The Polish army had demonstrated during
its maneuvers that it was in no way a modern army; the German
army demonstrated in its own exercises that it was the finest
army on the continent.   Although Seeckt deserves much credit
for the army's high quality, it was Groener who actually
oversaw the modernization of the Reichswehr. By 1933, all the
Germans needed to do to form a fully mechanized army was to
substitute tanks for horses.   This became possible only in
1935, after Hitler's abrogation of the Versailles disarmament
clauses.

NOTES

1.   Seeckt had to resign after it became known that he
had permitted the eldest son of the Hohenzollern crown prince
to participate in the exercises of the 9th Infantry Regiment,
which continued the tradition of the Prussian Foot Guards.
Gessler was forced to resign as a result of his being impli-
cated in a financial scandal involving secret subsidies to the
navy.   See F. L. Carsten, The Reichswehr and Politics, 1918-
1933 (Oxford: Clarendon Press, 1966), pp. 245-250.
2.   For a discussion of the "new realism" amongst German
officers, see Gaines Post, Jr., The Civil-Military Fabric of
Weimar Foreign Policy (Princeton, N.J.: Princeton University
Press, 1973), pp. 94-100.
3.   Chancellor Wilhelm Marx to the Prussian Minister
President, Berlin, 6 January 1927, Akten des auswärtigen Amtes
(Records of the German Foreign Office), hereafter AA, reel
4519, serial K951, frames K248 645-648.   In shorthand nota-
tion, AA/4519/K951/K248 645-648.
4.   Defense Minister Otto Gessler to Foreign Minister
Gustav Stresemann, no. 679/27, Berlin, 25 October 1927,
AA/3613/K6/K000 300-304.
5.   "Endlich Erläuterungen des Obersten Freiherrn von
Fritsch," AA/3613/K6/K000 305-308.
6.   Gerhard Köpke, "Aufzeichnung über die Pläne des
Reichswehrministeriums   betreffend   den   'Landesschutz',"
AA/3613/K6/K000 309-315.
7.   Colonel Werner Blomberg to State Secretary Schubert,
No. 678/27, Berlin, 12 November 1927, AA/3613/K6/K000 318.
8.   Dirk Forster, "Aufzeichnung über das Kriegsspiel der
Heeresleitung im Winter 1927/28," AA/3613/K6/K000 329-331.
9.   Colonel Blomberg to State Secretary Schubert, no.
42/28, Berlin, 14 January 1928, AA/3613/K6/K000 336-341.
10.   Unsigned, "Die Lage baut sich auf dem Winterkriegs-
spiels des Truppenamtes auf," no. IIF 453, AA/3613/K6/K000
347-350.
11.   Unsigned handwritten note, AA/3613/K6/K000 350.
12.   Unsigned "Vormerk," AA/3613/K6/K000 342-344.
13.   Chief of the army command Wilhelm Heye to Foreign
Office, no. 360/28, Berlin, 20 April 1928, AA/3613/K6/K000
374-377.
14.   Post, Civil-Military Fabric, p. 100.
15.   Seeckt's book Landesverteidigung was not published
until May 1930.   In this work, it was evident that Seeckt
still viewed national defense in a narrow military context.
He believed that there must actually be three forces for
defense: a standing army of 200,000 men, which, besides an
excellent infantry and a hard-hitting cavalry, must also be
strong in air assets and motor transport; a training army, to
prepare reserves for the standing army; and a people's levy,
consisting of millions of men.   This last force would take
care of rear-area security to free more troops of the standing
army for action.   See the review of Landesverteidigung in 12
Uhr Berliner Zeitung, reprinted and translated in United
States Military Intelligence Reports: Germany, 1919-1941
(Frederick, Md.:   University Publications of America, 1983),
military attache Colonel Edward Carpenter to War Department,
Berlin, 4 June 1930, reel 19, frames 0486-0487 (hereafter
USMI, 19, 0486-0487).

16.   See Groener's correspondence with the Reichsarchiv in the microfilmed copy of the Groener Papers, reel 8, National Archives, Washington, D.C.

17.   Erich Zechlin, "Aufzeichnung," Hiermit: Dirk Forster, Herbert von Dirksen, Berlin, 18 April 1928, AA/3527/9182H/E645 778-779.

18.   Dirksen, "Aufzeichnung," Berlin, 16 May 1928, AA/3527/9182H/E645 788.

19.   Colonel A. L. Conger to War Department, Report no. 8431, "Combat Estimate of the German Army," Berlin, 1 December 1926, USMI, 16, 0619-0625.

20.   Groener, Das Panzerschiff, Abdruck Nr. 15, Berlin, November 1928, Groener Papers, reel 25, pp. 1-29.

21.   Groener's speech to the Reichstag is found in the Groener Papers, reel 25, pp. 1-21.

22.   "Strategische Manöver 1923" and "Grundlagen für ein strategisches Manöver 1924 in der Ostsee," Records of the German Navy, Marineleitung, Flottenabteilung, serial PG 34065, "Kriegsaufgaben." A complete microcopy of interwar German naval records is on file at the University of Michigan, no. 13-132849, reels 28-32, 35.

23.   Post, Civil-Military Fabric, pp. 239-262.

24.   Dirk Forster, "Aufzeichnung über das Marinekriegsspiel in Kiel Mitte Dezember 1927," AA/3613/K6/K000 324-326.

25.   Admiral Erich Raeder, "Das Herbstmanöver 1928," Kiel, 1 January 1929, serial PG 34048/3.

26.   Admiral Raeder, "Schlussbetrachtung Herbstmanöver 1928," ibid.

27.   Truppenamt, "Studie Gdingen (Landunternehmungen)," 30 June 1928, serial PG 34101.

28.   Fleet Commander Oldekop to Truppenamt, Kiel, 2 February 1929, serial PG 34101.

29.   Truppenamt to Naval Command, Berlin, 23 June 1928, serial PG 34101.

30.   Truppenamt, "Übersicht: Vorbereiten zum Studie Gdingen," Berlin, 30 June 1928, serial PG 34101.

31.   Truppenamt to Defense District II, Berlin, 23 January 1930; Truppenamt to Naval Command, Berlin, 5 March 1930, serial PG 34102.

32.   Naval Command to Foreign Office, Kiel, 12 January 1933, serial PG 34102.

33.   "Kriegsspiel: Studie Ost, spring 1931," serial PG 34102.

34.   "Denkschrift des Flottenkommandos über die Durchführung der Studie 'O,'" Kiel, 22 July 1931, pp. 1-29, serial PG 34102.

35.   Admiral Raeder, "Geheime Kommandosache, Prüf. Nr. 50," Berlin, 25 November 1931, AA/3613/K6/K000 643-653.

36.   Groener, "Gedanken über die Entwicklung des Kriegswesens," Groener Papers, reel 25, pp. 1-29. See also, on the same reel, "Stichworte für grössere gemischte motorisierte Verbände."

37.   Groener to Prussian Minister of the Interior, no. 377/28, Berlin, 20 June 1928, AA/4519/K951/K248 769-771.

38.   "Abschrift zu Nr. 377/28," AA/4519/K951/K248 772-774.

39.   Groener to Chancellor Hermann Müller, no. 6196, Berlin, 13 August 1928, AA/4519/K951/K248 777-779.

40.   Groener to Foreign Minister Stresemann, no. 255/29, Berlin, 18 March 1929, AA/4041/L129/L026 609-610.

41.   See, for instance, Report no. 2006, Berlin, USMI, 24, 0724-0725. The report, entitled "German Fortifications in East Prussia," contained the claim of the Polish General Staff that fortification work in East Prussia was proceeding "without interruption."

42.   Quoted in military attache Edward Carpenter to War Department, Report no. 1772, Warsaw, 15 July 1932, USMI, 24, 0803.

43.   Ibid., 0804-0805.

44.   Acting military attache H. H. Zornig to War Department, Report no. 9003, Berlin, 8 October 1927, USMI, 14, 0845-0850. See especially "Confidential Appendix," USMI, 14, 0850.

45.   Military attache Edward Carpenter to War Department, Report No. f865, Berlin, 17 December 1928, reel 17, 0758-0819. See especially p. 9, "Comments on the Maneuvers."

46.   Ibid., II, "Blue: Situation for September 3/4."

47.   Ibid., III, p. 1, "Red: War Situation for September 3/4."

48.   Ibid., p. 4, "Attache's Comments."

49.   Ibid., VII, p. 1, "Orders for the Concentration of the 1st Reserve Brigade on September 6."

50.   Ibid., pp. 7-8, "Attache's Comments."

51.   Ibid., III, "Blue: Brigade Order for 7 September."

52.   Ibid., p. 8, Attache's Comments."

53.   Ibid., pp. 9-12, "Comments on the Maneuver." See especially the comments on cavalry, armored cars, and bivouacs.

54.   Post, Civil-Military Fabric, pp. 193-202.

55.   Rainer Wohlfeil, "Heer und Republik," in Handbuch zur deutschen Militärgeschichte, vol. 6 (Frankfurt am Main: Bernard & Graefe Verlag für Wehrwesen, 1970), pp. 228-229.

56.   Harald von Riekhoff, German-Polish Relations, 1918-1933 (Baltimore: Johns Hopkins Press, 1971), p. 342 n.

57.   Both the Tempo article and the Hindenburg speech are translated in H. H. Zornig to War Department, Report no. 11,193, Berlin, 19 December 1930, USMI, 19, 0376-0419. See especially pp. 30-33.

58.   P. W. Evans to War Department, Report no. 29,187, Berlin, 3 October 1930, USMI, 19, 0434-0438.

59.   Riekhoff, German-Polish Relations, p. 345.

60.   Lieutenant Colonel Jacob W. S. Wuest to War Department, Report no. 12,513, Berlin, 25 November 1932, USMI, 19, 0847-0875. See especially p. 4, "The Exercise."

61.   Ibid., Appendix B, "Organization of Major Tactical Units Which Took Part in the Maneuver," p. 1.

62.   Ibid., Appendix B, pp. 2-3.

63.   Ibid., pp. 5-12, "Statement of Problem" and "Development of the Exercise."

64.   Ibid., p. 10.

65.   Ibid., pp. 12-19, "Conduct of the Exercise."

66.   The maneuvers of the 2nd Division in Mecklenburg which took place in August-September 1932 gave further evidence of the German preference for maneuver warfare. During these exercises, the Reichswehr practiced "continuous moving warfare." The Germans, "handicapped by the size of their army, are attempting at present to increase the mobility of their infantry, at the same time not lessening the coordination between infantry and artillery." Wuest to War Department, Report No. 12,446, Berlin, 12 October 1932, USMI, Reel 19, 0841-0846.

5
Conclusion

In military affairs, the behavior of individuals is often decisive. Armies generally become as good as their commanders allow them to be. This was particularly true of the the German army in the interwar period. The story of German military rebirth in the 1920s is a tale of two generals, Hans von Seeckt and Wilhelm Groener. Both were highly capable officers, but each brought to his office different views of military affairs which gave German military policy his personal stamp. Seeckt was the builder. He reconstructed the Reichswehr from bits and pieces of the old imperial army, thereby ensuring that German military traditions were preserved. During Seeckt's tenure as army commander, he created an army which corresponded to his own tactical ideas. The new army was small, highly mobile, and contained a large contingent of horsed cavalry. It was schooled in offensive warfare. Even in the context of a strategic defensive, Seeckt's Reichswehr intended to repel invasions of the German East by vigorous counterattacks aimed at the enemy's flank. Apart from this general intention, however, it is apparent that the army gave little consideration to the forms which a war with Poland might take. Seeckt's most important task, creating an army out of nothing, left him little time for the larger questions of national strategy and military policy. This stress on purely military questions was the major difference between Seeckt's and Groener's tenures as army commander. During the Groener years, Germany's military leaders were free to concentrate specifically on war planning. The army which Groener inherited was a superb, if small, force. Consequently, his energy could be devoted to strategic concerns, as opposed to the tactical preoccupations of the Seeckt years. Under Groener, German military policy, particularly for an eastern conflict, developed into an all-encompassing strategy of Landesschutz. This strategy included renewed interest in the recruitment of border guards, the establishment of liaison between military planners and civilian officials in the Foreign Office, and a renewed stress on naval planning for a conflict with Poland. Under Groener, both army and navy conducted a series of maneuvers, wargames, and planning exercises designed to investigate the possibilities of a German-Polish war. Both services were imbued with an offensive spirit even more pronounced than that of the Seeckt

years.   The navy, in particular, planned for an offensive
strike against the Polish port of Gdynia.   This new offensive
spirit was reflected in the tactical doctrine and new equipment which Groener brought to the armed forces.   Whereas
Seeckt had been a great believer in the continued efficacy of
cavalry, Groener was a much more modern military thinker. He
saw the advantage of incorporating motorized and mechanized
units into the army.   During the maneuvers of 1932, for
instance, both forces were motorized to a large degree, even
to the point of including a motorized cavalry corps in the
order of battle.   With respect to naval armament, Groener was
instrumental in the construction of what came to be known as
the pocket battleships--fast, heavily armed, modern ships
which were a large step forward in terms of naval technology.
Although the Versailles treaty regulated the equipment of the
German forces, Groener ordered his officers to perform the
theoretical work which would allow a rapid modernization of
the Reichswehr when the international situation permitted it,
an action which was his greatest achievement as minister of
defense.
     German military achievements of the interwar period were
the result of the lost war and the treaty which followed it.
Victory breeds complacency, while defeat usually leads to a
reappraisal of past habits. This was what happened to Germany
in the 1920s.   No other state had more reasons than Germany to
rethink its entire military posture, from tactics to the
highest levels of strategy.   Both of Germany's primary enemies, France and Poland, had been victorious in recent wars,
France in 1918 and Poland in 1920.   Both states undertook
military reforms and modernization during the interwar years,
to be sure.   But these occurred half-heartedly, as for
instance in the confusing attempts to reorganize Polish
cavalry units after 1926.   France rested on its laurels by
retreating behind a strategy of passive defense and allowing
superannuated generals to remain on the rolls long after their
usefulness was gone.   Germany, however, saw its military
forces defeated and dismantled during and immediately after
the war.   The Versailles treaty contained military restrictions which apparently left Germany with little more than a
police force.   This tiny army, heavy in cavalry, was a natural
subject upon which Seeckt, Groener, and a host of bright
younger officers could conduct their experiments in mobile
warfare.   Likewise, the Allied stipulation that the German
army be made up of long-term volunteers ensured that each
soldier received superb training.   The Reichswehr became the
best-trained army in German history, as it demonstrated in its
maneuvers and battle exercises.   It would be an exaggeration
to suggest that Seeckt or Groener completely ignored the past.
Both men wanted to maintain a continuity with the old
Prussian-German army.   Yet the defeat in the war and the
draconian peace which followed gave Germany's military leaders
cause to search for new tactics and strategies.   This was the
backdrop against which we should view the development of
Blitzkrieg tactics.   Far from destroying the German army, the
Versailles treaty made it even more capable of fighting a war.
     What, then, was Germany's military posture in 1933? On
the eastern border, at least, Seeckt and Groener had solved
the problem of defending the borders with the small forces
allowed.   A combination of border guards, fortifications, and
highly trained Reichswehr units appears to have been capable

of repelling any Polish assault.   The elite formations of the
Reichswehr would have counterattacked and taken the Poles   in
the flank, while border guards provided local defense and
flank security for the regular forces.   If we compare the
performances of the Polish and German armies in their respective maneuvers,   we see clearly that the German forces
outperformed   their Polish adversaries in every aspect of war-
making.   Compared to the Poles,   the Germans marched faster,
concentrated their fire more effectively,   used covering
terrain more wisely,   and had superior leadership at all
levels.   It cannot be said that the Germans were better armed,
since treaty restrictions allowed Germany no tanks,   aircraft,
or heavy artillery.   Yet the Poles, who possessed all of these
weapons to some degree,   appear not to have gained any
advantage from them.   During Polish maneuvers, the failure to
exploit these modern weapons was conspicuous.   The lack of any
doctrine for the use of armor was especially noticeable.
While tanks were often wheeled out to impress foreign
visitors,   armor played no serious role in the exercises.   But
the lack of tanks and aircraft did not stop the Germans from
including armor and air power in their maneuvers.   Tanks and
armored cars were fully integrated into infantry and cavalry
formations in all German military exercises.   This incorpora-
tion of armor and infantry was the essence of the combined-
arms tactics with which the Wehrmacht would conquer Europe by
1940.   Despite its size,   it was obvious to most military men
that the Reichswehr was infinitely superior to the Polish
army.   Indeed, most observers believed that, man for man, the
German army was the finest in the world.   Seeckt and Groener
had indeed accomplished their mission.
     Looking back from our own modern perspective,   it appears
ironic that the eventual conquerors of the German army did
come from the East.   Thus,   despite the efforts of Seeckt and
Groener,   the attempt to guarantee Germany's security in the
east came to nothing.   For Germany, the long-awaited clash
with Poland finally occurred in 1939.   The result was a
stunning victory for a rearmed Germany and an utter debacle
for the Poles.   After less than one month of combat,   not a
single Polish division remained intact.   Further German campaigns in the east against the Red Army, however, had the
opposite result.   This time it was the German forces which
were annihilated.   The defeat of 1945 eclipsed that of 1918 in
its effects on the German nation.   The Reich was once more
divided.   Both halves of partitioned Germany are today satellite states of the superpowers.   In light of these facts,
perhaps we should ask whether Germany's eastern military
policy of the 1920s had any negative implications.   The ease
with which disarmed Germany regained military superiority over
Poland did have one unfortunate effect on German military and
political leaders.   The experience with Poland during the
Weimar era reinforced the traditional lack of respect which
German leaders had for the armies of Slavic nations.   Before
1914, of course, disdain for the Russian army was the basis of
the Schlieffen plan, which called for stripping Germany's
eastern defenses in order to defeat France before Russia could
mobilize.   During the 1920s, German military intelligence knew
of the many problems which beset the Polish army.   These
included poor leadership,   confused organization,   a haphazard
logistical network,   and outmoded equipment.   The Germans
viewed   these deficiencies as symptomatic of the Slavic

character.   The lightning conquest of Poland reinforced the
German idea of Slavic military inferiority. Not surprisingly,
the Wehrmacht carried this same contempt into its campaign
against the Soviet Union.   Despite their later   claims   that
Hitler had given the army a task beyond its capability, almost
all German officers felt in 1941 that the invasion of the
Soviet Union would be a repetition of the Polish campaign.
Hence they reacted to the stiff Soviet resistance with great
surprise, even panic.   The negative attitudes toward Slavic
soldiery developed or at least reinforced in the 1920s would
bear deadly fruit for Germany during the Second World War.

Bibliography

PRIMARY SOURCES

Two indispensable research guides for work with unpublished German sources are George O. Kent, ed., A Catalog of Files and Microfilms of the German Foreign Ministry Archives, 1920-1945, 4 vols. (Stanford: Hoover Institution Publications, 1962), and Christopher M. Kimmich, ed., German Foreign Policy, 1918-1945: A Guide to Research and Research Materials (Wilmington, Del.: Scholarly Resources Inc., 1981).

1. Records of the German Foreign Office (National Archives, Washington, D. C., Microcopy T120):

   Serial 2945. Büro des Reichsministers: Polen. Reels 1424-1431.
   Serial 3170. Büro des Reichsministers: Entwaffnung, Interallierte Kommissionen, und Ostfestungen. Reels 1605-1612.
   Serial 3177. Büro des Reichsministers: Militärwesen. Reels 1567-1574.
   Serial 4556. Büro des Staatssekretärs: Russland, Polen, Randstaaten. Reel 2302.
   Serial 9182H. Geheimakten 1920-1936: Polen, Deutscher Militärattache in Polen. Reel 3527.
   Serial 9285. Abteilung II F Militär und Marine: Auflösung der Selbstschutzorganisation, Einwohnerwehren. Reels 3496-3497.
   Serial 9476. Abteilung II F Militär und Marine: Garantie für das Landheer. Reel 3664.
   Serial 9537. Abteilung II F Militär und Marine: Schlussbericht der I. M. K. K. Reels 3685-3688.
   Serial 9622. Abteilung II F Militär und Marine: Frage des Kontrollrechts der durch die Genfer Beschlüsse von 12-12-1926 bei Zerstörung von Unterständen der Ostfestungen. Reel 3596.
   Serial 9854. Abteilung II F Militär und Marine: Bildung von Schutz- und Ortswehren in Ostpreussen. Sicherheitspolizei und Reichswehr in Ostpreussen. Reel 3623.

Serial K6.   Geheimakten 1920-1936:   Militärpolitik.
    Reel 3613.
Serial K7.   Geheimakten 1920-1936:   Besprechung mit
    der Marineleitung über Danzig (Studie Ost).   Reel
    3613.
Serial K190.   Geheimakten 1920-1936:   Polen, Mili-
    tärangelegenheiten.   Reels 3758-3760.
Serial K191.   Geheimakten 1920-1936:   Polen, Marine-
    angelegenheiten.   Reel 3761.
Serial   K950.   Alte   Reichskanzlei: Auswärtige
    Angelegenheiten; Entwaffnung.   Reels 4517-4518.
Serial   K951.   Alte   Reichskanzlei: Volkswehr   und
    Wehrpflicht; Reichswehr.   Reels 4519-4520.
Serial K952.   Alte   Reichskanzlei: Heeresorganisa-
    tion.   Reel 4521.
Serial   K953.   Alte   Reichskanzlei: Landesvertei-
    digung.   Reel   4521.
Serial   L129.   Abteilung   II F Militär   und   Marine:
    Anfragen der I.M.K.K.   wegen des Systems der Ost-
    befestigungen.   Reel 4041.
Serial   M342.   Geheimakten 1920-1936:   Militärische
    Nachrichten.   Reel 5487.

2.   Records of the German Navy (University of Michigan
     Library,   Ann   Arbor, Mich.), no. 13-132849, reels 28-32,
     35.

Serial PG 34048/3.   Marineleitung, Flottenabteilung:
    Herbstmanöver 1928; Gefechtsübung 1929.
Serial PG 34051.   Marineleitung,   Flottenabteilung:
    Manöver.
Serial   PG 34061.   Marineleitung,   Flottenabteilung:
    Admiralstabsfragen.
Serial PG 34065.   Marineleitung,   Flottenabteilung:
    Kriegsaufgaben.
Serial PG 34073.   Marineleitung,   Flottenabteilung:
    Kriegsspiele.
Serial PG 34073/1.   Marineleitung, Flottenabteilung:
    Kriegsspiele.
Serial PG   34076.   Marineleitung,   Flottenabteilung:
    Kriegsspiele.
Serial   PG 34089.   Marineleitung,   Flottenabteilung:
    Ostseeverteidigung Pillau.
Serial PG 34095.   Marineleitung,   Flottenabteilung:
    Heeresangelegenheiten.
Serial PG 34101.   Marineleitung,   Flottenabteilung:
    Studie "Gdingen."
Serial PG   34102.   Marineleitung,   Flottenabteilung:
    Studie "Gdingen."
Serial   PG   34117.   Marineleitung,   Flottenabteilung:
    Studie "Fall Danzig."
Serial   PG 34118.   Marineleitung,   Flottenabteilung:
    Studie Ost.
Serial PG 48898.   Marineleitung: Auslands-Berichte.
Serial PG 49031.   Archiv der Marine: Polen.

3. Personal Papers (National Archives, Washington, D.C.).

      Papers of General Hans von Seeckt.   Microcopy M132,
          28 reels.

      Papers of General Wilhelm Groener.   Microcopy M137,
          27 reels.

4. United States Military Intelligence Reports: Germany,
    1919-1941.   A Microfilm Project of University Publica-
    tions of America, Inc. Frederick, Md.: 1983. 28 reels.

SECONDARY SOURCES

Addington, Larry H. The Blitzkrieg Era and the German General
    Staff, 1865-1941. New Brunswick, N.J.: Rutgers Univer-
    sity Press, 1971.
Benoist-Mechin,   Jacques.   Histoire de l'Armee Allemande.
    Vols. 2 and 3. Paris: Editions Albin Michel, 1938.
Boehm, Max Hildebert. Die deutschen Grenzlande. Berlin: R.
    Hobbing, 1925.
Borgert, Heinz-Ludger.   "Grundzüge der Landkriegführung von
    Schlieffen bis Guderian." In Handbuch zur deutschen
    Militärgeschichte, 1648-1939, vol. 9. München: Bernard
    & Graefe Verlag für Wehrwesen, 1977.
Brackmann, Albert, ed. Deutschland und Polen: Beiträge zu
    ihren geschichtlichen Beziehungen. München und Berlin:
    Verlag von R. Oldenbourg, 1933.
Bretton, Henry L. Stresemann and the Revision of Versailles.
    Stanford: Stanford University Press, 1953.
Breyer, Richard. Das deutsche Reich und Polen, 1932-1937:
    Aussenpolitik und Volksgruppenfragen. Würzburg: Holzner-
    Verlag, 1955.
Broszat, Martin. Zweihundert Jahre deutsche Polenpolitik.
    Frankfurt am Main: Suhrkamp, 1972.
Carsten, F. L. The Reichswehr and Politics, 1918-1933.
    Oxford: Clarendon Press, 1966.
Castellan, Georges. Le Rearmament Clandestin du Reich, 1930-
    1935. Paris: Librairie Plon, 1954.
Craig, Gordon A. Germany, 1866-1945. New York: Oxford Uni-
    versity Press, 1978.
    _____. The Politics of the Prussian Army, 1640-1945.
    London: Oxford University Press, 1955.
Davies, Norman. White Eagle--Red Star: The Polish-Soviet
    War, 1919-1920. London: Macdonald & Co., 1972.
Debicki, Roman. The Foreign Policy of Poland, 1919-1939. New
    York: Praeger, 1962.
Deutschen Gesellschaft für Wehrpolitik und Wehrwissenschaften,
    ed. Generaloberst von Seeckt: Ein Erinnerungsbuch.
    Berlin: Verlag von E. S. Mittler & Sohn, 1937.
Diehl, James M. Paramilitary Politics in Weimar Germany.
    Bloomington: Indiana University Press, 1977.
Dirksen, Herbert von. Moscow, Tokyo, London: Twenty Years of
    German Foreign Policy, 1919-1939. New York: Hutchinson,
    1951.

Dülffer, Jost. "Der Reichs- und Kriegsmarine, 1918-1939." In Handbuch zur deutschen Militärgeschichte, 1648-1939, vol. 8. München: Bernard & Graefe Verlag für Wehrwesen, 1977.

Dupuy, T. N. A Genius for War: The German Army and General Staff, 1807-1945. Englewood Cliffs, N.J.: Prentice-Hall Inc., 1977.

English, J. A. A Perspective on Infantry. New York: Praeger, 1981.

Erfurth, Waldemar. Die Geschichte des deutschen Generalstabes, 1918-1945. Göttingen, Berlin, Frankfurt: Musterschmidt-Verlag, 1957.

Eyck, Erich. A History of the Wiemar Republic, 2 vols. Cambridge: Harvard University Press, 1962.

Fechner, Helmuth. Deutschland und Polen, 1772-1945. Ostdeutsche Beiträge aus dem Göttinger Arbeitskreise, vol. 27. Würzburg: Holzner-Verlag, 1964.

Feller, Jean. Le Dossier de l'Armee Francaise. Paris: Perrin, 1966.

Fiedor, K. "The Attitude of German Right-Wing Organizations to Poland in the Years 1918-1933." Polish Western Affairs 14, no. 2.

Gasiorowski, Zygmunt J. "Stresemann and Poland after Locarno." Journal of European Affairs 18: 292-317.

_____. "Stresemann and Poland before Locarno." Journal of European Affairs 18: 25-47.

Gatzke, Hans W. Stresemann and the Rearmament of Germany. Baltimore: Johns Hopkins Press, 1954.

Gayre, Gr. Teuton and Slav on the Polish Frontier. London: Eyre and Spottiswoode, 1944.

Gessler, Otto. Reichswehrpolitik in der Weimarer Zeit. Stuttgart: Deutsche Verlags-Anstalt, 1958.

Geyer, Michael. Aufrüstung oder Sicherheit: Die Reichswehr in der Krise der Machtpolitik, 1924-1936. Wiesbaden: Steiner, 1980.

Gleitze, Bruno. Ostdeutsche Wirtschaft: Industrial Standorte und volkswirtschaftliche Kapazitäten des ungeteilten Deutschland. Berlin: Duncker & Humblot, 1956.

Gordon, Harold J. The Reichswehr and the German Republic, 1919-1926. Princeton, N.J.: Princeton University Press, 1957.

Görlitz, Walter. History of the German General Staff, 1657-1945. New York: Praeger, 1959.

Groener, Wilhelm. Lebenserinnerungen: Jugend, Generalstab, Weltkrieg. Osnabrück: Biblio Verlag, 1972.

_____. Das Testament des Grafen Schlieffens. Berlin: E. S. Mittler & Sohn, 1927.

Groener-Geyer, Dorothea. General Groener: Soldat und Staatsmann. Frankfurt am Main: Societäts-Verlag, 1954.

Güth, Rolf. Die Marine des deutschen Reiches, 1919-1939. Frankfurt am Main: Bernard & Graefe Verlag für Wehrwesen, 1972.

_____. "Die Organisation der deutschen Marine in Krieg und Frieden, 1913-1933." In Handbuch zur deutschen Militärgeschichte, 1648-1939, vol. 8. München: Bernard & Graefe Verlag für Wehrwesen, 1977.

Guderian, Heinz. Panzer Leader. New York: Ballantine Books, 1965.

Guske, Claus. Das Politische Denken des Generals von Seeckt. Historische Studien, no. 422. Lübeck and Hamburg: Matthiesen Verlag, 1971.

Heis, Friedrich. Deutschland und der Korridor. Berlin: Volk und Reich Verlag, 1933.

Hiden, John. Germany and Europe, 1919-1939. London and New York: Longman, 1977.

Hogg, Ian. Artillery in Color, 1920-1963. New York: Arco Publishing, Inc., 1980.

Höltje, Christian. Die Weimarer Republik und das Ostlocarno-Problem, 1919-1934. Würzburg: Holzner-Verlag, 1958.

Hürten, Heinz, ed. Die Anfänge der Ära Seeckt: Militär und Innenpolitik, 1920-1922. Quellen zur Geschichte des Parlamentarismus und der politischen Parteien, series 2, vol. 3. Düsseldorf: Droste, 1979.

Jablonowski, Horst. "Probleme der deutsch-polnischen Beziehungen zwischen den beiden Weltkriegen." In Zu den deutsch-polnischen Beziehungen: Zwei Vorträge. Würzburg: Holzner-Verlag, 1969.

Kellermann, Volkmar. Schwarzer Adler--Weisser Adler: Die Polenpolitik der Weimarer Republik. Köln: Markus Verlag, 1970.

Kitchen, Martin. A Military History of Germany: From the Eighteenth Century to the Present Day. Bloomington: Indiana University Press, 1975.

Koch-Weser, Erich. Deutschlands Aussenpolitik in der Nach-kriegszeit, 1919-1929. Berlin-Grunewald: Kurt Vowinckel Verlag, 1929.

Korbel, Josef. Poland between East and West: Soviet and German Diplomacy toward Poland, 1919-1933. Princeton, N.J.: Princeton University Press, 1963.

Krummacher, F. A., and Albert Wuker, eds. Die Weimarer Republik. München, Wien, Basel: Verlag Kurt Desch, 1965.

Lloyd George, David. Memoirs of the Peace Conference. New Haven: Yale University Press, 1939.

Luckau, Alma. "Kapp Putsch: Success or Failure?" Journal of Central European Affairs 7: 398 ff.

Mason, Herbert Molloy, Jr. The Rise of the Luftwaffe. New York: The Dial Press, 1973.

Matuschka, Edgar Graf von. "Organisation des Reichsheeres." In Handbuch zur deutschen Militärgeschichte, 1648-1939, vol. 6. Frankfurt am Main: Bernard & Graefe Verlag für Wehrwesen, 1970.

Meier-Welcker, Hans. Seeckt. Frankfurt am Main: Bernard & Graefe Verlag für Wehrwesen, 1967.

Meurer, Christian. Die Grundlage des Versailles Friedens und der Völkerbund. Würzburg: Kabbitsch & Mönnich, 1920.

O'Neill, Robert J. "Doctrine and Training in the German Army." In The Theory and Practice of War. Edited by Michael Howard. Bloomington: Indiana University Press, 1965.

Pagel, Karl, ed. The German East. Berlin: Konrad Lemmer Verlag, 1954.

Phelps, Reginald. "Aus den Groener Dokumenten." Deutsche Rundschau 76: 616-625, 830-840.

Pilsudski, Jozef. Year 1920. London: Pilsudski Institute of London, 1972.

Post, Gaines, Jr. The Civil-Military Fabric of Weimar Foreign Policy. Princeton, N.J.: Princeton University Press, 1973.

Rabenau, Friedrich von. Seeckt. Leipzig: Gesellschaft der
    Freunde der deutschen Bücherei, 1942.
_____. Seeckt: aus seinem Leben, 1918-1936. Leipzig:
    von Hase und Koehler Verlag, 1940.
Rahn, Werner. Reichsmarine und Landesverteidigung. München,
    1976.
Rakenius, Gerhard. Wilhelm Groener als erster General-
    quartiermeister: Die Politik der Obersten Heeresleitung.
    Boppard am Rhein: Boldt, 1977.
Rhode, Gotthold. Die Ostgebiete des deutschen Reiches.
    Würzburg: Holzner-Verlag, 1955.
Riekhoff, Harald von. German-Polish Relations, 1918-1933.
    Baltimore: Johns Hopkins Press, 1971.
Rill, Bernd. Deutsche und Polen: Die Schwierige Nachbar-
    schaft. Puchheim: IDEA Verlag, 1981.
Roos, Hans. Geschichte der polnischen Nation, 1916-1960.
    Stuttgart: W. Kohlhammer, 1961.
_____. Polen und Europa: Studien zur polnischen
    Aussenpolitik, 1931-1939. Tübingen: Mohr, 1957.
Rosenthal, Harry Kenneth. German and Pole: National Conflict
    and National Myth. Gainesville: University Presses of
    Florida, 1976.
Rosinski, Herbert. The German Army. Washington: The Infan-
    try Journal, 1944.
Ryder, A. J. Twentieth Century Germany: From Bismarck to
    Brandt. New York: Columbia University Press, 1973.
Schmidt-Richberg, Wiegand. Die Entwicklung der militärischen
    Luftfahrt in Deutschland, 1920-1933. Beiträge zur
    Militär- und Kriegsgeschichte, vol. 3. Stuttgart:
    Deutsche Verlags-Anstalt, 1962.
Schneider, Paul. Die Organisation des Heeres. Berlin, 1931.
Schüddekopf, Otto. Heer und Politik: Quellen zur Politik der
    Reichswehrführung, 1918 bis 1933. Hannover und Frankfurt
    am Main: Norddeutsche Verlagsanstalt O. Goedel, 1955.
Schulze, Hagen. "Der Oststaat-Plan 1919." Vierteljahrhefte
    für Zeitgeschichte 19: 123-163.
Schützle, Kurt. Reichswehr wider die Nation: Zur Rolle der
    Reichswehr bei der Vorbereitung und Errichtung der
    faschistischen Diktatur in Deutschland, 1929-1933.
    Berlin (East): Deutscher Militärverlag, 1963.
Seeckt, Hans von. Gedanken eines Soldaten. Leipzig: von
    Hase und Koehler Verlag, 1935.
Skrzynski, Alexander. Poland and Peace. London: G. Allen
    and Unwin, 1923.
Tessin, Georg. Deutsche Verbände und Truppen, 1918-1939.
    Osnabrück: Biblio Verlag, 1974.
Völker, Karl-Heinz. Die Entwicklung der Militärischen Luft-
    fahrt in Deutschland, 1920-1933. Stuttgart: Deutsche
    Verlags-Anstalt, 1962.
Waite, R. G. L. Vanguard of Nazism: The Free Corps Movement
    in Postwar Germany, 1918-1923. Cambridge: Harvard Uni-
    versity Press, 1952.
Wandycz, Piotr S. France and Her Eastern Allies, 1919-1925.
    Minneapolis: University of Minnesota Press, 1962.
Watt, Richard. Bitter Glory: Poland and Its Fate, 1918-1939.
    New York: Simon & Schuster, 1979.
Werner, Karl. Fragen der deutschen Ostgrenze. Breslau:
    Verlag von Wilh. Gottl. Korn, 1933.

Wheeler-Bennett, John W. The Nemesis of Power: The German
    Army in Politics, 1918-1945. London: Macmillan & Co.,
    1964.
Winnig, August. Am Ausgang der deutschen Ostpolitik: Persön-
    liche Erlebnisse und Erinnerungen. Berlin: Staats-
    politischer Verlag, 1921.
Wohlfeil, Rainer. "Heer und Republik." In Handbuch zur
    deutschen Militärgeschichte, 1648-1939, vol. 6.
    Frankfurt am Main: Bernard & Graefe Verlag für
    Wehrwesen, 1970.
Wünsche, Wolfgang. Strategie der Niederlage: Zur
    imperialistischen deutschen Militärwissenschaft zwischen
    den beiden Weltkriegen. Berlin (East): Deutscher
    Militärverlag, 1961.
Zamoyski, Adam. The Battle for the Marchlands. Boulder:
    East European Monographs, 1981.
Zimmermann, Ludwig. Deutsche Aussenpolitik in der Ära der
    Weimarer Republik. Göttingen, Berlin, Frankfurt:
    Musterschmidt-Verlag, 1958.

Index

About the Author

ROBERT M. CITINO is Assistant Professor of History at Lake Erie College. He has worked as a civilian historian for the U.S. Army.